"Here is a groundbreaking ar
that will open up new vistas o
of Christ from the beloved tre_____ ___ ___ _____. . . . Professor Robertson has convincingly argued that there is a distinctive progression
across the five books of the Psalter. . . . What Robertson has done
for us is to include in this book five diagrams, along with his text, to
show how Torah Psalm 1 and messianic Psalm 2 supply us with the
major themes that are then developed across the whole Psalter with
the grouping of significant psalms along the way. . . . The impact
that this view of such a Psalter structure will have on New Testament
perspectives and studies should be enormous."
>   —**Walter C. Kaiser Jr.**, President Emeritus, Gordon-Conwell Theo-
>   logical Seminary

"What a pleasure to read! O. Palmer Robertson's scholarly but accessible *Flow of the Psalms* demonstrates that there is an orderly thematic
arrangement for the seemingly 'most miscellaneous of the sacred books'
(Augustine)—the Psalms. Showing us the genius of the book's structure
and the interconnections between structure and substance, Robertson
makes the overall theological message of the Psalms come to light. His
fresh and insightful work on this majestic book of Scripture is sure to
expand your mind, warm your heart, and open your mouth to join
with all creation in shouts of '*Hallelu-YAH*.'"
>   —**Douglas Sean O'Donnell**, Friends of QTC Senior Lecturer in
>   Biblical Studies and Practical Theology, Queensland Theo-
>   logical College, Brisbane, Australia

"The book of the Psalms: a random collection of individual poems
or a well-structured composition with a specific theological message?
While an average Bible reader gets the impression of the former, several biblical scholars in modern times have attempted to discover
the latter—but mostly in vain. This new book offers a courageous
and thought-provoking proposal to read the Psalter afresh. Palmer
Robertson argues that the Psalms exhibit a deliberate architectonic
structure and an organized development of thought progression from
the beginning to the end. Pivotal to his argument is a new evaluation

of the function of the two 'poetic pillars' (Pss. 1 and 2), with Torah and Messiah as organizing themes of the Psalter. In my opinion, the author is successful in defending the idea of a great number of interconnections in structure and theology in the Psalms. The redemptive-historical development of confrontation–communication–devastation–maturation–consummation is quite helpful, as is the emphasis on the function of memorization of the Psalms by means of, for example, acrostic psalms. This book is written in a lucid and attractive style and reads as the report of an exploratory expedition. Robertson's joy of discovery is contagious, as is his love for God's Word that inspired him. It is therefore my hope and expectation that the teaching of this book will enrich many readers, both laymen and scholars."

—**Eric Peels**, Professor of Old Testament Studies and Rector of the Theological University Apeldoorn, The Netherlands

"Very few evangelical scholars have mastered Old Testament studies to the level of O. Palmer Robertson. His expertise is evident in this work on the Psalms. More than this, he interacts with modern scholarship without compromising his commitment to the full authority of Scripture. And best of all, his work is easily understood and available to serve pastors and other church leaders as they preach and teach Christ from the Psalms. This book is undoubtedly one of the very best studies of this part of Scripture."

—**Richard L. Pratt Jr.**, Founder and President, Third Millennium Ministries

"With his customary clarity and insight, Robertson presents a Psalter that is at once theologically rich, historically relevant, and practically impactful. His approach is largely redemptive-historical and canonical, which provides him with multiple advantages as he explores the shape and coherence of the Psalter as a poetic anthology and its place within the larger biblical story of redemption. Robertson's often-creative interpretation is nevertheless attuned to contemporary scholarship, which he presents in a manner accessible to laymen and preachers."

—**John Scott Redd Jr.**, President and Associate Professor of Old Testament, Reformed Theological Seminary, Washington, D.C.

The
FLOW
OF THE
Psalms

THE
FLOW
OF THE
Psalms

DISCOVERING THEIR
STRUCTURE AND THEOLOGY

O. PALMER ROBERTSON

P U B L I S H I N G

P.O. BOX 817 • PHILLIPSBURG • NEW JERSEY 08865-0817

Unless otherwise indicated, all Scripture quotations either are the author's own or are taken from the HOLY BIBLE, NEW INTERNATIONAL VERSION®. NIV®. Copyright © 1973, 1978, 1984 by International Bible Society. Used by permission of Zondervan Publishing House. All rights reserved. Poetic indentions are the author's own.

Scripture quotations marked (ESV) are from the ESV® Bible (The Holy Bible, English Standard Version®), copyright © 2001 by Crossway, a publishing ministry of Good News Publishers. Used by permission. All rights reserved.

Italics within Scripture quotations indicate emphasis added.

Page design by Lakeside Design Plus

ISBN: 978-1-62995-133-1 (pbk)
ISBN: 978-1-62995-134-8 (ePub)
ISBN: 978-1-62995-135-5 (Mobi)

Printed in the United States of America

Library of Congress Cataloging-in-Publication Data

Robertson, O. Palmer.
  The flow of the Psalms : discovering their structure and theology / O. Palmer Robertson. -- 1st [edition].
      pages cm
  Includes bibliographical references and index.
  ISBN 978-1-62995-133-1 (pbk.)
  1. Bible. Psalms--Criticism, interpretation, etc. I. Title.
  BS1430.52.R63 2015
  223'.206--dc23
                                            2015001259

In memory of
Gwenette Phillips Robertson
1934–2014

With beauty outwardly and beauty inwardly, she displayed the grace of Christ through all her life. Her love of music, her love of singing, welled up from a heart filled to overflowing with the love of Christ.

CONTENTS

FOREWORD

It is a real joy and a privilege to write the foreword to *The Flow of the Psalms* by O. Palmer Robertson, for here is a groundbreaking and innovative piece of research and study that will open up new vistas of study and preaching to the whole body of Christ from the beloved treasury of the Psalter. Many of us over the years have come to appreciate the numerous books and articles that have come from the labors of Dr. Robertson. Currently, he divides his time between Uganda, where he serves as Director and Vice Chancellor of the African Bible University, and Cambridge, England, where he spends the balance of his time in study and research of the Scriptures. His new project on the Psalms will introduce us to a whole new avenue of thinking and ministering for the glory of our God.

The book of Psalms has been one of the great sources of blessing to the body of Christ. Yet for all too long now, the book of Psalms has been treated by many scholars and lay readers as a sort of hodge-podge collection of individual poems randomly placed together with no planned pattern of arrangement or purpose to the whole book. This is not to say that some have not attempted to see whether the five books into which the Psalms are divided offer some type of organization. Alas, the conclusion has usually been that if such an intentional structure exists, it is a mystery, or that the Psalter is a collection without any sort of rhyme or reason.

Recent introductions to the Old Testament have even gone beyond giving up on finding how all 150 psalms are linked together; these studies have insisted that a particular psalm is not even to be interpreted by the psalms that border it. Thus, every psalm is said to stand alone, its neighboring psalm having little or no impact on its meaning or its placement at that point in the book of Psalms. But Professor Robertson has convincingly argued that there is a distinctive progression across the five books of the Psalter.

This should not be a surprising turn of events for those who hold the Scriptures to be a revelation from God, for there is a divine unity, purpose, and plan to all that God has disclosed in his Word. Our God is not the author of randomness or confusion; he is the God of order. Nevertheless, the current trend is to place modern emphasis on the diversity, plurality, and isolated individualism of scriptural texts. The complaint is that there are just too many topics and that the picture is just too complex to argue for a deliberate flow of the biblical materials so that they form a picture moving toward a goal and purpose even though the materials might stretch, as is the case with the five books of the Psalms, over some five hundred years. But for that matter, the whole Bible was authored by some thirty-nine or forty writers over a period of fourteen to fifteen hundred years. Yet what they wrote was with a single plan, which I have elsewhere labeled the *promise-plan of God*.

In like manner, Professor Robertson has pointed to such structural items as the placement of acrostic psalms and the strategic coupling of a messianic psalm with a Torah psalm, but he has also gone on to point to the grouping of psalms by topics, such as the kingship psalms, innocent-sufferer psalms, specified-enemy psalms, *Yahweh Malak* ("Yahweh is King") psalms, Psalms of Ascents, and *Hallelu-YAH* psalms, along with specific messianic psalms that give further indication as to how the Psalter is structured.

Even though the flow of the Psalms is not purely chronological, there is a relative ordering in the time sequences marked out in this work. Slowly, a number of recent studies are beginning to show that the whole Psalter has an intentional structure. But what Robertson has done for us is to include in this book five diagrams, along with his text, to show how Torah Psalm 1 and messianic Psalm 2 supply us with the major themes that are then developed across the whole Psalter with the grouping of significant psalms along the way. His narrative moves from "Confrontation" in Psalms 1–41 (Book I), as David met a multitude of enemies while attempting to establish the Lord's kingdom of righteousness and peace, to "Communication" with foreign nations and peoples, with his use of *Elohim* as the name for God instead of *Yahweh* (Pss. 42–72; Book II). This led to the "Devastation" of the people for their lack of faith, as described in the seventeen psalms of Book III (Pss. 73–89). Book IV (Pss. 90–106) has at its core *Yahweh Malak* psalms (Pss. 92–100), which anticipate the rejuvenation of Yahweh's kingdom in the "Maturation" of God's plan in the flow of the Psalms' theology and narrative. Finally, Book V (Pss. 107–150), comprising the final forty-four psalms of the Psalter, gives us the "Consummation" of the flow of the Psalms. Psalm 118, a messianic psalm, is coupled with Psalm 119, a Torah psalm, to once again point to the major structural unit in the Psalms announced in Psalms 1 and 2. The *Hallelu-YAH* finale in Psalms 146–150 serves as the pinnacle of this climactic collection. Both Psalms 110 and 118, two focal messianic psalms, give us some of the best revelations of the sufferings and glory of the Messiah. Not surprisingly, the New Testament quotes these psalms, along with Psalm 2, more extensively than any others.

The Flow of the Psalms has a host of themes and avenues for further thought and reflection. Its coupling of the Torah and messianic themes throughout the Psalter points to the heart of the matter. The impact that this view of Psalter structure will have on New Testament perspectives and studies should be enormous. At the very least, this fresh reading of the Psalter in its structural flow should give a new insight into this poetic book of Scripture that has long been regarded as isolated collections of unrelated themes. The biblical-theological context of the book of Psalms calls us to heed it in our own thinking and to teach it to those to whom we minister.

Walter C. Kaiser Jr.
President Emeritus
Gordon-Conwell Theological Seminary
South Hamilton, Massachusetts

Editor's Preface

In a number of places throughout this work, the divine name *Yahweh*—יְהוָה—whose distinctly covenantal meaning was revealed to Moses in Exodus 3, is rendered COVENANT LORD or LORD OF THE COVENANT. This representation of *Yahweh* communicates the principal distinctiveness of this name for God.

The term *Yahweh* sounds awkward in English and communicates little to the reader. Substitutions such as the hybrid *Jehovah* and the capitalized LORD or LORD do little to communicate the uniqueness of this term. Yahweh is *distinctly* the LORD OF THE COVENANT, the COVENANT LORD.

P&R Publishing

Acknowledgments

I would like to express great appreciation to the following people for their contributions to the completion of this book:

To the Administration and Board of African Bible Colleges, Inc. Special thanks is due to the Administration and Board for allowing me time away from administrative and teaching duties that I might complete this work.

To the Administration, Faculty, and Staff of African Bible University of Uganda. How gracious have they all been in taking on many additional responsibilities during my absence.

To Tyndale House in Cambridge, England. The administration and staff have been a constant source of encouragement and helpfulness, and the daily interaction over tea with fellow researchers has provided stimulating fellowship.

To Steffen Jenkins. Steffen generously and graciously shared with me all his resources of knowledge about current studies in the Psalms and their structure.

To my wife, Joanna. Joanna has been my most loving critic, whose red-pen markings have contributed much to the final form of this book.

O. Palmer Robertson
Tyndale House
Cambridge, England
May 1, 2014

ANALYTICAL OUTLINE

1. Throughout this volume, the asterisk (*) indicates a grouping of psalms whose titles do not all specifically refer to David or some other individual.

1

INTRODUCTION

More often than not, people perceive the book of Psalms as a random collection of individual poems on a variety of topics. With this assumed framework for reading, it is understandable that little awareness exists in terms of a comprehension of the book's total message, its specific emphases, or any flow of the book's structure and theology from beginning to end.

The difficulty of grasping some structural order in the Psalter is by no means a modern problem. Augustine, Bishop of Hippo, after setting forth a commentary on the Psalms condensed to over six hundred pages, opens his treatment of Psalm 150 with the following acknowledgment:

> Although the arrangement of the Psalms, which seems to me to contain the secret of a mighty mystery, hath not yet been revealed unto me, yet, by the fact that they in all amount to one hundred and fifty, they suggest somewhat even to us, who have not as yet pierced with the eye of our mind the depth of their entire arrangement, whereon we may without being over-bold, so far as God giveth, be able to speak.[1]

Augustine proceeds to speak extensively of the significance of 150 as the number of the Psalms, of the difficulty of understanding the division into five books when there is actually only one book, and of the significance of the three groups of fifty psalms each that

1. Augustine, *Expositions on the Book of Psalms*, ed. A. Cleveland Coxe, in *Nicene and Post-Nicene Fathers*, ed. Philip Schaff (Peabody, MA: Hendrickson, 1994), 8:681.

advance from penitence (Ps. 50) to mercy and judgment (Ps. 100) to praise (Ps. 150).

In the middle of the nineteenth century, one insightful commentator who treasured the revelations of God in the book of Psalms anticipated more recent discussions. This particular author was fully aware of the challenge of a comprehensive understanding of the book of Psalms. He provides an honest summary of the problem by describing the book of Psalms as

> the most miscellaneous of the sacred books, containing a hundred and fifty compositions, each complete in itself, and varying in length, from two sentences (Ps. 117) to a hundred and seventy-six (Ps. 119), as well as in subject, style, and tone, the work of many authors, and of different ages; so that a superficial reader might be tempted to regard it as a random or fortuitous collection of unconnected and incongruous materials.[2]

Rejecting various efforts to reconstruct the psalms in some order that might provide greater coherence to the Psalter, this author suggests that studying the order in which the book presents itself will prove to be the most productive approach. Even if all the elements that link one portion of the book to another might not be immediately apparent, enough clues are evident to supply some overall awareness of the genius of the book's structure. As a matter of fact, the more a person studies the total message of the Psalms, the more convinced he becomes that a greater number of interconnections in structure and theology exist in the book than will ever be fully uncovered.

The authors of a recent commentary on the Psalms describe their approach to the Psalter, explaining in the process why their introduction to the whole book is being reserved until the third volume dealing with Psalms 1–50 has been completed:

2. Joseph Addison Alexander, *The Psalms: Translated and Explained* (Grand Rapids: Zondervan, 1864; repr., n.d.), 3. J. A. Alexander was the son of Archibald Alexander, the founding professor of Princeton Theological Seminary in 1812. In this commentary, J. A. Alexander acknowledges his indebtedness to the three-volume commentary of E. W. Hengstenberg on the Psalms.

Because we do not regard the Psalter, as some other commentators have, as nothing but a "storage cabinet" for individual psalms, but rather as a successively developed, but nevertheless compositionally structured entity whose form gives an additional dimension of meaning to each individual psalm, the "introduction" can be meaningfully composed only when we have analyzed all the individual psalms.[3]

Taking into account the structure of the Psalter makes two significant contributions to the interpretive process: (1) it has the potential of uncovering internal connections among the various psalms; and (2) it provides additional light to each individual psalm on the basis of this internal structuring. Both these elements have the potential of uncovering the richer meaning of the Psalter as a whole as well as with respect to its various parts.[4]

Obviously, it is impossible to know exactly how the final form of the Psalter came together. Yet we can be fairly certain of some things. Essentially all evidence points to the fact that David composed a great number of the psalms in about 1000 B.C. We know from their content that some psalms were composed as much as five hundred years later, since they describe responses to Israel's exile and restoration (Pss. 137, 126). We know that at least one earlier arrangement of the psalms was made before the final form of the Psalter, as indicated by the postscript of Psalm 72. This concluding notation of the psalm says, "The prayers of David the son of Jesse are ended" (Ps. 72:20), and yet the Psalter contains a number of psalms attributed to David after Psalm 72. We know that an editor or editors arranged the collection of 150 psalms into five "books" of significantly uneven size, with forty-one psalms in Book I (Pss. 1–41), thirty-one psalms in Book II (Pss. 42–72), seventeen psalms in Book III (Pss. 73–89), seventeen psalms in Book IV

3. Frank-Lothar Hossfeld and Eric Zenger, *Psalms 2: A Commentary on Psalms 51–100* (Minneapolis: Fortress Press, 2005), xi.

4. Raymond B. Dillard and Tremper Longman III, *An Introduction to the Old Testament* (Leicester, UK: Apollos, 1995), 227, propose that the "primary literary context" for the study of a psalm is "not the psalms that border it, but the psalms that are generically similar to it." They further observe: "Except under rare circumstances, it is inappropriate to exegete a psalm in the literary context of the psalms that precede and follow it." Yet the many structural elements within the Psalter encourage careful consideration of a particular psalm's setting in the context of the psalm grouping in which it is found.

(Pss. 90–106), and forty-four psalms in Book V (Pss. 107–150). We also know that someone selected and distributed certain Davidic psalms into four major groupings across the five books, and quite likely chose at some points to leave earlier groupings intact.[5] Further, we know that some person or persons put together the entirety of the book as we now observe it.[6]

So who was this final editor/author/organizer or group of editors who constructed the final form of the Psalter? How did he or they do this work? We cannot know with certainty the answer to these questions. But to make this procedure more concrete, let us imagine that this person was someone like Ezra the scribe. If not Ezra, it could well have been some person or group of persons similar to Ezra.

So let us imagine our "Ezra" or some grouping of individuals similar to Ezra in the exilic and/or postexilic period of Israel's redemptive history as the final organizer(s) and editor(s) of the Psalter.[7] We know some things about Ezra. Like Paul his New Testament counterpart, he was a scribe of the law. Ezra is described as a priest and a teacher "well

5. Gerald Henry Wilson, *The Editing of the Hebrew Psalter* (Chico, CA: Scholars Press, 1985), 5, makes the valid point that the "prior existence" of individual collections "must have inhibited the editorial exercise of freedom in the final shaping of the psalms." Given the limitations of current sources, it is virtually impossible to reconstruct the historical process that was involved in rearranging Psalter materials. But it may be assumed that the integrity of the various psalms was scrupulously maintained.

6. Hossfeld and Zenger, *Psalms 2*, 1, offer a much more detailed hypothesis of the formation of the Psalter, including references to numerous composers, editors, collectors, and redactors who placed and re-placed individual psalms according to certain ideas, created their own psalms, sharpened and deepened theological profiles, drew from several partial psalters put together at different times, and finally shaped the book of Psalms as we now have it by a many-layered process rather than in a single action. These authors suggest that the first collection resembling Psalms 3–41 might have originated in the "late preexilic period," which would be as much as three hundred years after David, while the "final redaction" may be dated between 200 and 150 B.C. While many of their proposals make significant contributions to the analysis of the Psalter's structure, conclusions about specifics in the process of the Psalter's development must generally be regarded as tendentious in character. Solid evidence of particulars that made up the process over the five hundred years of the Psalter's development is simply not available.

7. Various proposals have dated the Psalter's completion as late as the second century B.C. or into the first century A.D. Even John Calvin in his comments on Psalms 74 and 79 leaves open the possibility of Maccabean psalms. *Commentary on the Book of Psalms* (Grand Rapids: Baker, 1993), 2:159, 281. But nothing inherent in the Psalter compels a date later than the time of Israel's return from exile, down to about 400 B.C.

versed in the Law of Moses, . . . a man learned in matters concerning the commands and decrees of the LORD for Israel" (Ezra 7:6, 11). He was a man who had "devoted himself to the study and observance of the Law of the LORD, and to teaching its decrees and laws in Israel" (Ezra 7:10). By *Law* or *Torah* is not meant merely the five books of Moses. Even these books must not be perceived as codifications designed to dictate every thought and action of the pious. *Law* or *Torah* was an elastic word that could include history, prophecy, poetry, and wisdom. This person, whoever he was, must have loved the whole of the Torah of the Lord, including the Psalms.

So our imagined "Ezra" first appears during the exile in Babylon. He might have been taken into exile as a young man with the first captives, like Daniel and Ezekiel. Or he might have been born in exile. But by the divine appointment of his life course, he stands among the celebrated scholars of God's Word in his day. He might even have authored some of the sacred writings, such as the books of Chronicles. Some years later, he appears among the leaders of Israel's worship who return to the Land of Promise.

Now into his hands, or the hands of a person or people like him, is placed the responsibility of ordering services for seeking God's face in worship among the Judean exiles in Babylon, and later in Judea after the return from exile. At his disposal is the collection or collections of psalms that have been handed down to him. For four to five hundred years, from the days of David in about 1000 B.C. to the events of Israel's tragic exile and meager restoration in around 586 and 536 to 515 B.C., these precious psalms have led God's people through every imaginable experience.

His task may be compared to that of a modern-day friend of a bride who has been asked to arrange the flowers for a wedding ceremony. It will be a large gathering. A thousand people might be in attendance. So will the person responsible for this artistic presentation in behalf of his close friend thoughtlessly arrange his collection of flowers into a shapeless mass, place them into a commonplace clay pot, and be done with the job? Of course not. His floral arrangement must be carefully crafted to enhance the beauty of every lily, rose, and iris.

5

In a similar way, the final editor (or editors) of the Psalter would have been quite deliberate in the arrangement of the assembled treasury of psalms. Very likely he (or they) would have accepted some arrangements that traditional usage had already established. But then he/they would have been quite deliberate in the placement of every psalm and grouping of psalms.

In considering the present arrangement of the Psalter, we see that a large grouping of psalms known to be David's has been positioned in the forefront of the collection. This grouping reflects the confrontation of David with numerous and varied enemies as he seeks to establish his messianic kingship (Book I, Psalms 1–41). Next our editor presents psalms declaring the victories of the Lord over the nations, while also depicting communications with the nations that climax in the prospect of a worldwide reign of David's son Solomon (Book II, Psalms 42–72). Then he offers a realistic picture of the conflict with the mighty "horns" of foreign powers that ultimately ends with the devastation of his people and the casting of Messiah's crown to the dust (Book III, Psalms 73–89). In response to this tragic note, he situates the stately psalm of Moses as a pivotal centerpiece of the Psalter. This majestic psalm thus serves as his introduction to the fourth book of the Psalms that leads God's people into a more mature perspective on the coming of the kingdom (Book IV, Psalms 90–106):

> Lord, you have been our dwellingplace through all generations. Before the mountains were born or you brought forth the earth and the world, from everlasting to everlasting you are God. (Ps. 90:1–2)

Having affirmed the Lord's dominion across the ages, he then places together a grouping of psalms that chant a favored refrain: "*Yahweh Malak*" ("The LORD is King") (Pss. 93, 96, 97, 99). In his final book, he calls for expressions of thanks and praise that serve as his climactic theme (Book V, Pss. 107–150). In recognition of the ongoing significance of David's role as the original creator of the Psalter, he has reserved a select number of David's psalms suitable to the time of Israel's exile (Pss. 138–145), which is the moment of the nation's history in which this editor has done the majority of his work. Our imagined ultimate

Psalter editor concludes this last book with a *"Hallelu-YAH* finale" that brings the whole collection to its climactic end (Pss. 146–150).

This abbreviated analysis of the arrangement of the Psalter is obviously an oversimplification. But that the book of Psalms has a structure should not be disputed. All the constituent elements of its magnificent complexity might never be discovered. But the architectonic structure clearly deserves further investigation. First consideration may be given to the basic structural elements in the Psalms.

2

BASIC STRUCTURAL ELEMENTS IN THE PSALMS

To grasp something of the extent of the structure within the Psalter, it might be helpful to observe some of the basic elements that combine to construct this majestic book of Scripture. At least twelve different elements of basic structure may be detected.

The Five Books

Among its most basic structural elements is the division of the Psalter into five "books." Initially it might seem altogether arbitrary that Jewish tradition has compared this fivefold division to the five books of Moses.[1] Indeed, efforts to compare each of the five books of the Psalms consecutively with the books of Genesis through Deuteronomy prove to be altogether unfruitful. Yet a more basic comparison of the Psalms with the Pentateuch might have genuine worth. As a serious corrective to the personalized, subjective reading of the Psalms, perceiving these poems as Torah, as instruction, as teaching for God's people concerning their way of faith and life, might provide a much more enriching approach to the Psalms.[2]

---

1. Some effort has been made to relate the five books to a traditional lectionary reading of the Pentateuch in a three-year cycle. But evidence for this relationship between the Pentateuch and the Psalms is lacking. Cf. Gerald Henry Wilson, *The Editing of the Hebrew Psalter* (Chico, CA: Scholars Press, 1985), 200–203.

2. For recent studies advocating this approach, see J. Clinton McCann, *A Theological Introduction to the Book of Psalms: The Psalms as Torah* (Nashville: Abingdon Press,

Some quite remarkable structures emerge when the orderings of these five books of the Psalms are considered more carefully. It is generally recognized that each of the books ends with a doxology. The wording of the four doxologies concluding the first four books is quite similar:

> May the LORD be praised [בָּרוּךְ יְהֹוָה], the God of Israel,
>> from everlasting to everlasting.
>> Amen and Amen. (Ps. 41:13, ending Book I)

> May the LORD God be praised [בָּרוּךְ יְהֹוָה אֱלֹהִים], the God of Israel
>> who alone does marvelous deeds.
> May his glorious name be praised forever;
>> may the whole earth be filled with his glory.
>> Amen and Amen. (Ps. 72:18–19, ending Book II)

> May the LORD be praised [בָּרוּךְ יְהֹוָה] forever!
>> Amen and Amen. (Ps. 89:52, ending Book III)

> May the LORD be praised [בָּרוּךְ־יְהֹוָה], the God of Israel,
>> from everlasting to everlasting.
> Let all the people say, "Amen!"
> Praise the LORD. (Ps. 106:48, ending Book IV)

The fifth book concludes with five *Hallelu-YAH* psalms (Pss. 146–150), which bring to a climax the previous four doxologies concluding Books I through IV.

The ultimate source of this fivefold division of the Psalter cannot be determined. Suffice it to say that this division into five books has been part and parcel of the Psalter from antiquity until today.

Groupings by Reference in Titles to Specific Individuals

One of the most obvious indicators of deliberate arrangement in the Psalter is the grouping of certain psalms by reference in their

---

1993); Gordon J. Wenham, *Psalms as Torah: Reading Biblical Song Ethically* (Grand Rapids: Baker Academic, 2012).

titles to specific individuals.[3] Most prominent in this area are four collections of psalms attributed to David, as indicated by the "By David" or "For David" or "About David" (לְדָוִד) phrase in their titles. The authenticity of Davidic authorship has been regularly questioned.[4] But both internal and external evidence support David's authorship of at least half the Psalter. This evidence includes the following: (1) Israel's historical records repeatedly affirm David as a composer of psalms and organizer of choirs to be accompanied by musical instruments. The consistency of this biblical witness that

3. Wilson, *Editing*, 139, notes the editorial shaping through reference to the names of authors in many psalm titles. But he also indicates his surprise at the "almost total absence of any explicit statements of organizational intent" in the Psalter. He observes that the titles of the individual psalms are only "descriptive" and not "organizational." Ibid., 140. He further indicates that outside the single postscript of Psalm 72:20, "the explicit organization of texts" is not a feature of the Psalter. Ibid., 141. Yet the groupings by attribution to specific individuals in the titles provide a prima facie case for intentional arrangement.

4. In the nineteenth century, basic skepticism regarding Davidic authorship of the psalms prevailed in many academic circles. Julius Wellhausen asserted that the psalms were "altogether the fruit" of the postexilic period and so none originated with David. *Prolegomena to the History of Ancient Israel* (Cleveland: World Publishing, 1961), 501. S. R. Driver, *Introduction to the Old Testament*, 9th ed. (Edinburgh: T&T Clark, 1913), 374, says that some of the psalms attributed to David do not display the "*freshness* and *originality* which we should expect in the founder of Hebrew Psalmody." (Emphasis added.) On the other hand, he asserts that "if Deborah, long before David's time, had 'sung unto Jehovah' (Judg. 5:3), there can be no *a priori* reason why David should not have done the same; and in 2 Sam. 23:1 the expression 'the sweet singer of Israel' implies that David was the author of religious songs." Ibid., 380. Criteria such as absence of "freshness" and "originality" applied by Driver are rather subjective, and cannot outweigh the multiple testimonies of authentic Davidic authorship. With their focus on cultic and form-critical matters related to the psalms, twentieth-century scholars Hermann Gunkel and Sigmund Mowinckel were willing to locate some psalms in the preexilic period. Gunkel attempts to trace the historical development of his various genres across the centuries, and concludes that some forms may be dated into the preexilic period. Cf. Hermann Gunkel and Joachim Begrich, *Introduction to Psalms: The Genres of the Religious Lyric of Israel*, trans. James D. Nogalski (Macon, GA: Mercer University Press, 1998), 319–32. Sigmund Mowinckel, *The Psalms in Israel's Worship*, two vols. in one, Biblical Resource Series (Grand Rapids: Eerdmans, 2004), 1:77, acknowledges that the "By David" title was "undoubtedly taken as an indication of authorship" in later times. But he interprets the phrase to mean "For David" rather than "By David." On the other hand, he affirms that because of their cultic types, there can be "no doubt" that psalmography in Israel "dates back to very old times." Ibid., 2:150. More recently, advocates of the "canonical criticism" pioneered by Brevard Childs have presumed to treat various psalms "as though" they were written by David, or to propose that various psalms have been "davidized" in a later age to give them more credibility. But the conclusion that such a process has taken place actually weakens rather than strengthens their credibility.

features David from every possible perspective as a creative musician with leadership roles in Israel's worship practices cannot be minimized. This description of David in the historical books of Scripture corresponds very closely to the picture of him that can be deduced from the headings as well as the substance of the psalms attributed to him. As a young man, he was recognized for his ability to accompany himself in his own musical performances (1 Sam. 16:14–23). Several of his poems appropriate for various occasions appear in the historical books (2 Sam. 1:17–27; 3:33–34; 22:1–51; 23:1–7). The musicians appointed by David perform as he directs them (1 Chron. 6:31; 15:16; 16:7; 25:1). Decades and centuries after David, the tradition still continues (2 Chron. 29:30; Ezra 3:10; Neh. 12:24–46; Amos 6:5). (2) The titles of no fewer than seventy-three psalms are best understood as attesting to Davidic authorship. The *leDavid* title may be interpreted to mean "By David," "For David," or "About David." But other psalms with the *lamed* prefix cannot mean "For Asaph" or "About the Sons of Korah." The natural meaning of the phrase in these titles is "By David." Fourteen psalm titles include reference to a specific incident in the life of David, are in the first person, and clearly intend to affirm Davidic authorship by the *lamed* prefix. Little reason exists not to regard the titles as basically trustworthy witnesses to Davidic authorship.[5] (3) The New Testament identifies David as the author of specific psalms (Pss. 2, 16, 32, 69, 95, 109, 110). In several of these cases, the argument based on the quoted psalm hinges on Davidic authorship (cf. Matt. 22:41–46 and parallels; Acts 2:22–31; 13:32–37; Rom. 4:1–8).

With these considerations in mind, we may conclude that particularly psalms in the first person attributed to David by their titles were composed by him. A few psalms without this indicator in their titles are interspersed among some of these Davidic collections. It could be supposed that these collections were assembled willy-nilly without rhyme or reason. But other manifestation of overall design

5. Derek Kidner, *Psalms 1–72: An Introduction and Commentary on Books I and II of the Psalms* (London: Inter-Varsity Press, 1973), 32–33, notes that the titles are part of the canonical Hebrew text, and that the Lord Jesus built his arguments on their statements. He concludes: "We need look no further than this for their authentication."

11

in the book of Psalms argues in favor of editorial intention. The collections are as follows:

- Book I, Psalms 3–41*[6]
- Book II, Psalms 51–71*
- Book V, Psalms 108–110
- Book V, Psalms 138–145

Only a very few psalms attributed to David appear outside these collections, which include Psalms 86 (Book III), 101, 103 (Book IV), 122, 124, 131, and 133 (Book V). A further analysis of the four major collections of Davidic psalms will be provided later in this volume.

Further groupings may be seen in the attribution of psalms to other individuals throughout the Psalter. Book II opens with a collection of psalms attributed to the "Sons of Korah" that represent approximately a third of the book (Pss. 42–49*; cf. also Pss. 84–88* attributed to the "Sons of Korah," which represent approximately a third of Book III). This allusion could be to contemporaries of David. At the same time, the phrase "Sons of Korah" could be assuming a "generational" perspective, embracing psalms that might have been composed decades after David's lifetime.[7] Book II concludes with a psalm attributed to Solomon (Ps. 72), and Book III opens with several psalms attributed to Asaph, representing approximately two-thirds of the book (Pss. 73–83). In a further instance of Psalter authorship with structural significance, Book IV opens with a psalm attributed to Moses (Ps. 90).[8] The fact that the various books of the Psalter are demarcated by psalms specifically attributed to different authors indicates the likelihood of intentional placement of these psalms by the final editor of the Psalter.[9] A few

---

6. The asterisk (*) indicates a grouping of psalms whose titles do not all specifically refer to David or some other individual.

7. Kidner, *Psalms 1–72*, 6, describes the sons of Korah as "a hereditary guild of temple officials."

8. A clear distinction in frequency of authorship indication may be seen in the comparison of Books I–III (Pss. 3–89), where only six psalms have no author indicated. But in Books IV and V (Pss. 90–150), only nineteen of sixty-one psalms indicate authorship.

9. See Wilson, *Editing*, 157, who discusses this positioning of differing authors in terms of "seams" within the book of Psalms. He speaks of "conscious editorial activity" in the designations of authorship.

psalms attributed to other individuals are scattered throughout the book of Psalms. Psalm 127, for instance, is attributed to Solomon, and functions as the middle psalm of the fifteen Psalms of Ascents. These various groupings and placements attributing authorship appear to be intentional rather than accidental.

The Two "Poetic Pillars"

Of primary importance in Psalter structure are the two "poetic pillars" that escort the reader into the temple of the book of Psalms, Psalms 1 and 2. Taken together, these two very brief psalms anticipate major themes that permeate all five books.[10] First among these themes is the contrast between the righteous and the wicked as they are judged on the basis of their response to God's revealed Torah, the law, the teaching, the instruction of the Lord.

Focus on the Torah

According to Psalm 1, the downward slope of the ungodly leads from

> walking in the counsel of the wicked, to
>> standing in the way of sinners, to
>>> sitting in the seat of scoffers. (Ps. 1:1)

Contrariwise, an entirely different way of life with a totally different destiny marks the righteous who love the law of the COVENANT LORD.

---

10. Wilson considers only Psalm 1 as constituting the introduction to the entire book of Psalms. Ibid., 204–7. Brevard S. Childs, *Introduction to the Old Testament as Scripture* (London: SCM Press, 1979), 516, states that the question whether Psalm 2 was conceived as a formal part of the introduction to the Psalter should be left open, since the evidence "is not sufficient to press the point." But the permeating concepts of kingship and kingdom of Yahweh and Messiah throughout the remainder of the Psalter virtually demand that Psalm 2 be joined with Psalm 1 in providing a proper introduction to the Psalter. In support of perceiving both Psalms 1 and 2 as introductory to the whole Psalter, see among others Jamie A. Grant, "The Psalms and the King," in *Interpreting the Psalms: Issues and Approaches*, ed. Philip S. Johnston and David G. Firth (Downers Grove, IL: InterVarsity Press, 2005), 108.

Throughout the Psalms, this contrast of people, path, and prospect appears repeatedly. The "wicked" are the "enemies," the "foes" of the righteous, so that the struggle of the two "seeds" depicted in Genesis 3:15 continues unabated throughout the five hundred years spanned by the Psalms.

At two other crucial points in the structure of the Psalter, additional Torah psalms appear. Psalm 19 and Psalm 119 combine to underscore the centrality of the Torah throughout the whole of the Psalter.

The Centrality of the Messiah

The second major theme found in these two poetic pillars that runs throughout the book of Psalms is the person of God's Messiah, his perpetual dynasty and his permanent dwellingplace.[11] From a redemptive-historical perspective, the Lord's covenant with David provides the essential theological framework for understanding the Psalms.[12] Climaxing the covenants made with Adam, Noah, Abraham, and Moses is God's covenant with David (2 Sam. 7:4–17). According to Psalm 2, the nations rage

> against the LORD
> and against his Messiah. (Ps. 2:2)

But the Lord has established his messianic king on Zion his holy hill. The decree of Yahweh says, "You are my Son" in accordance with the

11. Both for alliterative purposes when coupled with the word *dynasty* and for emphasis, the untraditional one-word spellings of *dwellingplace* and *restingplace* are used in this volume. Repeatedly throughout the Psalter, these two promises of *dynasty* and *dwellingplace/restingplace* encapsulate the covenant that God made with David, the primary author of the Psalms.

12. Hans-Joachim Kraus, *Theology of the Psalms* (Minneapolis: Augsburg, 1986), 175–76, cites Karl Barth as indicating that the historical experience of Israel must have been the source of all the various elements of the Psalter, and adds that it is "specifically" the "history of David" that must be understood as providing the basis for interpreting the Psalms. Kraus notes that " '*David*' " "provides the origin and the goal in terms of which the Psalms must ultimately be understood." By deliberately placing "David" in italics, Kraus may intend to refrain from identifying "David's" experience reported in the Psalms as the actual experience of the son of Jesse. If this is the case, Kraus has lost the force of authenticity behind the realities of history that provide the foundation for a proper perspective on God's redemptive working in time and history as the basis of the Psalter's message. Yet he notes that perceiving the historical person of David as the center of the Psalter prepares the way for understanding redemptive truth as ultimately embodied in the coming Messiah.

precise wording of the Davidic covenant (Ps. 2:7; cf. 2 Sam. 7:14). The nations, the ends of the earth, will be his possession. Kings and rulers of this world receive clear advice on dual points: "Serve the LORD" and "Do obeisance to the Son" (Ps. 2:6–8, 10–12). This all-embracing decree regarding the reign of God and his Anointed One from their united thrones in Zion sets the stage for the full development of the Psalter.

So these two opening psalms present in condensed poetic fashion the overarching message of the Psalter. God's law, the contrary responses of two groups of people to that law, and the outworking of the consequence of their responses are interrelated themes that permeate the Psalter. At the same time, two kings and two kingdoms merge into each other through the repeating message of the Psalms. David and his descendants will be established in a perpetual kingship at a particular locale. Yahweh rules over heaven and earth from eternity and throughout all time. Eventually, Messiah's kingship must merge with Yahweh's kingship so that the kingdoms of earth and heaven, of time and eternity, are one. This merger of the two kings and the two kingdoms permeates the theology of the Psalter. This perspective alone can explain how the concept of kingship in Israel continues long after kings no longer exist in the nation. It also explains how the kingship of Jesus as Messiah could merge so perfectly with God's kingship over the world.[13]

Three Torah Psalms Coupled with Three Messianic Psalms

As has been noted, the Psalter begins with a pronouncement of blessing on the person who delights in the "Torah of Yahweh" (Ps. 1:2). The word *Torah* derives from a term having the basic meaning "to teach." The "Torah of Yahweh" is the teaching, the instruction, the

---

13. "Israel continued to celebrate the righteous rule of its king long after the institution of kingship had been destroyed because the earthly king from the line of David had become a type of God's Messiah. Especially in Ps. 2 the psalm has been given an eschatological ring by emphasizing the kingship of God which God's anointed ruler merely represents." Brevard S. Childs, *Biblical Theology of the Old and New Testaments: Theological Reflection on the Christian Bible* (London: SCM Press, 1992), 193. Except for the last phrase characterizing Messiah's rule as being able to "merely represent" God's rule, this statement has captured an essential tenet of the theology of the Psalms. Both David and Christ did more than "merely represent" the Lord's rule.

wisdom for life that comes from the Lord. A legalistic view of life is the furthest thing possible from the proper understanding of Torah. Indeed, rules for life are involved. But Torah is much more. It speaks of a wholesome approach to life that comes from a full apprehension of the will of God for the well-being of human beings made in God's image.

So it is not surprising to find additional Torah psalms that serve as pivotal points in the Psalter. In three prominent cases, the Torah psalm is coupled with a messianic psalm (Pss. 1–2; Pss. 18–19; Pss. 118–119). Each of these couplings provides a major structural element in the Psalter.

The Acrostic Psalms

Situated across Books I and V of the Psalter are eight acrostic psalms (Pss. 9/10, 25, 34, 37; 111, 112, 119, 145). These unique psalms follow the order of the Hebrew alphabet in their sequence of verses. Numerous variations of this pattern occur, but the actuality of versification essentially in the order of the Hebrew alphabet is quite obvious. The role of these psalms in the structure of the Psalter will be explored later.

Groupings Celebrating the Kingship of Yahweh and His Messiah

The union of the rule of God and Messiah is a focal truth that runs through the Psalter. Three separate collections in three different books unite these two kingships.

A distinctive collection of five psalms (Pss. 20–24) connects with pivotal Psalm 18 as it declares the "victories" of the Lord's anointed king (Ps. 18:50). These same messianic victories are the object of the prayers of God's people (Ps. 20:5) and the occasion for their rejoicing (Ps. 21:1, 5). The unanswered puzzling of this messianic king ("My God, my God, Why . . . ?") eventually concludes with international and generational worship of the Lord who rules over the nations (Ps. 22:1, 27–31). Even the king-Messiah finds comfort among shadows as deep as death because the Lord himself is his Shepherd-King (Ps. 23:1, 4). Consummatively, the ancient gates of glory must lift up, that the Covenant Lord Almighty, the King of Glory, may come in (Ps. 24).

16

Four consecutive psalms in Book II proclaim Israel's God and his Messiah as sovereign over all the nations of the earth. In a most startling proclamation, the psalmist first hails the messianic king as the eternal God who has been anointed by his God (Ps. 45:6–7). The next psalm in this grouping of kingship psalms declares that the Covenant Lord Almighty will be "exalted among the nations, . . . exalted in the earth" (Ps. 46:10). He is "the great King over all the earth" (Ps. 47:2, 7). This Sovereign God over the nations permanently resides on Mount Zion, the city of the Great King (Ps. 48:2).

A grouping of psalms in Book IV employs a distinctive phrase to proclaim the Lord's kingship: *Yahweh Malak* ("The Lord is King") (Pss. 93, 96, 97, 99). The phrase underscores the permanence of the Lord's universal rule across all ages. The phrase occurs only once in Scripture outside this distinctive collection in Book IV of the Psalter (1 Chron. 16:31). In this passage, David celebrates the bringing up of the ark of the covenant, symbolizing the throne of God, to Jerusalem so that it becomes permanently located alongside David's messianic throne. In this context, it may be joyfully proclaimed:

> Let the heavens rejoice,
> Let the earth be glad;
> Let them say among the nations,
>   "*Yahweh Malak!*" (1 Chron. 16:31; cf. Ps. 96:10)

Other groupings of kingship psalms may be noted. But these three collections in three different books indicate a purposeful arrangement of this type of psalm.

Psalms of Ascents

Each of these fifteen psalms (Pss. 120–134) contains the heading "A Psalm of Ascents" (שִׁיר הַמַּעֲלוֹת).[14] The collection includes psalms of David, a psalm of Solomon, and a psalm referring to Israel's return

14. The heading of Psalm 121 reads slightly differently, with a *lamed* instead of the regular *he* prefix.

17

from exile. Yet the group is united as songs suitable for pilgrims either ascending to Jerusalem or returning from national exile.

Psalms of Historical Recollection

Two psalms at the conclusion of Book IV (Pss. 105–106) provide lengthy historical recollections of the Lord's dealings with his people in the past. Both these psalms mirror portions of the historical description of David's bringing up the ark of the covenant to Jerusalem as reported in the book of Chronicles (1 Chron. 16:7–36). As a consequence, both histories may be seen as focusing on the significant moment in redemptive history when God's throne was joined to David's throne. Psalm 78 is also a psalm of historical recollection, concluding with the establishment of David as the shepherd-king of his people.

A second collection of psalms of historical recollection appears in Book V (Pss. 135–137). These three psalms serve as a transition in Book V from the Psalms of Ascents (Pss. 120–134) to the final Davidic collection (Pss. 138–145).

Focal Messianic Psalms

Certain psalms stand out as having a distinctive focus on the messianic king promised in the Davidic covenant. Psalm 2 introduces the figure of Yahweh's Messiah to the Psalter. Psalm 22 serves as the focal point of a grouping of five psalms uniting two psalms about Messiah's kingship with two psalms about Yahweh's kingship (Pss. 20–24). Psalm 45 presents Messiah as God just before the grouping of three psalms that depict the reign of God over the nations in Book II (Pss. 46–48). Psalm 69 is quoted by three different authors of the New Testament, indicating its significance in shaping New Testament theology. Psalm 72, attributed to Solomon, climaxes Book II with a description of Messiah's universal rule. Psalm 80 presents a Messiah *ben* Joseph at the midpoint of Book III as the only hope for a devastated northern kingdom. Psalm 110 in Book V presents a single messianic person who is doubly anointed as both king and priest. Psalm 118 receives special New Testament recognition as the "Psalm Most Quoted" with its identification of Jesus as the expected messianic king.[15] The positioning of these focal messianic psalms at crucial points in various books of the Psalter seems clearly intentional rather than having occurred by haphazard circumstance.[16]

Psalms Confessing Sin

The several psalms confessing sin could overwhelm the guilty if all were grouped together, though a collection of four psalms each including confession of sin concludes Book I (Pss. 38–41). At first sight, their appearance throughout the Psalter might seem to be a random scattering. A reversal of expected chronological order appears when David's rejoicing that he has been forgiven (Ps. 32) precedes his confession of sin as he seeks forgiveness (Ps. 51).

Yet the Psalm 51 confession naturally and properly follows God's formal issuance of a "summons" to heaven and earth so that he may "judge his people" (Ps. 50:4). David as guilty king is the first to be called forth for judgment. In another instance of deliberate placement of a confessional psalm appropriate to its context, Psalm 106 explicitly identifies the sins of the psalmist's contemporaries with the repetitive sins of the fathers, which has led to their chastening by exile (Ps. 106:6). He concludes by placing a plea on the lips of his repentant companions: "Save us, O LORD our God, and *gather* us from the nations" (Ps. 106:47). These words have been placed so that they conclude Book IV while simultaneously leading naturally into the opening phrases of the following psalm as it introduces the

15. Divergent countings may identify Psalm 2 or Psalm 110 as the "Psalm Most Quoted" in the New Testament. Suffice it to say that all three of these psalms play a critical role in the formation of the theology of the New Testament.

16. Wilson, *Editing*, 162, places a number of these psalms under the usual category of "royal psalms." He notes that they are "widely distributed through the Psalter" and "show no editorial concern to group or otherwise mark them out." Yet though appearing individually rather than as a group, these focal messianic psalms have a structural role to play by their strategic placement. They might have been somewhat overpowering if they had all been assembled into one section of the Psalter. As they stand, they are scattered across various books of the Psalter.

fifth and final book of the Psalter: "Let the redeemed of the LORD say so—. . . those he *gathered* from the lands, from east and west, from north and south" (Ps. 107:3). The confession of sin by the psalmist has been critical in bringing about the restoration of the people.

Each of the five books of the Psalter contains its quota of psalms with serious confession of sin, though significantly more appear in Book I than in subsequent books. To a greater or lesser extent, the following psalms present the plea for forgiveness by the penitent sinner: Psalms 6, 25, 32, 38, 39, 40, 41 (Book I); Psalms 51, 65 (Book II); Psalms 78, 85 (Book III); Psalms 103, 106 (Book IV); Psalm 130 (Book V).

"Poetic Pyramid" Psalms

Distributed across various books of the Psalter are several groupings of psalms arranged in a symmetrical pattern with an equal number of psalms balancing one another on either side of a centralized psalm. The number of psalms included in these groupings varies from five to fifteen. These collections may be envisioned in the shape of a pyramid, with the central psalm serving as the pinnacle of the grouping. A fuller presentation of this psalm structure will be found in an excursus to Book V at the end of chapter 9.

Hallelu-YAH Groupings of Psalms

Three distinctive groupings of psalms introduce for the first time in the Bible the celebrative ejaculation *Hallelu-YAH*. The phrase means "All of you, Praise Yahweh," with the poetically abbreviated *YAH* substituting for *Yahweh*. This spontaneous declaration of praise to the Lord occurs in the Old Testament only in the book of Psalms. In the first instance, three *Hallelu-YAH* psalms have been situated so that they conclude Book IV of the Psalms (Pss. 104–106). Psalms 104 and 105 end with *Hallelu-YAH*, while Psalm 106 begins and ends with *Hallelu-YAH*.

A collection of seven psalms in Book V forms the second *Hallelu-YAH* grouping (Pss. 111–117). This collection has been placed so that it concludes the first portion of Book V immediately before the pivotal third Messiah-and-Torah coupling (Pss. 118–119). Jewish tradition has called the bulk of this collection the "*Hallel* of Egypt" because of the reference to Israel's coming out of Egypt in the central psalm of this grouping (Ps. 114). Only Psalm 114 of these seven psalms does not have the *Hallelu-YAH* formula of praise. Three *Hallelu-YAH* psalms precede Psalm 114 (Pss. 111–113), and three *Hallelu-YAH* psalms follow Psalm 114 (Pss. 115–117).

Without question the five concluding psalms (Pss. 146–150) that begin and end with a triumphant *Hallelu-YAH* have been deliberately placed as an appropriate finale to the entire Psalter. No more fitting collection could be imagined to climax this "Book of Prayers and Praises."

Conclusion regarding Basic Structural Elements

So the initial impression of a helter-skelter, discombobulated assembly of a variety of psalms must be reviewed in light of the obvious arrangement of psalms into various collections. Taken together, these various groupings just listed account for a large segment of the Psalter. Other groupings or interconnections bind the entire book of Psalms into a well-organized composition.

Acknowledging all these various structural elements of the Psalter does not mean that the book should be perceived as though it were a theological treatise setting forth its various topics in a predetermined logical order. The development across decades and centuries invariably meant fresh additions along the way. One author has offered an appropriate image of the Psalter's superstructure:

> Its structure is perhaps best compared with that of a cathedral built and perfected over a matter of centuries, in a harmonious variety of styles, rather than a palace displaying the formal symmetry of a single and all-embracing plan.[17]

Indeed, from the perspective of human production, "a single and all-embracing plan" that devised the whole of the book of Psalms could hardly have been possible. The very creation and collection of the

---

17. Kidner, *Psalms 1–72*, 7.

Psalter over a five-hundred-year span of history denied to any single person or a contemporaneous group the privilege of structuring the whole according to a predetermined plan. Yet by the "singular care and providence" of the Lord's sovereign purposes (Westminster Confession of Faith [WCF] 1.8), the awesome structure and substance of the Psalter is exactly what it is. To God be the glory for the incomparable majesty of his perfected Word.

3

THE REDEMPTIVE-HISTORICAL
FRAMEWORK OF THE PSALMS

Many studies have been made of various theological topics related to the Psalms.[1] It would be quite possible to construct a "theology of the Psalms" based on the principal *loci* of systematic theology. A doctrine of God, man, sin, salvation, and eschatology could be derived from the teaching of the various psalms. A study of this nature could prove to be quite useful.

But a more inductive approach to the theology of the Psalms would consider the message of the book in terms of its redemptive-historical framework. At first glance, it might appear that an approach to the Psalms from the perspective of the progress of redemptive history would not be very effective. It might be assumed that the Psalms concentrate essentially on one point in redemptive history, the time frame of David the king.

Even if that presumption were true, it could be quite productive to study the book of Psalms from the perspective of its locale in the period of King David. For that epoch climaxed the forward movement of God's redemptive purposes in history, so far as the Old Testament is concerned. After God's covenant with David, no further covenants were realized. The promise of a "new covenant" came through the Lord's prophets (Jer. 31:31–34; Ezek. 37:21–28). But it never was the intent of the Lord to institute any covenants for his Old Testament people as a national

1. See, for instance, the collection of essays in Philip S. Johnston and David G. Firth, eds., *Interpreting the Psalms: Issues and Approaches* (Downers Grove, IL: InterVarsity Press, 2005). Topics include "The Psalms and Distress," The Psalms and Praise," The Psalms and the King," "The Ethics of the Psalms," and "The Evangelists and the Psalms."

entity beyond the covenant with David. In David, the king had come and the kingdom had come. By the merger of God's throne with David's throne, Old Testament experience of redemption reached its apex. All the remainder of redemptive history in the Old Testament era throughout the critical days of Israel's succession of kings and prophets, including its exile and restoration, was lived out under God's covenant with David. Indeed, God's previous covenantal relations with his people had their continuing significance, as the psalms themselves demonstrate. But in terms of a redemptive-historical perspective, a major distinctive of the book of Psalms is its unfolding of the central aspects of God's covenant with David, which may be characterized as the "covenant of the kingdom."[2]

At the same time, it needs to be remembered that the material in the book of Psalms spans almost five hundred years of redemptive history. From the time of David in 1000 B.C. to the return from exile in 537 B.C., many events of redemptive history transpired. Not least among these was the establishment of the Davidic monarchy and its continuation across twenty generations, the destruction of both the northern and southern kingdoms of Israel and Judah, the exile into Assyria and Babylon, and the eventual return to the Land of Promise under the Medo-Persian Empire. It would actually be quite surprising if the book of Psalms did not reflect on many aspects of this lengthy historical process. For the people of God never wholly abandoned the worship of the God of their fathers, which would invariably have involved continual usage of the Psalms.

One clear insight into the worshipful awareness of the people of God across these five hundred years is the unabated appeal to the various covenants that preceded God's oath to David regarding the king and his kingdom.[3] The vital role in the Psalms of these sover-

---

2. The proposal of Gerald Henry Wilson, *The Editing of the Hebrew Psalter* (Chico, CA: Scholars Press, 1985), 143, that the addition of concrete historical circumstances in the life of David to particular psalms enables these psalms to function on a "more personal level" has some merit, so long as the connection with David is not regarded as fictitious. Wilson's legitimate observation could be enhanced by considering the increased richness of personal application if David is regularly perceived as the covenantal head of the community. Transference of value in the Psalms is not simply a matter of one person (David or the psalmist) to another person (the contemporary reader), but primarily from covenantal head to the people he represents.

3. Raymond B. Dillard and Tremper Longman III, *An Introduction to the Old Testament* (Leicester, UK: Apollos, 1995), 228, recognize the centrality of the covenant idea as a

eignly established relationships between God, humanity, his people, and the world that climaxed in the covenant with David may be summarized as follows:[4]

God's Covenant at Creation[5]

The prophet Jeremiah speaks of God's covenant "with the day and with the night" (Jer. 33:20; cf. Jer. 31:35), referring to his purposeful ordering of the original cosmos. So the psalmist affirms:

> The day is yours,
>> and yours also the night;
>> you established the sun and moon. (Ps. 74:16)

Not only day and night, but summer and winter, along with all the boundaries of the earth, are acknowledged to be his handiwork (Ps. 74:17). He formed the mountains by his power (Ps. 65:6). The heavens and the earth are his, for he created north and south, including specifically mounts Tabor and Hermon (Ps. 89:11–12). Indeed:

> In his hand
>> are the depths of the earth,
>> and the mountain peaks
> belong to him.

---

principal focus of the Psalter. They affirm that covenant "is a concept that ties together many strands of the theology of the Psalms."

4. The term *berith* occurs twenty-one times in the Psalms, not including the two instances of its apparent reference to musical tunes in two psalm titles (Pss. 60, 80). Twenty instances refer to divine covenants, while Psalm 83:5 refers to a human covenant. The uses of the word are fairly evenly divided among the five books. Only in Psalm 105:8–10, 42 does the term refer specifically to the Abrahamic covenant. In a number of psalms it refers to the Mosaic covenant. For a fuller discussion of the nature of a divine covenant in Scripture, see O. Palmer Robertson, *The Christ of the Covenants* (Phillipsburg, NJ: Presbyterian and Reformed, 1980), 3–15.

5. It may be objected that the term *covenant* is never used in the early chapters of Genesis to describe the relation of God to the creation. Yet the scattered references in Scripture are enough to justify the application of the term to the creational order (cf. Isa. 24:4–6; Jer. 33:19–21; Hos. 6:7). Cf. the discussion in Robertson, *The Christ of the Covenants*, 18–25.

The sea is his,
    for he made it,
and his hands
    formed the dry land. (Ps. 95:4–5)

Other gods are idols, but the Lord made the heavens (Ps. 96:5). He set the earth on its foundations. He covered it with the deep, and the waters stood above the mountains. At his rebuke, the waters fled. They flowed over the mountains and went down into the valleys (Ps. 104:5–8). Five times over in five different psalms of Book V, the refrain describes God as "Maker of heaven and earth" (Pss. 115:15; 121:2; 124:8; 134:3; 146:6). In all these expressions, the psalmist affirms the beauty and order of God's work in creation.

The original *creational ordinances of labor, marriage, and Sabbath* appear repeatedly as central themes in the Psalms. In noting the role of mankind as ruler over the earth, the psalmist declares, "The highest heavens belong to the LORD, but the earth he has given to man" (Ps. 115:16). He can only marvel at humanity's responsibility from the time of creation to "rule over the fish of the sea and the birds of the air and over every living creature that moves on the ground" (Gen. 1:28b):

When I consider your heavens, the work of your fingers,
the moon and the stars which you have set in place,

what is man that you are mindful of him,
the son of man that you care for him?

You made him a little lower than the heavenly beings
and crowned him with glory and honor.

You made him ruler over the works of your hands;
you put everything under his feet:
    all flocks and herds,
        and the beasts of the field,
    the birds of the air,
        and the fish of the sea,
        all that swim the paths of the seas. (Ps. 8:3–8)

This particular psalm (Ps. 8) functions significantly when the various messages of the psalms to "Everyman" are being considered. Numerous psalms come from the pen of David as Israel's messianic king, which explains the large number of psalms in the first person. But if "Everyman" is ruler over all of God's creation, if according to Psalm 8 "Everyman" is a king in his own right, then the various messages of the various psalms by King David may be variously applied to "Everyman."

The psalmist also celebrates the sustaining powers of the Creator God, climaxing with the provision of food for all his creatures, including humanity, as ordered at creation:

> He makes springs pour water into the ravines;
> it flows between the mountains.
>
> They give water to all the beasts of the field;
> the wild donkeys quench their thirst.
>
> The birds of the air nest by the waters;
> they sing among the branches.
>
> He waters the mountains from his upper chambers;
> the earth is satisfied by the fruit of his work.
>
> He makes grass grow for the cattle,
> and plants for man to cultivate—
>> bringing forth food from the earth:
>> wine that gladdens the heart of man,
>> oil to make his face shine,
>> and bread that sustains his heart. (Ps. 104:10–15)

Yet humanity's enjoyment of this bountiful provision depends on man's labor to "subdue" the earth, as indicated at creation (Gen. 1:28):

> The lions roar for their prey
> and seek their food from God.

The sun rises, and they steal away;
they return and lie down in their dens.

Then man goes out to his work,
to his labor until evening. (Ps. 104:21–23)

In similar fashion, the *creational mandate of marriage* to "multiply and replenish the earth" (Gen. 1:28) provides an additional cause for celebration by the psalmist:

Sons are a heritage from the LORD,
    children a reward from him.
Like arrows in the hands of a warrior
    are sons born in one's youth.
Blessed is the man whose quiver is full of them. (Ps. 127:3–5)

Your wife will be like a fruitful vine
    within your house;
Your sons will be like olive shoots
    around your table. (Ps. 128:3)

So the Psalms celebrate marriage and procreation as instituted at creation. The repeated emphasis on the role of the genealogical principle in the Psalms underscores the continuing significance of the creational ordinance of marriage.[6]

The third *creational mandate of the Sabbath* arises from the fact that God "blessed" the Sabbath day and "sanctified" it (Gen. 2:3). Humanity is the particular beneficiary of this blessing and sanctifying of the Sabbath by God. The "rest" from work every seventh day is one of God's greatest blessings. Alongside the blessing of rest is the sanctifying of the day, which means that it has been set apart for God and for God alone. This focusing on God alone for a whole day each week indicates that he must be worshiped on that day, for how can God be contemplated in all his goodness and glory without worshiping him? "Come, let us worship and bow down,

6. For further consideration of the role of the generational principle in the Psalter, see the treatment later in this chapter of God's promise regarding the "seed" in the Abrahamic covenant.

let us kneel before the LORD our Maker" (Ps. 95:6) joins man's role as worshiper to God's role as Creator. The whole of the Psalter is designed to provide a framework for God's people to approach the Lord properly in worship, whatever may be their outward or inward life circumstance.

Yet the psalmist is also fully aware of the "eschatological" character of the Sabbath principle. He declares that the "rest" of God in creation continues as a consummating factor in redemption. Because Israel hardened its heart during the days of its wilderness wandering, God declared in his justified wrath, "They shall not enter into my Rest" (Ps. 95:11). This rest of redemption, symbolized in the peaceful possession of the Land of Promise, existed as a prospect for God's people in the days of Moses and Joshua. At the same time, God's rest ("my" rest) continues until today. With rich biblical-theological insight, the writer to the Hebrew Christians in the days of the New Testament concludes that "there remains a rest for the people of God" on the basis of this statement in Psalm 95 (Heb. 3:7–4:11). It may be correctly observed that little or nothing is specifically said in the Psalms about the fourth commandment regarding Sabbath observance despite all the emphasis on worship. Yet the broader dimensions of the Sabbath principle find explicit expression in the Psalms through its constant summons to worship.[7]

In terms of *rest* as a larger dimension of the Sabbath principle, the psalmist joins the indicative with the imperative to show that *rest* is a present possession while also being a blessing yet to be experienced. Even as he undergoes assault intended to topple him, the psalmist declares:

> My soul finds rest in God alone;
> my salvation comes from him. (Ps. 62:1)

7. Cf. Gordon J. Wenham, *Psalms as Torah: Reading Biblical Song Ethically* (Grand Rapids: Baker Academic, 2012), 103. Wenham expresses puzzlement that the fourth commandment is "completely ignored" by the Psalms. He makes no mention of the foundational rooting of the *rest* concept in the Sabbath, which finds significant exposition in the Psalms. The interconnections among the creational rest of the Sabbath, the conquest-rest of Joshua, the Psalter's rest of Psalm 95, and the consummate rest that remains for the people of God are brilliantly explored by the New Testament writer of the letter to the Hebrews (Heb. 3:7–4:11). For a discussion of the intimate interplay of these various biblical concepts of *rest*, see O. Palmer Robertson, *God's People in the Wilderness: The Church in Hebrews* (Fearn, Ross-shire, Scotland: Christian Focus Publications, 2009), 66–71; 106; *The Christ of the Covenants*, 68–74.

But simultaneously he must admonish himself:

> Find rest, O my soul, in God alone;
>   my hope comes from him. (Ps. 62:5)

In a psalm that offers a sevenfold encouragement to those who trust God that they will enter the "rest" of inheriting the land, the poet declares:

> A little while, and the wicked will be no more; . . .
> But the meek will inherit the land
>   and enjoy great peace. (Ps. 37:10–11; cf. vv. 3, 9, 22, 27, 29, 34)

Even the self-testimony of the psalmist that he will "lie down and sleep in peace" despite all the machinations of his enemies (Ps. 4:8; cf. Ps. 3:5) may be read as fulfillment of the blessing pronounced in anticipation of the inheritance of the Promised Land: "I will grant peace in the land, and you will lie down and no one will make you afraid" (Lev. 26:6). It may be assumed that in his observance of the commandments, statutes, and ordinances of the law, the psalmist would have respected the worshipful rest of one day in seven (Ex. 20:8–11; 31:12–17; Deut. 5:12–15). He would have rejoiced whenever someone invited him to "rest in the shadow of the Almighty" (Ps. 91:1b; cf. Ps. 122:1). But in the larger dimensions of the forthcoming "rest," he would have regularly affirmed that there remained a "rest" for the people of God (Ps. 95:11; cf. Heb. 4:3–11).

So the Psalms display ample knowledge of the foundational ordinances arising from creation. The Sabbath, marriage, and labor are all regularly celebrated by the psalmist. The authors of the various psalms indicate that these orderings of creation deserve to be constantly rehearsed among the worshiping community.

God's Covenant Initiating Redemption

Immediately upon opening the book of Psalms, the reader is struck with the intensity of a struggle between the *righteous* and the *wicked*.

Particularly as a person reads through Book I (Pss. 1–41), he finds himself confronted constantly with this conflict between God's people and their evil foes. By the time the reader gets to Book III (Pss. 73–89), the adversary has swollen to the point of being identified with international armies invading the sacred lands and places of God's people.

How is this conflict to be understood? Is David a person with an imbalanced personality who sees all people who disagree with him as his "enemies"? Or is this aspect of the Psalter to be discarded as irrelevant to the modern reader, particularly in places where the psalmist calls down curses on his enemies?

"I shall put enmity between you and the woman, and between your seed and her seed" clearly indicates the source of this enmity among humans. As a primary factor in his redemptive initiatives, God himself declares that he is the One who will initiate this enmity. For warfare with Satan and his seed is essential to the causes of redemption (Gen. 3:15a). This God-initiated enmity offers the first ray of redemptive hope. This hope will be realized only through a prolonged "struggle of the seeds." This struggle must ultimately focus on a singular seed, a "he" who will crush the archenemy's head even as the archenemy crushes his heel (Gen. 3:15b).

In this original context of the "struggle of the seeds" may be found the key to the unending conflict between the *righteous* and the *wicked* that permeates the Psalms. According to the psalmist:

> Even from birth the wicked go astray;
> from the womb they are wayward and speak lies.
>
> Their venom
> Is like the venom of a snake,
> like that of a cobra that has stopped its ears. (Ps. 58:3–4)

Among the sons of men, "there is no one who does good. . . . All have turned aside, they have together become corrupt; there is no one who does good, not even one" (Ps. 14:1, 3).

Quite interestingly, the psalmists develop the concept of the original degeneracy and total depravity of humanity with an intensity comparable to the denunciations of Israel's prophets. So much so that when the apostle Paul wishes to present a montage of humanity's inherent corruption, he collects several passages from the Psalms (Rom. 3:10–14, quoting Pss. 14:1–3; 5:9; 140:3; and 10:7), while citing only one passage from the Prophets (Rom. 3:15–18, quoting Isa. 59:7–8).

At the same time, the psalmist could almost be said to have a fixation on "death" as the consequence of the violation of the original bond between God and humanity. "In the day you eat of it, you shall surely die" (Gen. 2:17c) finds its solemn echo throughout the Psalms.[8] Death is the last great enemy (1 Cor. 15:26) and finds ample room to make its bittering presence known in each of the five books of the Psalms.

Recognizing the brevity of human life inevitably ushers in the waiting specter of death. The psalmist even pleads for a realistic perspective on the length of his own life:

> Show me, O LORD, my life's end and the number of my days;
> let me know how fleeting is my life.
>
> You have made my days a mere handbreadth;
> the span of my years is as nothing before you.
>> Each man's life is but a breath. *Selah*
>
> Man is a mere phantom as he goes to and fro.
>> He bustles about,
>>> but only in vain;
>> he heaps up wealth,
>>> not knowing who will get it. (Ps. 39:4–6)

---

8. J. Clinton McCann, *A Theological Introduction to the Book of Psalms: The Psalms as Torah* (Nashville: Abingdon Press, 1993), 158, asserts that "it is not at all clear that the humans would have lived forever if they had not sinned. . . . The punishment for sin was not physical death." He concludes: "If we accepted our lives as a gift of God, . . . then physical death would be no problem." Ibid., 159. The ramifications of his assertion are rather large, affecting views of incarnation, atonement, and resurrection. Jesus took on mortal flesh—flesh so that he might die physically in the place of sinners who deserved physical death (Heb. 2:14–15). For the apostle Paul, deliverance from the curse of sin comes only with the resurrection of Christ's body: "And if Christ has not been raised, your faith is futile; you are still in your sins" (1 Cor. 15:17). From a pastoral perspective, it is rather difficult to imagine a circumstance in which the pastor would attempt to comfort the bereaved by explaining that the death of a wife, a child, a mother, or a brother is "no problem."

On the one hand, death appears as the just deserving of the wicked. The psalmist prays: "Let death take my enemies by surprise; let them go down alive to the grave" (Ps. 55:15). He is confident that God will bring down the wicked by a premature death to the pit of corruption: "Bloodthirsty and deceitful men will not live out half their days" (Ps. 55:23).

On the other hand, the psalmist has experienced deliverance from death, and anticipates further divine interventions. From his youth he has faced the prospect of death (Ps. 88:15). The cords of death entangled him; the anguish of the grave overwhelmed him. But he called on the Lord, who delivered his soul from death, his eyes from tears, his feet from stumbling, so he could continue to walk before the Lord in the land of the living (Ps. 116:3–4, 8–9).

These verses represent only a smattering of the many passages in the Psalms that deal with the subject of death.[9] This unnatural conclusion to every human life can be understood only in the context of the original threat to the original man: "In the day you eat of it, you shall surely die" (Gen. 2:17c).

The prospect of redemption introduces the hope of ultimate deliverance from death. Indeed, the constant dread of death in the Psalter has been interpreted by some to mean that the psalmist saw no hope beyond the grave. But a review of these passages that express a sense of hopelessness in the face of death makes it apparent that many of the passages allude to premature death, or death at the hands of violent enemies. Yet the psalmist may also say, "Even though I walk through the valley of the shadow of death, I shall fear no evil" (Ps. 23:4).

Beyond this repeated expression of concern over death is the hope sometimes expressed of resurrection into life, body and soul. The psalmist draws a vivid contrast between the end of those who trust in themselves, and those who trust in God:

9. References to death are scattered throughout all five books of the Psalter, underscoring its significance in the thought of the psalmist. The following passages may be noted: Book I—Pss. 6:5; 9:13, 17; 13:3; 18:4–5; 22:15; 23:4; 30:3, 9; 33:19; 39:4–6, 11. Book II—Pss. 49:10, 14, 17; 55:15, 23; 56:13; 68:20. Book III—Pss. 73:19; 86:13; 88 (many references). Book IV—Pss. 90:3, 5, 7, 9–10; 94:17, 21; 102:3–11, 20, 23–26; 103:15–16. Book V—Pss. 107:18, 20; 115:17; 116:3, 8, 15; 141:8.

Like sheep [those who trust in themselves] are destined for the grave,
and death will feed on them.

The upright will rule over them in the morning;
their forms will decay in the grave, far from their princely mansions.

But God will redeem my life from the grave;
he will surely take me to himself. (Ps. 49:14–15)

Elsewhere the psalmist declares, "You will not allow your holy one to see corruption" (Ps. 16:10); "In righteousness I will see your face; when I awake, I will be satisfied with seeing your likeness" (Ps. 17:15). Though struggling seriously with the prosperity of the wicked in this life, the psalmist reaches a positive conclusion:

I am always with you;
    you hold me by my right hand.
You guide me with your counsel,
    and afterward you will take me into glory. (Ps. 73:23–24)

So the anticipation of redemption from the grave overcomes the permeating awareness of the inevitability of death. The psalmist is fully conscious of his need for total deliverance from the last great enemy, and attests to his expectation of this deliverance.

God's Covenant with Noah

Only Psalm 29 alludes to God's covenant with Noah by an explicit mention of the flood.[10] But this singular reference establishes dramati-

---

10. The term *mabbul* is found only here and in the record of Noah's flood in Genesis 6–11. In the pointing of the Massoretes, it is "the" flood, not "a" flood. Cf. Joseph Addison Alexander, *The Psalms: Translated and Explained* (Grand Rapids: Zondervan, 1864; repr., n.d.), 128: "The God whose voice now produces these effects is the God who sat enthroned upon the deluge, and this same God is still reigning over nature and the elements, and is able to control them for ever." Says Artur Weiser, *The Psalms: A Commentary* (London: SCM Press, 1959), 265: "Just as he did in the days when the great flood of waters came upon the earth and all men died, so today, too, the Lord still sits enthroned in sublime imperturbability as the victor over the powers of chaos—and as the King he will continue to do so in all eternity."

cally a framework both of fear of divine judgment for the wicked and of unshakable confidence for the righteous, as did the floodwaters of Noah.[11] A violent thunderstorm sets the stage in which the "voice of Yahweh" speaks through repeated explosions of thunder. Seven times over, *kol Yahweh* (קוֹל יְהוָה), the "voice of Yahweh," speaks by the thunder. His voice breaks the cedars, shakes the desert, and strips the forests bare (Ps. 29:5–9). Climactically the psalmist recalls that momentous event of flood-destruction, characterized in the Septuagint (LXX) as "the cataclysm" (τὸν κατακλυσμὸν—Ps. 29:10). By a distinction of verbal forms, the psalm declares, "Yahweh *sat* [enthroned] at the flood [יָשָׁב], and *continues to sit* [enthroned] [וַיֵּשֶׁב] forever."[12] The

11. Early treatments of proposed parallels between Psalm 29 and Canaanite and Ugaritic materials may be found in Harold Louis Ginsberg, "A Phoenician Hymn in the Psalter" (paper presented at Atti del XIX Congresso Internazionale degli Orientalisti, Rome, 1935), 472–76; Theodor Gaster, "Psalm 29," *Jewish Quarterly Review* 37 (1946): 55–65. Though affirming the Canaanite origin of Psalm 29, Ginsberg concludes by appropriately asking the "most obvious question," which is "how in the world" (!) did a Canaanite psalm "find its way into the Israelite liturgy?" Ginsberg, "Phoenician Hymn," 475. He falters in his several hypothetical answers to his own query. Hans-Joachim Kraus, *Psalms 1–59: A Commentary* (Minneapolis: Augsburg, 1988), 346, supports the "probability" that a Canaanite Baal hymn was handed down to Israel without radical revision. See ibid., 347, for further bibliography promoting this view. For a thorough treatment of the possibility of parallels between Ugaritic materials and Psalm 29, see Yitzhak Avishur, *Studies in Hebrew and Ugaritic Psalms* (Jerusalem: Magnes Press, 1994). After a detailed analysis of the relevant texts and secondary literature, his conclusions are that "there is no justification for assuming that Canaanite psalms are found in the Bible.... Similarly, we conclude that Ps. 29 is not a Canaanite psalm (in contrast to the regnant scholarly view)." Ibid., 7. He specifically rejects Ginsberg's claims regarding the pagan elements in Psalm 29 (ibid., 44), as well as his assertions that the praise for God's voice in Psalm 29 was adapted from praise for the voice of the Syrian storm god (ibid., 45), and that the toponyms *Lebanon* and *Sirion* "cannot serve as conclusive proof" of the psalm's Canaanite provenance (ibid., 47). After over seventy pages of detailed analysis of Psalm 29 in terms of its possible relationship to Canaanite materials, Avishur concludes that despite the affinities, Psalm 29 differs from Ugaritic literature in that (1) some words of fundamental importance in Psalm 29 do not occur in the known vocabulary of Ugaritic or Phoenician; (2) roots corresponding to the central theological concepts appear in Ugaritic, "but not in the same forms or usages as in Ps. 29"; and (3) the stylistic patterns and literary forms in Psalm 29 are "far more complex and well-developed than those appearing in Ugaritic literature." Ibid., 110. The "glorification of Yahwe's voice (thunder)" (Ginsberg, "Phoenician Hymn," 472) is much better understood as originating in connection with the manifestation of Yahweh's lordship over the flood, as indicated in the psalm itself (Ps. 29:10), than of pagan images of Baal's roars.

12. For the distinction of tenses in the Hebrew text, see Derek Kidner, *Psalms 1–72: An Introduction and Commentary on Books I and II of the Psalms* (London: Inter-Varsity Press, 1973), 127. S. R. Driver, *A Treatise on the Use of the Tenses in Hebrew* (Oxford:

term for "flood" (מַבּוּל) occurs only here in the Old Testament and also repeatedly in the narrative of Noah's flood (Gen. 6–11). As Noah's "storm of all storms" struck terror into the hearts of the wicked, so thunderstorms ever since continue to strike terror into the hearts of unbelievers. At the same time, the thunder that terrifies the unrepentant sinner in its display of the unrestrainable power of the Almighty can offer comfort to the believer. According to one commentator:

> Psalm 29 has often been used as the psalm for the first Sunday after Epiphany, when the focus is on the baptism of Jesus. The choice is a profound interpretation of the occasion. The liturgical setting connects the psalm's mighty theophany with the quiet epiphany in the waters of the Jordan. The voice of the LORD in the thunderstorm is paired with the voice from heaven saying, "This is my Son." The storm says, "This is my cosmos"; the baptism, "This is my Christ." The two go inseparably together. The Christology is not adequate unless its setting in cosmology is maintained. The Old Testament doxology is necessary to the gospel.[13]

Psalm 29 concludes this dramatic witness to the power of Yahweh by reference to the "calm after the storm." His concluding blessing of "peace" reminds of the rainbow arching the flood. The Lord pronounces his refreshing benediction:

> Yahweh gives strength
>   to his people;
> Yahweh blesses his people
>   with [all-embracive] *shalom*. (Ps. 29:11)[14]

Clarendon Press, 1892), 90–91, discusses the use of the imperfect with waw consecutive in which "the action, or its results, continues into the writer's present." Yahweh "sat" at the deluge, and "continues sitting" as King forever. Says John Goldingay, *Psalms, Volume 1: Psalms 1–41* (Grand Rapids: Baker, 2006), 420f.: "the psalm asserts that there was such a moment [when Yahweh asserted his sovereignty], and that it had permanent consequences. That assertion of authority would then last 'forever.'"

13. James Luther Mays, *Psalms*, Interpretation, A Bible Commentary for Teaching and Preaching (Louisville: John Knox Press, 1994), 138.

14. Cf. Franz Delitzsch, *Biblical Commentary on the Psalms* (Grand Rapids: Eerdmans, 1959), 1:373: "He . . . blesses with peace, while the tempests of His wrath burst over their

So the psalmist offers his ongoing testimony to the biblical-theological significance of Noah's flood. God forever reigns as King over every storm and tsunami that sweeps the face of this earth. God's covenant with Noah ensures both consummative devastation for the wicked and all-encompassing blessing for the righteous.

God's Covenant with Abraham and the Patriarchs

As in the narrative of Genesis, so in the Psalms the covenant with Abraham and his descendants begins with the sovereign choice of God. From among all the idol-worshipers on the other side of the River, Abraham is the one person divinely chosen (Gen. 12:1; Josh. 24:2–3). He is God's servant, and his seed are the "chosen" ones (Ps. 105:6). With Abraham and his seed God took the initiative to "cut a covenant" (Ps. 105:9–10). This solemn life-and-death commitment of the Almighty to his "chosen ones" embraces "a thousand generations" (Ps. 105:8). Consequently, this covenant extends down from Abraham across five hundred years of passing time to Moses, who is also identified as his "chosen one" (Ps. 106:23). The term also embraces the nation as a whole:

He brought out his people with rejoicing,
his chosen ones with shouts of joy. (Ps. 105:43)

Praise the LORD, for the LORD is good;
sing praise to his name, for that is pleasant.
For the LORD has chosen Jacob to be his own,
Israel to be his treasured possession. (Ps. 135:3–4)

Eventually David emerges as the one "chosen" by God to be Israel's king, and Mount Zion is designated as his "chosen" dwellingplace. The LORD OF THE COVENANT declares:

---

foes. How expressive is *shalom* as the closing word of this particular Psalm! It spans the Psalm like a rainbow. The opening of the Psalm shows us the heavens opened and the throne of God in the midst of the angelic songs of praise, and the close of the Psalm shows us, on earth, His people victorious and blessed with peace . . . in the midst of Jahveh's voice of anger, which shakes all things. *Gloria in excelsis* is its beginning, and *pax in terris* its conclusion."

> I have cut a covenant with my chosen one,
>> I have sworn to David my servant,
> I will establish your line forever
>> and make your throne firm through all generations. (Ps. 89:3–4)

> For the LORD has chosen Zion,
>> he has desired it for his dwelling:
> "This is my restingplace for ever and ever;
>> here I will sit enthroned, for I have desired it." (Ps. 132:13–14)

In his turn, the psalmist offers a personal plea that he, too, may experience the divine grace of inclusion among God's "chosen ones":

> Remember me, when you show favor to your people,
> help me when you save them,
>> that I may enjoy the prosperity of your chosen ones,
>> that I may share in the joy of your nation
>> and join your inheritance in giving praise. (Ps. 106:4–5)

As various people read the Psalms in faith, they in their turn may join in this plea for themselves.

Appropriately rendered as the "elect" of God by the Septuagint, this covenantal choice of Abraham becomes the basis for the threefold promise of land, seed, and blessing to the patriarch and his descendants (Gen. 12:1–3). These three mainstay promises of the covenant continually reappear in the Psalms. To Abraham, Isaac, Jacob, and the nation of Israel the promise of the land remains secure (Ps. 105:8–11). Seven times over in one psalm, "inheriting the land" promised to Abraham becomes the focus of blessing for the Lord's covenant people (Ps. 37:3, 9, 11, 22, 27, 29, 34). God's promise for the weak and threatened is that he will eventually bless him "in the land" (Ps. 41:2).

In terms of God's promise to Abraham regarding the "seed," the generational focus of the Psalms permeates the hope of the future. The psalmist composes his poem to be sure that the current generation will tell the "next generation" the Lord's work in establishing Jerusalem as the city of the Great King (Ps. 48:12–13). In anticipating his rehearsal of the "mighty acts of God" across the centuries, the psalmist expects his message to span at least three or possibly four generations:

> I will utter hidden things, things from of old—
>> what we have heard and known,
>> what our fathers have told us.
> We will not hide them from their children;
> we will tell the next generation
>> the praiseworthy deeds of the LORD,
>> his power, and the wonders he has done.
> He decreed statutes for Jacob and established the law in Israel,
>> which he commanded our forefathers to teach their children,
>>> so the next generation would know them,
>>> even the children yet to be born,
>>> and they in turn would tell their children.
> Then they would put their trust in God
>> and would not forget his deeds
>> but would keep his commands. (Ps. 78:2–7)

This expectation of the seed climaxes with the promise given to King Messiah regarding his offspring:

> Your sons will take the place of your fathers;
> you will make them princes throughout the land. (Ps. 45:16)

The psalmist then declares his commitment to extend this message regarding the promised Messiah to the generations to come:

> I will perpetuate your memory through all generations;
> therefore the nations will praise you for ever and ever. (Ps. 45:17)

In terms of the *blessing* promised to and through Abraham, the various psalmists pronounce their benedictions throughout the book.[15] One distinctive merger of covenantal blessing occurs when a psalmist unites the Lord's covenantal promise that in Abraham

---

15. The term for "blessed" (אֶשֶׁר) occurs twenty-five times in the Psalter in twenty-five different psalms, covering a number of circumstances.

39

all the nations would be blessed with the priestly benediction of the Mosaic covenant. First the psalmist quotes the opening lines of the Aaronic blessing:

> May God be gracious to us and bless us
> and make his face shine upon us. (Ps. 67:1; cf. Num. 6:24–25)

But then he broadens the recipients of the blessing so that it reaches beyond Israel to all nations:

> That your ways
>   may be known on earth,
> your salvation
>   among all nations. (Ps. 67:2)

Then the psalmist extends his benedictory pronouncement in a manner that anticipates Paul the apostle's profound undulation of blessing that moves from Israelite to all nations and then back again to Israelite (Rom. 11:11–36). The blessing of Israel is pronounced over the nations so that "all the peoples" may praise God. As a consequence of this blessing on the nations:

> *Then* the land will yield its harvest,
> and God, our God, will bless us.
>   God will bless us,
>   and all the ends of the earth will fear him. (Ps. 67:6–7)

How glorious is this universal, good-news gospel that first blesses Israel, then all the nations, and then again Israel! The one who comprehends the length and breadth and depth and height of God's great purposes for all nations will be compelled to break out in doxological praise, as did the apostle Paul:

> Oh the depth of the riches
>   of the wisdom and knowledge of God!
> How unsearchable are his judgments,
>   and his ways past finding out! (Rom. 11:33)

God's Covenant with Moses

Both history and law constitute the Torah of Moses, and both the history and the law of Moses play a vital role in the celebrations of the Psalms. The miraculous works of the Lord in the complete redemption of his people provide a skeletal backbone for the legal dimension that runs through the Psalms. From the wandering of the patriarchs, the descent into Egypt, the plagues, the exodus, wilderness wanderings, conquest, judges, until finally climaxing with David, the history of Yahweh's redemptive wonder-working calls forth repentance from sin, trust in God's providential ordering, obedience to his revealed will, and hope in a future consummation.[16] Major passages in which a bulk of the psalm rehearses the history of Israel's redemption under Moses include:

Psalm 78, which traces the history of "a stubborn and rebellious generation, whose hearts were not loyal to God, whose spirits were not faithful to him" (Ps. 78:8).

Psalm 105, which reminds the people of the Lord's covenantal faithfulness from the word promised to Abraham through the inheritance of the land.

Psalm 106, which opens by declaring, "We have sinned, even as our fathers did," then rehearses the many times God's covenant people forgot him, and finally pleads with the Lord to "save us, . . . and gather us from the nations" (Ps. 106:6, 47).

Particularly the covenantal relationship of God with Israel in Moses' day serves as a major theme of the psalmists:

Psalm 66:6, 9. "He turned the sea into dry land, they passed through the waters on foot." In like manner, "he has preserved our lives and kept our feet from slipping."

16. Regarding the role of the narrative materials in the Psalms, Wenham, *Torah*, 119, says: "These retellings of the past are not merely historiographic, written to record events; their purpose is to educate the user of the psalms in both theology and ethics."

Psalm 68:1, 21. "May God arise, may his enemies be scattered," which quotes the words of Moses that were spoken each time the ark began to move across the wilderness (Num. 10:35). In like manner, "surely God will crush the heads of his enemies."

Psalm 74:13, 22. "You split open the sea by your power." In similar fashion, "Rise up, O God, and defend your cause."

Psalm 77:16, 10. "The waters saw you . . . and writhed; the very depths were convulsed." So in times of distress, "To this I will appeal: the years of the right hand of the Most High."

Psalm 114:1, 3, 7–8. "When Israel came out of Egypt, . . . the sea looked and fled." So: "Tremble, O earth, at the presence of the Lord . . . , who turned the rock into a pool, the hard rock into springs of water."

Psalm 135:8–9, 14. "He struck down the firstborn of Egypt, the firstborn of men and animals. He sent his signs and wonders into your midst, O Egypt, against Pharaoh and all his servants." So it may be expected that "the LORD will vindicate his people and have compassion on his servants."

Psalm 136:1, 16, 23, 25. "Give thanks to the LORD, . . . to him who led his people through the desert, . . . who remembered us in our low estate . . . and who gives food to every creature."

This "actualization" in the Psalms of previous events in the days of Moses as recorded in the Torah does not merely have the result of recalling these earlier occurrences of God's saving interventions. By celebrating them in the worship of Israel, their reality comes to life once more as a consequence of the regenerated faith of his people.

In addition to the reminders of God's mighty acts of redemption in history, the active review in the Psalms of the legal dimensions of the Torah of Moses also has a vital impact on the lives of God's people. The placement of the three Torah Psalms (Pss. 1, 19, 119) in Book I and Book V indicates the ongoing role of the "law," the "teaching," the "instruction" of the Lord in the worship and life of God's people:

- Psalm 1 introduces the law as one of the two primary pillars of the life of God's people.
- Psalm 19 notes the role of the law as revealing the way of the Lord alongside the revelation embedded in creation.
- Psalm 119 magnifies the law in all its various applications to life.

This inclusion of the law in the Psalms embraces the ceremonial as well as the moral aspects of the COVENANT LORD'S law. A few illustrations may suffice:

The Priestly Benediction

Regularly, appeal is made in the Psalms to the priestly benediction prescribed for Aaron and his descendants: "The LORD bless you and keep you, the LORD make his face shine upon you and be gracious to you; the LORD lift up his countenance upon you and give you peace" (Num. 6:24–26). This priestly benediction becomes the basis of covenantal blessing on God's people throughout the five hundred years of the Psalter's formation, reaching to almost a thousand years beyond the days of Moses. It is ritually pronounced at least ten times over in the book of Psalms.[17] A climax is reached in Psalm 80 when the middle phrase of the benediction appears as the middle line of a refrain that crescendoes with an expanding use of the divine name. In the original Mosaic setting, the threefold repetition of the name *Yahweh* was the manner by which the priest formally "set [Yahweh's] name on the sons of Israel, and [he would] bless them" (Num. 6:27). So in the day of national devastation, the psalmist elaborates on this formula by the threefold repetition of his refrain:

> Cause us to return;
> *let your face shine on us,*
> and we shall be saved. (Ps. 80:3, 7, 19)

A more elaborate form of the divine name appears each time the refrain is repeated, so that the benediction moves from *Elohim* (Ps. 80:3), to

17. The passages are as follows: Pss. 4:6; 31:16; 37:6; 67:1; 80:1, 3, 7, 19; 94:1; 104:15; 118:27; 119:135; 139:12. Cf. also the role of four key words from the Aaronic benediction in the Psalms of Ascents as treated in chapter 9 of this volume.

Elohim of Hosts (Ps. 80:7), to *Yahweh Elohim of Hosts* (Ps. 80:19). In this climactic way, God's "name" is "set" on his people as they suffer from devastating international invasion.

The collection of psalms identified in their titles as the "Songs of Ascents" (Pss. 120–134) make extensive use of the Aaronic benediction. "The LORD bless," "keep," "be gracious," and give "peace" that permeate these particular psalms all derive from the blessing of Israel's priests. One can imagine the growing anticipation of these blessings as the pilgrim approached Jerusalem.

The Role of Sacrifices

At first, it seems that the psalmists are rather ambivalent regarding the proper role of sacrifices. On the one hand, the psalmist reports a negative attitude:

> Sacrifice and offering
> you did not desire . . . ;
> Burnt offerings and sin offerings
> you did not require. (Ps. 40:6)

Again, God declares through the psalmist:

> I have no need of a bull
> from your stall,
> or of goats
> from your pens. (Ps. 50:9)

But then this same psalm affirms:

> He who sacrifices thank offerings
> honors me,
> and he prepares the way
> so that I may show him the salvation of God. (Ps. 50:23)

In an earlier day, negative biblical critics would seize on this apparent tension point to establish either a contradiction in the Scriptures or a rivalry between prophet and priest in the Old Testament. But more

44

recent considerations indicate that the psalmist wishes to encourage a pure heart in true worshipers without minimizing the offering of sacrifices according to the law of Moses.

The Cultic Festivals

The psalmist also recognizes the ongoing significance of the cultic festivals as prescribed by the Mosaic law:

> Sound the ram's horn at the New Moon,
> and when the moon is full, on the day of our feast.
> This is a decree for Israel,
> an ordinance of the God of Jacob. (Ps. 81:3–4)

Even in Israel's exilic and postexilic period, the cultic laws were viewed by the psalmists as directives from the Lord:

> Jerusalem is built like a city . . .
> . . . where the tribes go up, . . .
> according to the statutes given to Israel. (Ps. 122:3–4)

So for the psalmists, the cultic regulations of Moses continue to play a prominent role in their concept of worship. Though denied formal activity of the cult during their exile because of their displacement from the Land of Promise and the devastation of the temple, they continued to hold in highest regard the specifications of the Mosaic cult-laws. By the orderings of the Sovereign Lord, their denial of cultic access prepared the path to a better way of worship, and ensured the ongoing significance of all the Psalms.

The Moral Law

More critical for the psalmist is the moral law, particularly as summarized in the Ten Words.[18] In one psalm, the eighth, the seventh, and the ninth commandments are specifically mentioned:

---

18. Wenham, *Torah*, 98–110, provides a helpful overview of each of the Ten Commandments as they appear in the Psalms.

To the wicked, God says:

"What right have you
　　to recite my laws
　　or take my covenant on your lips?

You hate my instruction
and cast my words behind you.

When you see a thief,
　　you join with him [eighth commandment];
　　you throw in your lot with adulterers [seventh commandment].
　　You use your mouth for evil
　　　　and harness your tongue to deceit.
　　You speak continually against your brother
　　　　and slander your own mother's son [ninth commandment].

These things you have done and I kept silent.
You thought I was altogether like you.

But I will rebuke you
　　and accuse you to your face." (Ps. 50:16–21)

In another instance, the psalmist specifically recalls the central focus of the Decalogue as revealed at Sinai:

You shall have no foreign god among you;
you shall not bow down to an alien god.
I am the LORD your God,
who brought you up out of Egypt. (Ps. 81:9–10; cf. Ex. 20:1–3)

The Lord pleads with his people to take heed to his words:

Hear, O my people, and I will warn you—
if you would but listen to me, O Israel!
. . . .
But my people would not listen to me;
Israel would not submit to me.

So I gave them over to their stubborn hearts
to follow their own devices.

If my people would but listen to me,
if Israel would follow my ways,

how quickly would I subdue their enemies
and turn my hand against their foes! (Ps. 81:8; 11–14)

So the covenantal law of Moses in all its different dimensions
is recognized by the various psalmists as having ongoing relevance
for the lives of God's people. The fact that the covenant with David
represented the climax of covenants in the Old Testament did not in
any way minimize the ongoing role of the Mosaic covenant of law.
Yet at the same time, the key role of the Davidic covenant must never
be overlooked for its unique place in the book of Psalms.

God's Covenant with David

The climax of this "covenantal chorale" in the book of Psalms, in
terms of the progression of redemptive revelation, focuses on the Davidic
covenant with the Lord's two specific promises to him regarding *dynasty*
and *dwellingplace*. Both these promises are encapsulated in the key
word *house* (בַּיִת) as it recurs in its original covenantal formulation. On
the one hand, God promises that he will build a "house" for David,
referring to the perpetual "dynasty" that he will establish for David and
his descendants (2 Sam. 7:11). On the other hand, David's son will build
a "house" for the Lord, referring to the Lord's permanent "dwellingplace" on Mount Zion in Jerusalem (2 Sam. 7:13). So perpetual *dynasty*
and permanent *dwellingplace* summarize the essential core of the Lord's
covenant with David. The COVENANT LORD declares that the "son" of
David who will rule forever for God on David's throne will also be
God's "son," and God will be his "father" (2 Sam. 7:14).

These two all-embracive themes of the Davidic covenant play a
major role throughout the whole of the book of Psalms.[19] David as

19. Jamie A. Grant, "The Psalms and the King," in *Interpreting the Psalms: Issues and
Approaches*, ed. Philip S. Johnston and David G. Firth (Downers Grove, IL: InterVarsity

47

the Lord's anointed, the messianic king, is constantly assaulted by the "wicked," the "enemies" of his righteous kingdom. But David's dynasty will be preserved from extermination by death at the hands of his foes, though the threat remains perpetually present. At the same time, the Lord's chosen dwellingplace on Mount Zion in Jerusalem will be established as the permanent locale from which he will rule over his people, as well as over all the nations of the world. The significance of a divinely designated "place" from which God and his appointed Messiah would rule dates back to the time of Moses with its many specific references to the "place" that the Lord will choose as a dwelling for his name (Deut. 12:4–7, 11, 14, 18, 21, 26; 14:23–25; 15:20; 16:2, 6–7, 11, 15–16; 17:8, 10; 18:6; 26:2, 9; 31:11). But now, consummatively in the Psalms, the Lord's throne will be merged with David's messianic throne in this single "place" of God's choice.[20] God dwells on Mount Zion (Pss. 9:11; 132:13–14); at the same time, his throne is in heaven (Pss. 11:4; 103:19; 123:1). Yet according to one author, "These two concepts . . . are not mutually exclusive."[21] Psalm 11:4 underscores these two dwellingplaces of God by declaring both in a single sentence: "The LORD is in his holy temple; the LORD's throne is in heaven." By this double dwellingplace, God "breaks through the limits of space."[22] God in all his fullness is enthroned in the temple on Mount Zion in Jerusalem, and God in all his fullness is enthroned in the midst of the glories of his heavenly dwelling.

Press, 2005), 102, understates the justification for his article when he affirms that "there is a sense in which [the Davidic king] subtly dominates the book of Psalms."

20. The suggestion of McCann, *Theological Introduction*, 146, that the centrality of Jerusalem in the Psalms may be replaced with the centrality of Jesus in the Christian profession blurs the distinction well preserved in Scripture between the "person" of the Messiah and the "place" of his enthronement. Both of these elements are essential to the Davidic covenant and its consummate fulfillment in the Christ and the heavenly Mount Zion (Gal. 4:26; Heb. 12:22).

21. Hans-Joachim Kraus, *Theology of the Psalms* (Minneapolis: Augsburg, 1986), 76.

22. Ibid., quoting J. Maier (no bibliographical information supplied). In further quoting Maier, Kraus approves of the concept that this idea rests on a "mythological" understanding of space. But mythological concepts by their very nature deny the reality of the biblical references to God's dwellingplace. "Figurative" representations of God's dwelling in heaven may be an appropriate way of understanding the biblical conceptions, but not "mythological."

Psalm 2 intertwines these two themes of *dynasty* and *dwelling-place* in a manner that anticipates much that follows in the Psalter. In this second psalm, the "wicked" are not restricted to personal "enemies" of David. Instead, it is "nations" and "peoples" that set themselves against the COVENANT LORD and his Christ. They are very real enemies posing very real threats. But the Lord scorns these determined and powerful enemies by setting his Messiah on his throne in Mount Zion. As a final admonition to the nations, they are told to "worship the LORD" with fear and rejoicing. The phrase translated "worship the LORD" (עִבְדוּ אֶת־יְהוָה) is distinctive in its use of the verbal root for "to be a servant, a slave," and conveys the idea of "take up the position of servanthood to Yahweh." Says one author:

> To "serve" means to orient one's whole life and existence to a sovereign master—literally, to be the "servant" or "slave" of a king. The term always occurs in the Psalter in relation to a royal figure, either human or divine.[23]

Simultaneously, they must "kiss the Son" in homage and entrustment (Ps. 2:11–12). Only then can they expect the covenantal "blessing" of the Lord. For this "blessed" status is reserved for those who delight in the Torah of the Lord (Ps. 1) and adore the Son of the Lord (Ps. 2).[24]

Much more could be said of these two themes of *dynasty* and *dwellingplace* with their permeating role throughout the book of Psalms. But the central place of these realities as promised in the Davidic covenant will become more and more apparent as the present study progresses.

---

23. McCann, *Theological Introduction*, 65.

24. Kraus, *Theology*, 180–85, provides a thoroughgoing treatment of Psalm 2, particularly as it finds fullest realization in the new covenant Scriptures.

4

The Flow of the Book

Is there such a thing as a "flow of the book" of Psalms? Is it possible to trace an organized development of thought progression from beginning to end? Much discouragement has been heaped on any effort to analyze the Psalter in terms of an intentional development of order and theme. Typical is the perspective of Franz Delitzsch:

> Among the Fathers, Gregory of Nyassa has attempted to show that the Psalter in its five books lead upward as by five steps to moral perfection, . . . and down to the most recent times attempts have been made to trace in the five books a graduation of principal thoughts, which influence and run through the whole collection. *We fear that in this direction, investigation has set before itself an unattainable end.*[1]

More recent psalm studies have even gone so far as to suggest that perhaps the "skepticism of ever bringing significant order to the Psalter as a whole" fostered the modern form-critical approach to the Psalms.[2]

---

1. Franz Delitzsch, *Biblical Commentary on the Psalms* (Grand Rapids: Eerdmans, 1959), 1:19 (emphasis added).
2. Gerald Henry Wilson, *The Editing of the Hebrew Psalter* (Chico, CA: Scholars Press, 1985), 1–2. Wilson's opening comments indicate a new direction in Psalter studies. Instead of concentrating on the literary form of individual psalms and then grouping them in genre categories such as "royal psalms," "lamentation psalms," "thanksgiving psalms" *à la* Hermann Gunkel, or "enthronement psalms" *à la* Sigmund Mowinckel, the trend is now to concentrate on the "final form," the "canonical form," of the book of Psalms as it appears in its wholeness. This trend is helpful from two perspectives: (1) it frees the church from being bound to follow a process (which is sometimes but not always helpful) of categorizing and classifying each psalm according to its genre and *sitz im leben*; and (2) it opens the door to consider carefully an area in which "canonical criticism" may

Instead of looking for meaning in the Psalms in the context of the Psalter as a whole, unity and meaning has been sought in the relation of various psalm genres to their cultural circumstance.[3]

Significantly, Delitzsch himself proceeds in his following sentence to acknowledge that the Psalter collection "bears the impress of one ordering mind."[4] Subsequently he notes:

> There is on the whole an unmistakable progress from the earliest to the latest; and we may say . . . that the real kernel of Davidic, and, generally speaking, older hymns is contained in Psalms 1–41 [Book I], that it is mainly hymns of the middle period that are found in Psalms 42–89 [Books II and III], and that the great mass of later and very late hymns must be sought in Psalms 90–150 [Books IV and V].[5]

Numerous additional collections or groupings may be observed among the Psalms in addition to the five books, as has been previously noted. These deliberate groupings with similar form, substance,

---

find its most legitimate function. When canonical criticism is applied to the Pentateuch or the book of Isaiah, it generally ends up producing what may be called a "Let's Pretend" theology. That is, the student of the Bible is asked to "pretend" that Moses wrote the Pentateuch and that Isaiah ben Amoz wrote all sixty-six chapters of his prophecy, even though (as a modern biblical critic) he may not believe they actually did, and then analyze the theology that takes shape as a consequence. The result is a theology that cannot be genuinely believed or trusted, since it makes the Pentateuch a Mosaic pretense and makes Isaiah no better than the dumb idols he criticized for not being able to predict the future. But because the book of Psalms actually did develop over a period of five hundred years with many editorial phases, studying the Psalms in their "final form," their "canonical status," could prove to be a very enriching approach. At the same time, the integrity of the various psalms must be maintained. It is sometimes proposed that many psalms began as "cultic" and then were later "davidized" so that these psalms took on a form more helpful to the individual in his personal reading of the Psalms. But if David did not actually originate these psalms, then the perspective of a "Let's Pretend" theology has injected itself once more.

3. John Goldingay, *Psalms, Volume 1: Psalms 1–41* (Grand Rapids: Baker, 2006), 36, concludes that "the Psalter as a whole does not have a structure that helps us get a handle on its contents." He looks instead to the "more traditional critical approach" of seeking to understand the Psalms in terms of the various types that recur frequently. Ibid., 37.

4. Delitzsch, *Psalms* (Eerdmans), 1:19.

5. Franz Delitzsch, *Biblical Commentary on the Psalms* (London: Hodder & Stoughton, 1894), 1:23.

or author attest to an intentional arrangement of the Psalms at more than one point during the five-hundred-year history of the creation and collection of the various psalms.[6] These groupings, which also manifest a progression across the scope of the Psalter, will now be considered more fully as they occur within the framework of the traditional five books of the Psalms.[7] In terms of the broadest possible themes, these five books may be categorized as follows:

Book I   Confrontation
Book II   Communication
Book III   Devastation
Book IV   Maturation
Book V   Consummation

The various structural and theological elements of these five books of the Psalter will now be explored in the remainder of this volume.

6. Significant direction for the exploration of intentional structure within the Psalter as a whole was provided by Wilson, *Editing*. Wilson searched for clues of the Psalter's overall structure by concentrating on the titles of the psalms, their genre, and their authorship indicators, as well as the psalms located at the "seams" of the five books of the Psalter. A major effort to exegete the various psalms in terms of the larger structures of the book is found in the commentaries of Hossfeld and Zenger (see select bibliography at the end of this volume). In his brief article, John H. Walton, "Psalms: A Cantata about the Davidic Covenant," *Journal of the Evangelical Theological Society* 34 (March 1991): 21–31, explored the structure of the Psalter by concentrating more directly on the content of the Psalms. His proposal that psalm content should function as a major key in uncovering Psalter structure, together with his focus on the Davidic covenant, has provided significant insight into the overall shaping of the Psalms. His effort to trace specifics in the history of David alongside the development of the Psalter fostered strained connections between the scriptural record of David's life and the various portions of the Psalms. In any case, structures in the Psalter should be sought in the substance of the Psalter, and not merely through the analysis of titles, authors, and genres.

7. Nancy L. deClaisse-Walford, *Reading from the Beginning: The Shaping of the Hebrew Psalter* (Ann Arbor, MI: UMI Dissertation Services, 1996), offers a number of insights in her analysis of the Psalter. Her methodology, however, has a limiting factor in that she focuses on the first and last psalm of each book of the Psalter to determine the flow of the book as a whole. Yet developments across the five books cannot be properly determined without analysis of the larger substance of each book.

5

BOOK I (PSALMS 1–41): CONFRONTATION

The Lord God Almighty rules eternally over heaven and earth. But the "mystery of iniquity" has arisen to challenge his sovereignty among humanity. In response to this challenge, through covenant and promise God has committed himself to redeem an innumerable host from every tribe, kindred, language, and people to be his own. The instrument by which this redemption will be accomplished is a "singular saving hero" who in the fullness of time will enter into mortal conflict with Satan himself (cf. Gen. 3:15). As a consequence, *confrontation* will characterize the whole of human history until the consummation.

In the days of Israel's kingship, this confrontation manifested itself through the struggle of Israel's messianic king to establish his kingdom of righteousness and peace. David the son of Jesse was the man chosen by God to fulfill this redemptive role. As the head of the line that would ultimately lead to the Royal Redeemer, he must enter into mortal conflict with the many enemies of his messianic kingdom. Particularly as he sought to establish for the first time this kingdom of righteousness, mercy, and peace, he would experience constant confrontation with his many enemies. Book I of the Psalms reflects this opening framework of confrontation.

This investigation of Book I will focus on the principal elements that structure the book. Four elements in particular will be considered: (1) the foundational role of Psalms 1 and 2 for the whole of the Psalter; (2) the first collection of Davidic psalms; (3) the structural significance of messianic Psalm 18 and Torah Psalm 19; and (4) the contribution of acrostic psalms to the structure of Book I.

The Foundational Role of Psalms 1 and 2

The introductory role of these two psalms has already been discussed. But their significance across the whole Psalter deserves further consideration. Taken together, these two psalms define the substance of essentially all that will follow throughout the remainder of the Psalms. The first psalm declares the critical character of the law; the second psalm presents the Son appointed by the Lord who will ultimately extend the messianic kingdom to the ends of the earth. Torah and Messiah, law and gospel—both are equally essential for the fulfillment of Yahweh's covenants and the advancement of Yahweh's kingdom.

Not only as psalms that introduce the whole book of Psalms, but also as introduction to a significant element in the structure of the Psalter, these two psalms join each other in a symbiotic relationship.[1] Subsequently, the coupling of a Torah psalm and a messianic psalm provides internal structuring within the two largest books of the Psalter. In Book I proper (Pss. 3–41), messianic Psalm 18 is coupled with Torah Psalm 19 at the major point of transition within the book. Materials regarding Torah and Messiah are treated differently in Book I before and after these two transitional psalms, as will be seen later. In a similar way, messianic Psalm 118 coupled with Torah Psalm 119 in Book V (Pss. 107–150) provides structure for the largest and concluding book of the Psalter. Significantly different groupings of psalms appear before and after these two pivotal psalms in Book V. In this context, the unique role of Torah Psalm 1 and messianic Psalm 2 deserves special consideration.

1. Cf. Jamie A. Grant, *The King as Exemplar: The Function of Deuteronomy's Kingship Law in the Shaping of the Book of Psalms* (Atlanta: Society of Biblical Literature, 2004). Grant's main thesis is that Psalms 1–2, Psalms 18–21, and Psalms 118–119 represent three groupings of Torah psalms with messianic psalms based on the kingship theology of Deuteronomy 17:14–20, which provide the focal identity of the Psalter as a whole. Says Grant: "the placement of the kingship psalms alongside torah psalms was a deliberate editorial act through which the Psalter's redactors intended to reflect the theology of the Deuteronomic Law of the King in the Book of Psalms." Ibid., 2.

Psalm 1

The positioning of Psalm 1 as the principal introduction to the whole of the Psalter makes a clear statement regarding the substance of the material that will follow. As has been observed,

> the ensuing Book of Psalms is to be treated as torah itself. The reader is to meditate on all that follows as instruction from God and to seek to live by its teaching as much as by the teaching of the Pentateuch.[2]

Far from being simply a collection of subjective reflections by various pious individuals, every part of the Psalter should be viewed as teaching, as divine revelation intended to function as the Lord's directions regarding what to believe and how to live. Whether it be instruction, praise, lament, thanksgiving, or confession, the whole book and all its parts should be reverenced as Yahweh's inspired teaching, which is the essential significance of the term *Torah*.[3] Yet Psalms 1, 19, and 119 are distinctively dedicated to the subject of Torah.

More specifically, Psalm 1 identifies two groups of people on the basis of their relation to God's law. The wicked despise God's Torah, while the righteous delight in his law. The righteous are like a tree transplanted by refreshing waters, bringing forth fruit throughout this life. Contrariwise, the wicked are like dried chaff blown about by the wind in all their earthly endeavors. In the end, the wicked will perish, and will be excluded from the assembly of God's people. But the righteous will be vindicated by the Lord who knows and loves them. This

---

2. Ibid., 53.

3. Providing a precise definition for *Torah* in the Psalms is a difficult task. The "meditation" (הָגָה) on the Torah recommended by Psalm 1 includes the idea of "muttering," "musing," "vocalizing," which assumes solid concept or word-content as over against mystic meditation. The term implies a written body of material that can be memorized, recited, and meditated on. Hans-Joachim Kraus, *Psalms 1–59: A Commentary* (Minneapolis: Augsburg, 1988), 116, says that the "center" of the Torah "is and remains the law of God transmitted by Moses . . . . Torah in this sense is the authoritatively valid 'Sacred Scripture.'" But what Scripture? The Pentateuch? The book of Deuteronomy? All canonical writings up to the time of the composition of the psalm using the term? If the latter is the case, then the *Torah* referred to by David in his psalms would be quite different from the *Torah* of the author of Psalm 119. Cf. Grant, *King as Exemplar*, 253–73, for an extensive discussion of optional identities of *Torah*.

contrast between the wicked and the righteous appears in each of the five books of the Psalter. The basic root for *wicked* (רָשָׁע) occurs about ninety times in the Psalms, with approximately half these instances appearing in Book I. Similarly, the basic root for *righteous* (צַדִּיק) occurs about fifty times in the Psalms, with approximately half these instances occurring in Book I. Quite clearly, the concentration on conflict between the righteous and the wicked in the Psalms is located in Book I. Yet the contrast between the two kinds of people in relation to God's law continues throughout the Psalter.

Psalm 19 as the second Torah psalm speaks only in a positive way regarding people's attitude toward the Torah of Yahweh. This psalm employs six different phrases for the *law* of the Lord in three verses. The distribution of these varied terms for *Torah* across the Psalter may be summarized as follows:

- *Torah/law of Yahweh*: Psalms 1, 19, 37, 40, 78, 89, 94, 105, 119
- *Testimony/statute of Yahweh*: Psalms 19, 25, 78, 81, 93, 99, 119, 122, 132
- *Precept of Yahweh*: Psalms 19, 103, 111, 119
- *Commandment of Yahweh*: Psalms 19, 78, 89, 112, 119
- *Fear of Yahweh*: Psalms 19, 34, 111, 119
- *Judgment/ordinance of Yahweh*: Psalms 19, 81, 89, 119, 147

As many as twenty separate psalms contain at least one of these representations of the Torah of Yahweh.[4] But as the listing above demonstrates, only Psalms 19 and 119 employ all six of these law-terms. This factor underscores the closeness of relationship between these two psalms.

Psalm 119 as the third and climactic Torah psalm reinforces the contrast of attitudes between embracing and repudiating God's law. Considering all the various designations for the wicked ("enemies," "evildoers," "oppressors," "arrogant," "foes," "faithless," etc.),

4. James Luther Mays, *The Lord Reigns: A Theological Handbook to the Psalms* (Louisville: Westminster John Knox Press, 1994), 153n12, lists fourteen psalms that give expression to Torah theology in addition to Psalms 1, 19, and 119: Psalms 18, 25, 33, 78, 89, 93, 94, 99, 103, 105, 111, 112, 147, 148. Additional psalms employing Torah terminology not mentioned by Mays include Psalms 34, 37, 40, 81, 122, 132.

sixteen of the twenty-two stanzas in Psalm 119 contrast the lifestyle of the righteous with the ungodly.

In any case, the role of Psalm 1 as an opening foundational psalm for the entirety of the Psalter is clearly established by this extensive usage of Torah terminology throughout the book. The Torah, the teaching, the instruction of the Lord must be viewed as a key factor in understanding the Psalms.

Psalm 2

Psalm 2 stresses four major themes derived from the Davidic covenant that also permeate the Psalter, establishing the foundational role of this introductory psalm. These four themes are: (1) the kingship of Yahweh over all the nations; (2) the locale of his rule in Mount Zion of Jerusalem; (3) the permanent establishment of the Davidic dynasty; and (4) the merger of Yahweh's throne with David's throne. These four permeating themes will be introduced only briefly at this point.

The Kingship of Yahweh over All the Nations

According to Psalm 2, the nations and kings of the earth rebel against Yahweh's lordship, but only in vain (Ps. 2:1). Enthroned in heaven, Yahweh first scoffs and then terrifies them in his wrath (Ps. 2:4–5).

This theme of Yahweh's kingship over the nations permeates the Psalms. A sample passage from each of the five books may serve to establish the point:

- "Yahweh is King forever and ever; the nations will perish from his land" (Ps. 10:16—Book I).
- "How awesome is Yahweh Most High, the great King over all the earth" (Ps. 47:2—Book II).
- "The sparrow has found a home . . . near your altar, O LORD Almighty, my King and my God" (Ps. 84:3—Book III).
- "Yahweh is the great God, the great King above all gods" (Ps. 95:3—Book IV).

57

- "I will exalt you, my God the King; . . . your kingdom is an everlasting kingdom, and your dominion endures through all generations" (Ps. 145:1, 13—Book V).

This psalm sampler drawing from each of the five books of the Psalter unites in declaring Yahweh to be Sovereign King over all. Beginning with the affirmation of Yahweh's rule over the nations in Psalm 2, the Psalter regularly declares him to be Lord over all.

The Locale of His Rule in Mount Zion of Jerusalem

Clearly, certain passages in the Psalms refer to heaven as the place of the Lord's enthronement.[5] In Psalm 2 itself, the psalmist declares that Yahweh is "enthroned in heaven" (Ps. 2:4). Yet in this same opening psalm, the Lord himself refers to "Zion, my holy mountain" (Ps. 2:6). Throughout the Psalter, Zion is identified as the locale of Yahweh's kingship.[6] This seeming dichotomy creates no problem for the Scriptures. An essential factor of the Davidic covenant was that David's offspring would build a "house" for the Lord, where he would dwell in the midst of his people, anticipating the construction of Solomon's temple (2 Sam. 7:13). As Solomon dedicates his temple, he refers to God's dwellingplace as being in Zion even as he rules from heaven. Solomon pleads that the Lord, whom the heaven of heavens cannot contain, will hear from heaven as prayer is directed to this "place" where his name dwells (1 Kings 8:27–30). It is not simply a matter of the "Name-dwelling," since the "Glory" of the Lord had already filled the temple before Solomon's prayer, indicating Yahweh's abiding presence within the Most Holy Place on Mount Zion (1 Kings 8:10–11).

So Psalm 2 anticipates a significant theme that runs throughout the Psalter by referring to Zion as the Lord's dwellingplace, while recognizing that his throne also is simultaneously in heaven. Integral

---

5. For passages establishing Yahweh's rule from heaven, see Psalms 11:4; 20:6; 33:13; 53:2; 57:3; 76:8; 89:2; 102:19; 113:4–5; 138:6; 144:5, 7; 150:1.

6. Sample passages from each of the five books of the Psalter are Psalms 9:11; 48:2; 76:2; 99:2; 132:13.

to the basic elements of the Davidic covenant as developed in the Psalter is the Lord's residing in the midst of his people. Yet he never relinquishes his sovereign rule from the exalted heights of heaven.

The Permanent Establishment of David and His Dynasty

Already it has been observed that all the various covenants initiated by the Lord manifest their ongoing significance in the Psalms. But climaxing them all in its prominence throughout the Psalter is the Lord's covenant with David, the covenant of the kingdom. Psalm 2 presses the centrality of this covenant to the forefront with its rehearsal of the "decree of Yahweh" addressed to David: "You are my Son; today I have become your Father" (Ps. 2:7; cf. 2 Sam. 7:14). Each subsequent book of the Psalter repeats or amplifies this commitment of the Lord to maintain David and his dynasty, with the significant exception of Book IV:

- Book I: "He shows to his anointed unfailing kindness, to David and his descendants forever" (Ps. 18:50). "Now I know that the LORD saves his anointed" (Ps. 20:6). "O LORD, the king rejoices in your strength" (Ps. 21:1).
- Book II: "Your sons will take the place of your fathers; you will make them princes throughout the land" (Ps. 45:16). "Increase the days of the king's life, his years for many generations. May he be enthroned in God's presence forever" (Ps. 61:6–7). "May his name endure forever; may it continue as long as the sun. All nations will be blessed through him, and they will call him blessed" (Ps. 72:17).
- Book III: "He chose David his servant and took him from the sheep pens . . . to be the shepherd of his people Jacob . . . . And David shepherded them with integrity of heart; with skillful hands he led them" (Ps. 78:70–72). "You said, 'I have made a covenant with my chosen one, I have sworn to David my servant, "I will establish your line forever and make your throne firm through all generations"'" (Ps. 89:3–4; cf. vv. 20, 29, 35–36, 49).

59

- Book V: "Yahweh said to Adonai, 'Sit at my right hand until I make your enemies a footstool for your feet' " (Ps. 110:1). "For the sake of David your servant, do not reject your anointed one. . . . One of your own descendants I will place on your throne" (Ps. 132:10–11; cf. v. 17).

By its specific repetition of the Lord's words in his covenant with David, Psalm 2 lays the foundation for this continuing, expansive reaffirmation of expectations regarding the Lord's maintenance of the Davidic line across the five-hundred-year span of the Psalter's history. The absence of any direct reference to the Davidic kingship in Book IV may be due to its exilic setting, when the people had no anointed king. As a consequence of the devastations of the exile, Israel's hope had to undergo a serious maturing process. Though the promise to David never disappeared, as seen in Psalms 101, 110, and 132, the people without a messianic king on the throne had to concentrate on the kingship of Yahweh over the whole world of time and space (Pss. 90, 92–100).

The Merger of Yahweh's Throne with David's Throne

Psalm 2 opens the Psalter with the imagery of this merger already in place. The messianic king is installed by Yahweh "on Zion," which the Lord himself describes as "my holy mountain" (Ps. 2:6). This declaration of the Psalter brings to expression the full significance of David's determination to bring the ark of the covenant up to Jerusalem, where his own throne was located (2 Sam. 6:12–19). By this action, David was insisting that Yahweh's throne be merged with his own throne. This intention he expected to see realized across the generations, and found a dramatic fulfillment at Solomon's inauguration as king in David's place. At the critical moment of transition, "Solomon sat on the throne of Yahweh as king in place of his father David" (1 Chron. 29:23). Messiah's throne is effectively merged with Yahweh's throne. The perfections of this merger appear in the many passages in the Psalms in which Zion, the place of David's enthronement, is presented as Yahweh's place of enthronement even while

Yahweh's lordship continues to be recognized as residing in heaven. Many of the references to God's dwellingplace in heaven are coupled with references to his dwellingplace in Zion (cf. Pss. 11:4; 20:2, 6; 53:2, 6; 57:1, 3; 76:2, 8; 102:16, 19; 110:1–2; 138:2, 6), which has the effect of merging the kingship of Yahweh with the kingship of David. For the Davidic Messiah rules for God.[7]

Because the major themes of Psalm 2 find extensive and continual elaboration in the remainder of the Psalter, this opening psalm may be viewed as foundational to the whole of the book. Along with Torah Psalm 1, messianic Psalm 2 provides an appropriate introduction to the whole of the Psalter.

The First Collection of Davidic Psalms (Psalms 3–41*[8])

So the Psalter opens with Psalms 1 and 2 serving as pillars marking the entrance to the temple of the Psalter. God's law and God's Messiah provide a dual source of blessing for God's people as they enter this temple. Two groups of people with a radically different faith and lifestyle respond differently to Yahweh's Torah and Yahweh's Messiah. Yahweh and his Messiah enter into inescapable conflict with the wicked, the unrighteous, the ungodly who oppose the rule of God. Book I of the Psalter presents the first collection of psalms that trace the development of this conflict.[9] Some individuals and nations set themselves against Yahweh and his Messiah, while others gratefully serve them both.

7. Cf. Gary N. Knoppers, *I Chronicles 10–29: A New Translation with Introduction and Commentary*, Anchor Bible (New York: Doubleday, 2004), 673: "Most extraordinary is that the Chronicler associates the kingdom or kingship of David with the kingdom or kingship of God on no fewer than four separate occasions (1 Chron. 17:14; 28:5; 29:11; 2 Chron. 13:8)." Knoppers cites Japhet to the effect that the Chronicler "equates monarchy with theocracy—the Israelite monarchy is Yhwh's kingship over Israel."

8. As in other chapters, the asterisk (*) after a listing of psalms indicates that the titles of that collection might not specifically attribute all those particular psalms to the same person.

9. Nancy L. deClaisse-Walford, *Reading from the Beginning: The Shaping of the Hebrew Psalter* (Ann Arbor, MI: UMI Dissertation Services, 1996), 144, says that Psalm 2 in particular and the royal psalms in general "address the postexilic community's questions" about the loss of a king. From this perspective, Psalm 2 is presumed to have taken its current shape after the exile. Much to the contrary, Psalm 2, originating in David and maintaining its Davidic integrity, defined the history of Israel's expectations from

All the psalms of Book I proper (Pss. 3–41*) are attributed to David as their author in their titles with only two exceptions, which shows the intensity of David's personal involvement in this cosmic confrontation.[10] Additional psalms in the Psalter collection without the "By David" indicator in their titles were also composed by David, as seen by the direct testimony of the New Testament. In reacting to the threats of the Jewish leaders before the assembled disciples, Peter acknowledges that God spoke "by the Holy Spirit through the mouth of [his] servant, our father David" (Acts 4:25). He then quotes from Psalm 2, even though no title exists to affirm David as its author. In similar fashion, the writer to the Hebrews indicates that God spoke "through David" about the consummate "rest" in Psalm 95 (cf. Heb. 4:7). Yet this psalm has no heading to affirm David as its author.

How many more of the untitled psalms throughout the Psalter were written by David cannot be known. But clearly David had a great deal to do with the composition of the Psalms as a consequence of his personal experiences as messianic king. Of the thirty-seven psalms attributed to David in Book I, only five have no singular personal pronoun (Pss. 12, 14, 15, 24, 29).

David's day until the appearance of the Christ in the person of Jesus. The apostle Peter significantly strengthens his argument when he affirms David's authorship of Psalm 2 (Acts 4:25–29). For now Jesus' experience of opposition by national powers must be seen as corresponding to David's identical experience as the Old Testament messianic figure. Rather than discrediting his messiahship, the opposition to Jesus, overcome stunningly by his resurrection, aids in identifying him as the consummate realization of Old Testament messianism. A similar case in point that underscores the Davidic authorship of certain psalms is the New Testament citation of Psalm 16. Peter's appeal to David's tomb as proof that David could not be the "Holy One" who could never see corruption (Ps. 16:10) would be totally irrelevant to the issue of Jesus' resurrection if David were not the author of the cited psalm (cf. Acts 2:25–32). But because the grave of David as the author of Psalm 16 is "here to this day" (perhaps accompanied by Peter with an appropriate directional gesture), he as the author of Psalm 16 could not have been speaking of himself. Instead, he had to be speaking of the consummate Messiah, who is now established as the resurrected Christ Jesus.

10. The only two psalms in Book I beyond the "introductory pillars" (Pss. 1–2) not specifically attributed to David in their titles are Psalms 10 and 33. Psalm 10 completes the acrostic poem begun in Psalm 9, which explains the absence of a title. The two are treated as one psalm in the LXX. Psalm 33 is a quasi-acrostic, with twenty-two verses but not arranged in alphabetic order. This psalm finds the community of God's people expressing their corporate trust in the Lord: "We wait in hope for the LORD; . . . we trust in his holy name[;] . . . we put our hope in you" (Ps. 33:20–22).

But why did this single person David have such a massive role to play in the production of the Psalter? Why are so many of his psalms written in the first person?

It would be too facile an explanation to say that by this form the Psalter intends to assist each individual across the ages in articulating his personal prayers before God. Instead, David's first-person addresses to God in the Psalms should be understood in terms of the climactic covenant of Old Testament redemptive history that God made with David. This climactic covenant of the kingdom was made specifically with David as messianic king. As a single individual, he received God's promises in the covenant regarding a perpetual dynasty. No wonder he exclaimed in utter amazement:

> Who am I, O Sovereign LORD, and what is my house, that you have brought me this far? And as if this were not enough in your sight, O Sovereign LORD, you have also spoken about the distant future of the house of your servant. So this is the Torah for humanity, O Sovereign LORD. (2 Sam. 7:18–19)

This distinctive role of David as God's anointed Messiah explains the centrality of his person in the Psalms.[11] These *I*-psalms describe the various situations in life faced by this singular servant of the Lord. Indeed, each of these psalms contains a message for the individual believer. But to understand these *I*-psalms in their fullest significance for the individual, they must first be appreciated for their role in speaking for God's anointed servant, the messianic king. Then a principle regularly at work in the Psalter will become clear in its significance: *As it fares with the messianic king, so it fares with each member of the messianic kingdom.*

The first psalm in Book I proper (Ps. 3) gives clear expression to this principle. Throughout the substance of this psalm, David speaks in the first person as he deals with the tragic situation in which his own son Absalom is leading a coalition of his own nation against him.

---

11. J. Clinton McCann, *A Theological Introduction to the Book of Psalms: The Psalms as Torah* (Nashville: Abingdon Press, 1993), 43, asserts that the choice of a Messiah is "simply one means by which the Lord exercises sovereignty," which tends to minimize the significance of the role of Messiah in the Psalter. Yet the merger of God's rule with Messiah's rule serves as a critical factor throughout the Psalter.

The conclusion of the psalm points to David's deep concern for God's people even though the challenge is directed to him personally. For as their messianic king fares, so his people fare:

> Arise, O Yahweh!
> Deliver *me*, O my God!
> . . . .
> May your blessing be *on your people.* (Ps. 3:7–8)

On a subsequent occasion, God's people declare their solidarity with their messianic king: "*We* will shout for joy when *you* are victorious" (Ps. 20:5). Again, the plea of the messianic king concludes:

> Guard *my* life and rescue *me*;
> . . . .
> Redeem *Israel*, O God, from all *their* troubles! (Ps. 25:20, 22)

Still again, after a concentrated prayer for his personal deliverance, the messianic king concludes:

> Yahweh is the strength of his people,
>   a fortress of salvation for his Anointed One.
> Save your people and bless your inheritance;
>   be their shepherd and carry them forever. (Ps. 28:8–9)

Even after his passionate plea for God's mercy as he confesses his great sin of adultery with Bathsheba, David climaxes his petition by asking for God's blessing on the nation:

> In your good pleasure
>   make Zion prosper;
>   build up the walls of Jerusalem.
> Then there will be
>   righteous sacrifices,
>   whole burnt offerings to delight you;
>   then bulls will be offered on your altar. (Ps. 51:18–19)

From the example of David as messianic king, God's people in every age may learn a valuable lesson about the most acceptable way to pray in times of great personal distress. Whenever the believer today feels a need for the Lord's special intervention, let him focus on the well-being of all of God's people as the proper framework for seeking personal deliverance. Even the extremely personal matter of receiving forgiveness for sins may be best formulated in the context of a consideration of the blessing that may come on all of God's people as the individual experiences forgiveness.

So the large number of psalms in Book I appearing in the first person by no means points to an egocentric perspective in which David can think of only his own personal problems. Instead, Davidic centrality in these psalms rests firmly on the reality that as the anointed king fares, so the totality of God's chosen people fare.

The large introductory collection of psalms attributed to David in Book I (Pss. 3–41*) is also noteworthy because of the permeation of references to "the wicked," "enemies," or "foes." No fewer than thirty of the forty-one psalms that constitute Book I make specific reference to these enemies of the psalmist. Of the remaining eleven psalms, three imply the presence of enemies (Pss. 15, 16, 20), and five refer to death (Pss. 16, 23, 30, 33, 39), which even under the old covenant may be regarded as the last great enemy (1 Cor. 15:26). A uniting element of this early collection of psalms may be identified as David's constant struggle with his enemies to establish the messianic kingdom of righteousness and peace. On this basis he expresses his confidence in ultimate victory over all his foes through the intervention of the LORD OF THE COVENANT. These central themes of constant confrontation and ultimate victory reflect the unending struggle of the "seed of the woman" with the "seed of Satan" that characterizes the whole of redemptive history.

The role of David in these psalms as God's anointed king struggling to establish the messianic kingdom of righteousness, mercy, and peace may be illustrated by a further consideration of Psalm 3. This psalm's title refers to the time when David fled from his son Absalom. So it may be asked: Why should a psalm related to this particular incident be positioned first in this collection in which many psalms deal with David's struggle with his enemies?

The answer to this question may be that David's conflict with his son must have been the most agonizing of all his struggles. He could endure attacks from enemies outside the bounds of his nation. He could accept the pain of enemies within his community. But his own son? A son who has dethroned his father? A son organizing a military troop that seeks to take his own father's life?

In this context, David first appeals to the Lord's ancient care as demonstrated to the primary patriarchal father at the time of the formal establishment of his covenant with Abraham. God revealed himself to Abraham as his "shield" and his "very great reward" (Gen. 15:1). The same Lord had made a covenant with David and now serves as a "shield" around him (Ps. 3:3). David then reminds the Lord of the two focal promises of his own covenant: a dynasty for himself and a dwellingplace for God in the midst of his people. "You bestow glory on me and lift up my head," alluding to the promise of his kingship (Ps. 3:3). The threatened Messiah cries to the Lord, who answers him "from his holy hill," the locale of God's dwellingplace among his people (Ps. 3:4). Because of the Lord's settled dwellingplace in their midst, the king can rest in peace even though tens of thousands are drawn up against him (Ps. 3:6). In the end, he expresses his confidence that deliverance comes not only for himself but equally for his people, so that he can confidently anticipate the Lord's blessing resting on his people (Ps. 3:8).

From a new covenant perspective, the believer must learn to pray his own first-person prayers in the same way as David. Petitions must ultimately aim at the good of the whole people of God. Otherwise, prayers can degenerate into self-seeking longings concerned only for personal advantage. By following David's example to the full, the blessing of the Lord will come to the full.

The Structural Role of Psalms 18 and 19 in Book I

Within Book I, Psalms 18 and 19 play a key role in structuring this first collection of Davidic psalms. These two psalms present the coupling of a messianic psalm with a Torah psalm. In this regard, they mirror the two opening psalms of the Psalter, Psalms 1 and 2: a Torah psalm and a messianic psalm.

The title of Psalm 18 indicates that David wrote this psalm "when the LORD delivered him from the hand of all his enemies and from the hand of Saul." It represents with little modification the psalm recorded in 2 Samuel 22, which has essentially the same heading (2 Sam. 22:1). This chapter in Samuel is placed just before a poetic recording of the "last words of David" (2 Sam. 23:1–7). But even as these "last words" are only poetically speaking David's "last" words, so it is most likely that the poem in 2 Samuel 22/Psalm 18 was not composed at the point in time at which each and every enemy of David was defeated. The very order that lists first the defeat of "all his enemies" followed by the defeat of Saul in the title suggests instead that this poem could have been composed shortly after Saul fell on the battlefield and all Israel then assembled in Hebron to anoint David as king over a united empire (2 Sam. 5:1–3). David at that point, being thirty years of age (2 Sam. 5:4), had many more enemies to face. As the scriptural notation states in this same context, "When the Philistines heard that David had been anointed king over Israel, they went up in full force to search for him" (2 Sam. 5:17). Yet shortly thereafter, Scripture reports that "the king was settled in his house and the LORD had given him rest from *all his enemies*" (2 Sam. 7:1; cf. Ps. 18 title). This was the time at which the Lord formally instituted his covenant with David and his seed (2 Sam. 7:11b, 16; cf. Ps. 18:50).

The placement of this poem in Book I of the Psalter, conjoined with Psalm 19 as the second Torah psalm, suggests an intentional arrangement of materials in Book I that has a direct relationship to the message of these two pivotal psalms. In comparing the two groupings formed by this placement within Book I (Pss. 3–17 and Pss. 18–41), several factors may be noticed that suggest a purposeful ordering of these two groupings in relation to Psalms 18 and 19. A number of considerations reinforce the significance of this key structural element in Book I.

Messianic-Kingship Terminology Before and After Psalms 18/19

Psalm 2 as a foundational pillar of the Psalter refers explicitly to the messianic *"King,"* the Lord's *"Anointed,"* Yahweh's *"Son"* (Ps. 2:6, 2, 7, 12). This messianic-kingship terminology does not appear again throughout Psalms 3–17.[12] But Psalm 18 concludes:

> He gives his *king* great victories;
> he shows unfailing kindness to his *anointed*,
>> to David and his *descendants* forever. (Ps. 18:50)

Once the solid establishment of David as messianic king by the defeat of all his enemies and Saul has been announced in Psalm 18, the psalmist makes significant use of this messianic-kingship terminology:

> Now I know the LORD saves his *anointed*. (Ps. 20:6)

> O LORD, save the *king*! (Ps. 20:9)

> O LORD, the *king* rejoices in your strength. (Ps. 21:1)

> The *king* trusts in the LORD. (Ps. 21:7)

> The LORD is . . . a fortress of salvation for his *anointed one*. (Ps. 28:8)

Not once is any use made of this messianic-kingship terminology before the Psalm 18 declaration of David's being established as king other than in foundational Psalm 2. Yet immediately after Psalm 18 has reported the defeat of "all [David's] enemies and . . . Saul," the Psalter presents several psalms that refer to David as "king" and "anointed one." So a recognizable difference exists in the use of messianic-kingship terminology before and after Psalm 18.

---

12. Psalm 16:10 declares that the Lord's "Holy One," the *hasid* (חָסִיד), will not see decay. This person is subsequently identified by both the apostle Peter and the apostle Paul as God's "Messiah" who cannot experience decay (Acts 2:24–32; 13:34–37). Yet Psalm 16:10 does not apply the specific terminology of "king," "anointed one," or "Son" to the person in this passage.

Five Kingship Psalms Immediately After Psalms 18/19

Not only the appearance of this messianic terminology right after Psalms 18 and 19 but the grouping of five kingship psalms immediately after this messianic-Torah coupling supports a structural role for Psalms 18/19. Psalms 20–24 contain two psalms presenting Messiah's kingship (Pss. 20–21) and two psalms celebrating Yahweh's kingship (Pss. 23–24), with Psalm 22 vividly depicting both these kingships.[13] The following aspects of this grouping of kingship psalms may be noted.

The prayers of the people for their messianic king in Psalm 20, the first psalm of this collection of five kingship psalms, resound with a note of "victory" for the Lord's anointed king, echoing the "victories" of Psalm 18:50:

> We will shout for joy
> over *your victory* . . . .
> May Yahweh fulfill all your petitions.
> Now I know Yahweh saves his anointed;
> he answers him from his holy heaven. (Ps. 20:5–6)

Psalm 21, the next kingship psalm of this collection, continues this theme of the victories of the messianic king:

> O Yahweh, in your strength
> the king delights,
> and in *your victory*
> he rejoices in ecstasy.
>
> . . . .
>
> Great is his glory
> in *your victory*;
> with splendor and majesty
> you have clothed him. (Ps. 21:1, 5)

13. Patrick D. Miller, "Kingship, Tora Obedience and Prayer," in *Neue Wege der Psalmenforschung*, ed. Klaus Seybold and Erich Zenger (Freiburg: Herder, 1995), 127–41, argues for a grouping of Psalms 15–24. Cf. Grant, *King as Exemplar*, 73–74. While this hypothesis has some merit, its structural straddling of pivotal Psalms 18 and 19 weakens its case.

No psalm in the first collection of Book I proper (Pss. 3–17) presents David as the "anointed one," the "king," who has won great "*victories*." But these two psalms that follow immediately after transitional Psalms 18 and 19 speak clearly of David the messianic king and his *victories*, just as they had been introduced in the concluding verse of Psalm 18.

This collection of five kingship psalms also presents Yahweh in his distinctive role as King (Pss. 23–24). Generally, readers of Psalm 23 have been fully taken up in the personalized images of the Lord as their tender Shepherd so that they have failed to recognize Yahweh's kingly status in this psalm. Yet the concept of God as Shepherd-King goes back almost a thousand years before David. Jacob the patriarch anticipates Yahweh's kingship when he speaks of "the God who has shepherded me all my days" (Gen. 48:15–16). In his prophetic pronouncement regarding the tribe of Joseph, Jacob speaks of the "Mighty One of Jacob," the "Shepherd, the Rock of Israel" (Gen. 49:24). Then climactically at the point of David's being anointed king over all Israel, the tribes previously loyal to Saul recalled the Lord's appointment of this man to be their shepherd-king:

> Yahweh said to you, "You will shepherd my people Israel, and you will become their ruler." (2 Sam. 5:2)

This same imagery is subsequently applied to Yahweh in his exaltation as King over his people at a time when the nation was in desperate need of the Lord's intervention:

> Hear us, O Shepherd of Israel,
> you who lead Joseph like a flock;
> you who sit enthroned between the cherubim,
> shine forth. (Ps. 80:1)

So the picture in Psalm 23 of Yahweh as David's Shepherd inevitably recalls the Lord's kingship. Psalm 23 may be viewed as an integral part of this collection of five kingship psalms that follow the declaration of David's being established in his kingship according to pivotal Psalm 18.[14]

The next psalm of this collection, Psalm 24, repeatedly acknowledges Yahweh's role as King:

> Lift up your heads, O gates,
> and be lifted up, you ancient doors,
>   and the King of Glory shall come in.

> Who is this King of Glory?
>   The LORD strong and mighty,
>   The LORD mighty in battle. (Ps. 24:7–8)

Five times over, the concluding verses of this psalm herald the "King of Glory" (Ps. 24:7–10). Twice the psalmist propounds the rhetorical question concerning the identity of this "King of Glory," the second time even more emphatically: "Who is He, this King of Glory?" (v. 10). Precisely as the psalmist answers antiphonally, Yahweh is this King of Glory.

This collection of kingship psalms following just after messianic Psalm 18 (coupled with Torah Psalm 19) supports the transitional role of these two psalms. They mark a clear transition point in Book I. Messianic terminology as well as a collection of messianic and divine-kingship psalms follows this joint marker in the first book of the Psalter.

Psalm 22 as the focal center of this collection of five kingship psalms plays a significant role in joining these two kingships. Psalm 22 functions significantly as a mediating psalm that brings together Messiah's kingship and Yahweh's kingship. The opening words of Psalm 22 raise an unanswered question as David the messianic king cries in

---

14. See the comments of John H. Stek on Psalm 23 in "Psalms," in *The NIV Study Bible* (London: Hodder & Stoughton, 1985). Stek develops quite effectively the identity of David's "shepherd" as Yahweh his "Shepherd-King." Stek describes Psalm 23 as a "profession of joyful trust in the Lord as the good Shepherd-King." Ibid., 790. He explains the term *shepherd* in Psalm 23 as a "widely used metaphor for kings in the ancient Near East, and also in Israel. . . . Here David the king acknowledges that the Lord is his Shepherd-King. . . . The heavenly Shepherd-King receives David at his table as his vassal king." Ibid., 790–91.

puzzled agony: "My God, my God, why have you forsaken me?" (Ps. 22:1). The psalmist suffers at the hands of brutal bulls, lions, dogs, and the horns of oxen (Ps. 22:12–13, 20–21). Scripture regularly employs this imagery of powerful bulls, lions, and the horns of oxen to indicate international powers. This conglomeration of international enemies indicates that it is the king, the Lord's anointed, who is the subject of the suffering at their hands. For these international forces would not target the "ordinary Israelite." The king himself is the subject of their assault. All his bones are out of joint. His tongue clings to the roof of his mouth. He lies in the dust of death. People stare and gloat over him. They divide his garments among them, and cast lots for his clothing (Ps. 22:14–15, 17–18). This vivid description clearly anticipates the sufferings of the messianic king (cf. Matt. 27:35, 46; Mark 15:34; John 19:34).

But the second portion of this mediating psalm speaks in the most glorious terms of Yahweh's kingship. His rule is universal and perpetual:

> All the ends of the earth
>> will remember and turn to Yahweh.
>
> All the families of the nations
>> will bow down to him.
>>
>> For dominion belongs to Yahweh,
>> and he rules over the nations.
>
> . . . .
>
> Posterity will serve him;
> Future generations will be told about the Lord.
>> They will proclaim his righteousness to a people yet unborn,
>> for he has done it. (Ps. 22:27–28, 30–31)

The stunning predictions about the Christ's sufferings in the first portion of Psalm 22 have tended to "restrain the eyes" of believers from fully absorbing the glories of the final portion of this psalm. But seen in the context of these five psalms of kingship, it becomes clear that the first portion of this mediating psalm (Ps. 22:1–21) relates to Messiah's kingship as just presented in Psalms 20 and 21. Then the second portion of this same psalm

(Ps. 22:22–31) depicts Yahweh's kingship over the nations, in anticipation of Psalms 23 and 24 that celebrate the Lord's kingship. Before Psalm 18, terminology of messianic kingship was not present except in Psalm 2. But after the pronouncement regarding David's kingship in Psalm 18, this grouping of five kingship psalms surfaces with great prominence.[15] The introduction of this impressive collection of kingship psalms at this point strongly underscores the transitional role of Psalm 18, coupled with Psalm 19, in Book I.

The Terms for *Law* Before and After Torah Psalm 19

A third evidence for the pivotal role of Psalms 18 and 19 in Book I may be seen by a comparison of the usage of the various terms for God's *law*. Except for the single reference to the Lord's "laws" that are far from the wicked (Ps. 10:5), the multiple terms for Yahweh's Torah, his law, and his testimonies, precepts, commands, and ordinances as introduced in Torah Psalm 19 do not appear in the first section of Book I (Pss. 3–17). But the various *Torah* terms appear a number of times in the second section of Book I (Pss. 18–41). Five of the six specific designations for *Torah* in Psalm 19 occur beyond the first section of Book I (Pss. 3–17):

All his *ordinances* are before me;
I have not turned away from his *statutes*. (Ps. 18:22)

All the ways of the LORD are loving and faithful
for those who keep his covenant and his *testimonies*. (Ps. 25:10)

I will teach you the *fear of the LORD*. (Ps. 34:11)

The *law* of God is in his heart. (Ps. 37:31)

Your *law* is within my heart. (Ps. 40:8)

---

15. Other groupings of kingship psalms may be found in each of the first four books of the Psalms: Psalms 45–48 (Book II); Psalms 75–76 (Book III); Psalms 92–100 (Book IV). It is not clear why a collection of specifically kingship psalms is absent from Book V. Could it be that the *Hallelu-YAH* psalms serve this role in Book V? See the discussion of this possibility in the treatment of Book V.

While these terms are absent from Psalms 3–17 apart from the single reference to God's laws as being far from the wicked (Ps. 10:5b), they appear with some regularity in Psalms 18–41, once pivotal Psalms 18 and 19 have introduced for the first time the multiple usage of these terms.

"Teaching" Before and After Psalms 18/19

A fourth evidence of the pivotal role of Psalms 18 and 19 appears when references to "teaching" in the sections before and after these two psalms are compared. No specific mention is made of "teaching" the way in Psalms 3–17, though two psalms refer to God's "leading" or "making known" the path of life to his people.[16] But following Torah Psalm 19, a number of references to "teaching" surface in the second section of Book I (Pss. 18–41):

> Show me your ways, O LORD,
> *teach* me your paths;
> guide me in your truth
> and *teach* me. (Ps. 25:4–5)

> *Teach* me your way, O LORD;
> lead me in a straight path
>   because of my oppressors. (Ps. 27:11)

> I will instruct you and *teach* you
>   in the way you should go;
> I will counsel you and watch over you. (Ps. 32:8)

> Come, my children, listen to me;
> I will *teach* you the fear of the LORD. (Ps. 34:11)

Teaching and instruction by the Lord belong to the essence of Torah. "Teaching" by the Lord would always be appropriate. Yet this divine tutelage is more readily promoted in the time after the

---

16. Psalm 5:8 states, "Lead me . . . in your righteousness . . .—make straight your way before me." Psalm 16:11 declares, "You have made known to me the path of life." Yet the basic terms meaning "to teach" (יָרָה. לָמַד) are absent from these passages..

Lord has given David some respite by the defeat of all his enemies, as indicated in the heading of transitional Psalm 18, coupled as it is with Torah Psalm 19. So quite appropriately, Psalm 25, coming just after the grouping of five kingship psalms (Pss. 20–24), responds to Torah Psalm 19 by a tenfold reference to the Lord's instruction: "show me," "teach me," "guide me," "teach me," "he instructs," "he guides," "he teaches;" "he will instruct," "he confides," "he makes known" (Ps. 25:4, 5, 8, 9, 12, 14). Once more, the transitional character of coupled Psalms 18 and 19 is indicated.

References to Confession of Sin

A second impact of the Lord's Torah beyond "teaching" the way is the conviction of sin and consequent confession. No explicit confession of sin by the psalmist is recorded in Psalms 3–17.[17] But Psalm 25 responds to Torah Psalm 19 with no fewer than four explicit acknowledgments of personal sin:

Remember not the sins of my youth and my rebellious ways. (Ps. 25:7)

The LORD . . . instructs sinners in his ways. (Ps. 25:8)

Forgive my iniquity, though it is great. (Ps. 25:11)

Take away all my sins. (Ps. 25:18)

Once the delicate matter of confessing personal sin has been broached by Psalm 25 in its response to Torah Psalm 19, a number of psalms confessing sin appear in this second major portion of Book I. Focal among these is the classic confession by David in Psalm 32:

Blessed is he
 whose transgressions are forgiven,
 whose sins are covered.
. . . .

17. In Psalm 6:1, the psalmist pleads, "Do not rebuke me in your anger, or discipline me in your wrath," which could imply guilt. But the psalm falls short of an actual confession of sin.

> I said, "I will confess my transgressions to the LORD"—
> and you forgave the guilt of my sin. (Ps. 32:1, 5)

An additional collection of four psalms confessing sin concludes this second and final section of Book I (Pss. 38:3–4, 18; 39:8, 11; 40:12; 41:4). Yet before Torah Psalm 19, no explicit confession of sin appears.

So the *Torah*, the "teaching," of the Lord accomplishes two things: (1) it "teaches" the way of the Lord; and (2) it convicts of sin. Though essentially absent in Psalms 3–17, both these elements are manifestly prominent in Psalm 25 as it responds directly to Torah Psalm 19. Beyond Psalm 25, a number of psalms include "teaching" and confession, supporting the transitional role of Torah Psalm 19.

References to Yahweh as the "Rock" of Stability

A final evidence for the transitional role of Psalms 18 and 19 may be seen in the references to Yahweh as the "Rock" of his people. The opening lines of Psalm 18 apply for the first time in the Psalms this ancient poetic imagery of a "Rock," representing divine stability residing in David's covenantal Lord:

> Yahweh is my Rock [סַלְעִי] . . . ; my God [אֵלִי] is my Rock [צוּרִי].
> (Ps. 18:2)

Not during the times that David wandered as a vagabond in the desert, or lived as a fugitive in a cave, or languished as a captive in the hands of alien Philistines could this image of stability be meaningfully employed in its fullest sense. But now that God has delivered David from "all his enemies and from . . . Saul," the Lord is portrayed as "the Rock," the Rock of stability on which the messianic kingship rests. In this regard, Psalm 18 coupled with Psalm 19 may be seen once more as a primary point of transition in Book I.

This ancient imagery of the Lord's unshakable stability goes back to the prophetic pronouncement of the patriarch Jacob over his favored son Joseph. The "Rock" of Israel steadied Joseph's bow in the face of all his opponents (Gen. 49:24). Moses' final song also hails the unwavering faithfulness of God as "the Rock" whose ways are always just, a God who does no wrong (Deut. 32:4). Israel erred greatly when the nation rejected "the Rock" their Savior (Deut. 32:15). They deserted the "Rock" who had fathered them (Deut. 32:18). In no way could they lose a battle, unless their "Rock" abandoned them (Deut. 32:30). For the "rock" of other nations cannot compare to Israel's "Rock" (Deut. 32:31). Again, Samuel's mother Hannah anticipates her son's role when the time comes for God to give strength to his king and exalt the horn of his anointed (1 Sam. 2:10c). With that future prospect before her, she delights to declare, "There is no Rock like our God" (1 Sam. 2:2).

So when David opens Psalm 18 by declaring that God is his "Rock," he draws on a proven imagery of God's immovable fidelity. Not one time only, but several times over in this psalm, he declares the Lord to be his "Rock":

> The LORD is my Rock . . . .
> My God is my Rock.
> Who is the Rock except our God?
>
> . . . .
> Praise be to my Rock! (Ps. 18:2, 31, 46)

Not surprisingly, David returns to this ancient imagery in his final poetic composition as recorded in 2 Samuel to capture the concept of the stability of a kingly rule based on righteousness:

> The God of Israel spoke,
> the Rock of Israel said to me:
>> when one rules over men in righteousness,
>> when he rules in the fear of God,
>>> he is like the light of the morning at sunrise on a cloudless morning,
>>> like the brightness after rain that brings the grass from the earth. (2 Sam. 23:3–4)

Never had this imagery been employed in the Psalter before Psalm 18. But then in the portion of Book I that begins with Psalm 18 (Pss. 18–41), the picture is used several times over:

O Lord, my Rock and my Redeemer. (Ps. 19:14)

To you I call, O Lord my Rock. (Ps. 28:1)

Come quickly . . . ; be my Rock of refuge. (Ps. 31:2)

You are my rock and my fortress. (Ps. 31:3)

In addition, the image of God's setting his messianic servant on a "rock" as a place of security and stability occurs in two other psalms in this collection:

He will . . . set me high upon a rock. (Ps. 27:5)

He set my feet on a rock. (Ps. 40:2)

The repeated use of this strong imagery of Yahweh as a Rock for his anointed one beginning with pivotal Psalm 18 corresponds to David's situation after God has defeated "all his enemies and . . . Saul," as expressed in the title of Psalm 18. This distinctive deployment of the "Rock" imagery strongly suggests a deliberate flow in the structure of the Psalter. The message of the book moves from David's struggle to establish his messianic kingship to the founding of a permanent dwellingplace in Jerusalem and a perpetual kingship according to God's covenant with David.

These several indicators support the concept that the coupling of messianic Psalm 18 with Torah Psalm 19 has been intentionally arranged to serve as a structural marker indicating development within Book I. Contendings to establish and maintain the messianic throne of David will continue. According to the narrative of 2 Samuel, the establishment of David as king over all Israel after the death of Saul only served to provoke the nation's ancient enemy to even greater efforts to overthrow the Messiah and his kingdom. David almost lost his life in a battle with the Philistines that occurred much later in his career as king. This incident led his men to take an oath: "Never again will you go out with us to battle, so that the lamp of

Israel will not be extinguished" (2 Sam. 21:17). But the two sections of Book I envision a definite change of circumstance for Israel's king, with messianic Psalm 18 coupled with Torah Psalm 19 serving as the pivotal point of transition.

The Structural Role of Acrostic Psalms in Book I (Psalms 9/10,[18] 25, 34, 37)

The alphabetic acrostics in the Psalter provide a further major indicator of intentional structure within the Psalter, and particularly in Book I.[19] These acrostic psalms are distinctive in their poetic form in that subsequent though not always consecutive verses begin with

18. Psalms 9 and 10 are treated as a single psalm in the LXX, which most likely would be dated sometime in the third or second century B.C. The Masoretic text separates the two psalms. A manuscript from Qumran with a proposed dating of A.D. 50–68 also attests to this separation by a blank line that precedes the first verse of Psalm 10. Cf. James Charlesworth et al., *Miscellaneous Texts from the Judaean Desert XXXVIII* (Oxford: Clarendon Press, 2007), 143, 148. The absence of a title for Psalm 10 supports the original unity of the two chapters, as attested to by the LXX. Worth noting also is the fact that Psalm 10 opens with the next letter of the alphabetic acrostic after the first eleven letters had been covered in Psalm 9. In addition, the conclusion of Psalm 10 with the sequential use of the final four letters of the alphabetic acrostic strongly supports the unity of the two psalms. The circumstances surrounding the division into two psalms are buried in the dark shadows of the past.

Generally, Psalms 9 and 10 are regarded as a "broken" acrostic, since six letters of the Hebrew alphabet are missing in Psalm 10. Yet the connection in substance between the nonalphabetic section (Ps. 10:2–11) and the alphabetic conclusion (Ps. 10:12–18) suggests that nothing has "gone missing" from the psalm. In terms of flow of thought, the opening verse of Psalm 10 begins with a cry of distress (Ps. 10:1). The following nonalphabetic verses define the reason for the distress, which has arisen because an oppressor ambushes, murders, lurks, and stalks (Ps. 10:2–11). Then in the alphabetic conclusion, the psalmist asks the Lord to intervene in behalf of the poor and the helpless, affirming that the God who "sees" will call this oppressor to account, contrary to his brash declaration that God does "not see" and will not call him to account (Ps. 10:11, 13–14). The final verses of Psalm 10 conclude with a clear echo of the substance of Psalm 9. Yahweh is King (Ps. 9:4, 7, 8, 11, 19, 20; cf. Ps. 10:16); and "[mere] humans" should recognize that fact (Pss. 9:20; 10:18). The thought pattern progresses in an orderly fashion across alphabetic and nonalphabetic sections, strongly supporting the idea of a unified rather than a "broken" poem.

19. For further exploration of the structural function of the four acrostic psalms in Book I, see this author's article "The Alphabetic Acrostic in Book I of the Psalms: An Overlooked Element of Psalter Structure," which is scheduled to appear in the December 2015 (volume 40, 2) issue of the *Journal for the Study of the Old Testament*.

a word whose first letter follows the order of the Hebrew alphabet. Various irregularities appear that are not consistent with the exact pattern of the alphabet. Sometimes a letter is omitted; at other times more than one verse opens with the same letter. Occasionally an additional verse not in alphabetical sequence concludes the poem. Yet the acrostic pattern is readily recognizable.

This first book of the Psalter (Pss. 1–41) contains four of the eight acrostic psalms. The remaining four acrostics all occur in Book V, the largest of the books of the Psalter, with forty-four psalms (Pss. 107–150).

These acrostic psalms function in a variety of ways. Being carefully spaced, they divide these two largest books of the Psalter into smaller sections. Often they provide structural framework for the books. As previously noted, acrostic Psalm 25 responds to Torah Psalm 19 by containing no fewer than ten references to the "teaching" function of the Torah. Acrostic Psalms 34 and 37 bracket four psalms of the innocent sufferer (Pss. 34–37). These four psalms are then followed immediately by four psalms of the guilty sufferer (Pss. 38–41). As a consequence, a pastor who is aware of the bracketing function of acrostic Psalms 34 and 37 could be significantly helped in counseling persons struggling with either innocence or guilt in response to their suffering.

A rather striking additional element of the acrostic poems of Book I is their relationship to creation psalms. Only three psalms in Book I mention the Lord's creation of the world. Yet in each case, the creation psalm immediately precedes an acrostic psalm:

- Creation Psalm 8 precedes acrostic Psalm 9/10
- Creation Psalm 24 precedes acrostic Psalm 25
- Creation Psalm 33 precedes acrostic Psalm 34

It might be assumed that this arrangement occurs as a purely random phenomenon. But it seems far more likely that the editor(s) of the Psalter deliberately placed each of the creation psalms just before an acrostic psalm.

The reason for this arrangement is difficult to determine. Could it be that psalms describing the creativity of the Lord in his shaping the *world* find a reflection in the creativity of the Lord in shaping the *word*?

A further matter of structural significance is the "quasi-acrostic." These psalms contain twenty-two verses in accord with the twenty-two letters of the Hebrew alphabet. But the verses do not give any hint of intending to follow an alphabetic order.

Once more, the reason for this arrangement is not apparent. Yet the intentional nature of this phenomenon receives support by the shaping of the longest acrostic poem of the Scriptures—the book of Lamentations. The first four chapters of Lamentations clearly conform to the classic acrostic pattern, with twenty-two verses arranged alphabetically in chapters 1, 2, and 4, and sixty-six verses arranged alphabetically in chapter 3. Chapter 5 of Lamentations has twenty-two verses, but without a hint of alphabetic arrangement. The acrostic structure of the first four chapters clearly shows that the number of twenty-two verses in chapter 5 is altogether intentional as a reflection of the acrostic form.

Three instances of quasi-acrostic psalms appear in the Psalter: Psalms 33, 38, and 103. In terms of their placement in Book I, Psalms 33 and 38 "bracket the brackets" of acrostic Psalms 34 and 37. Once more, the reason for this arrangement is difficult to discern. Yet their positioning clearly seems to be intentional.

Despite unanswered questions surrounding the acrostic psalms of Book I, two factors appear to be quite clear. First, it seems evident that the acrostic psalms were deliberately positioned as structural factors in this collection. They divide the second-largest book of the Psalter (Book I) into smaller segments. Second, their form seems clearly intended to aid in the memorization of these particular psalms. For by memorizing these four psalms (Pss. 9/10, 25, 34, 37) along with an awareness of their positioning in the Psalter, the student of the Psalter has immediate access to many additional psalms. He knows that Psalms 8, 24, and 33 are creational psalms that precede acrostic Psalms 9/10, 25, and 34. He knows that Psalms 34–37 are psalms of the innocent sufferer while Psalms 38–41 are psalms of the guilty sufferer. He knows that quasi-acrostic Psalms 33 and 38 "bracket the brackets" formed by Psalms 34 and 37. By appreciating the placement of the four acrostic psalms of Book I, he has immediate access to no fewer than fourteen of the forty-one psalms of Book I, or one-third of the total number of the psalms in the book.[20]

In conclusion, a recognition of the structural role of the acrostic psalms in the Psalter could serve as a great blessing for the church of Jesus Christ today. Perhaps a new generation of believers will respond to the challenge of memorizing the acrostic psalms in the language of inspired Scripture as a way of grasping something of the structural order of the Psalter. The results of this memorization of these acrostic psalms would be instantaneous access to a significant portion of an "inspired abbreviation" of the whole Bible. Martin Luther summarized this perspective on the Psalms. His words are worth quoting in full:

> The Psalter ought to be a precious and beloved book, if for no other reason than this: it promises Christ's death and resurrection so clearly—and pictures his kingdom and the condition and nature of all Christendom—that it might well be called a little Bible. In it is comprehended most beautifully and briefly everything that is in the entire Bible. It is really a fine enchiridion or handbook. In fact, I have a notion that the Holy Spirit wanted to take the trouble himself to compile a short Bible and book of examples of all Christendom for all saints, so that anyone who could not read the whole Bible would here have anyway almost an entire summary of it, comprised in one little book.[21]

If Luther is correct in his statement that the whole Bible is contained in the Psalms, what a blessing it would be for the individual as well as for God's people as a whole if a serious effort were made to memorize a strategic selection of psalms, including the eight carefully positioned acrostic psalms.

20. The structural positioning of the four acrostic psalms in Book V is even more apparent, and will be discussed in the treatment of Book V.

21. Martin Luther, *Luther's Works* (Philadelphia: Muhlenberg Press, 1960), 35:254. In a similar vein, John Calvin describes the book of Psalms as "An Anatomy of all the Parts of the Soul." *Commentary on the Book of Psalms* (Grand Rapids: Baker, 1993), 1:xxxvii.

Conclusion to Book I

Book I concludes with a personalized psalm of Messiah in which he suffers the betrayal of a close friend:

> Even my close friend, whom I trusted,
>> he who shared my bread,
>> has lifted up his heel against me.
>>> (Ps. 41:9; cf. Matt. 26:23; Luke 22:21; John 13:18)

Even though the whole of this psalm may not be directly applied to Jesus Christ as the ultimate Anointed One, particularly in its confession of sin (Ps. 41:4), the basic anticipation of betrayal of God's Messiah by a close friend who has turned into his archenemy is clearly a messianic motif harking back to the life-and-death struggle between the singular saving seed of the woman and Satan himself, the ultimate enemy of God's people (Gen. 3:15).[22]

As the Psalter progresses, this animosity between the two seeds is viewed from various perspectives. At one point, *communication* with the enemy includes an invitation to join in the worship of the LORD OF THE COVENANT (Book II). At another point, the Lord's people experience *devastation* at the hands of international enemies (Book III). Still further, the people of the Lord undergo *maturation* as they focus on Yahweh's kingship despite the displacement enforced by their enemies (Book IV). Finally, God's people experience *consummation* as they shout "*Hallelu-YAH*" when ultimate victory is achieved over all their enemies (Book V).

---

22. Cf. O. Palmer Robertson, *The Christ of the Covenants* (Phillipsburg, NJ: Presbyterian and Reformed, 1980), 99–103.

6

BOOK II (PSALMS 42–72): COMMUNICATION

Confrontation with enemies has been the dominant theme of Book I. David as the Lord's anointed has experienced unending struggle with the opponents of his kingdom. Even though a distinctively messianic psalm (Ps. 18) coupled with a second Torah psalm (Ps. 19) forms a transition in Book I in which it is declared that the Lord had delivered David "from all his enemies and from Saul," the struggle continues.

Book II consists of thirty-one psalms (Pss. 42–72), which are divided essentially one-third and two-thirds between a collection of psalms by the "Sons of Korah" (Pss. 42–49[*1]) followed by a single psalm of Asaph (Ps. 50), and a second collection of the psalms of David (Pss. 51–71[*]), followed by a single psalm of Solomon (Ps. 72). The psalms of the Sons of Korah set a new tone at the opening of Book II. A progression in perspective has clearly taken place over the situation prevailing in Book I. Constant ups and downs in the struggle to realize Yahweh's kingdom of righteousness and peace will continue. Yet immediately after introductory Psalm(s) 42/43 and Psalm 44, four psalms celebrate the kingship of Elohim and his Messiah over the nations (Pss. 45–48).[2] After the next two psalms issue a formal

1. Again, throughout this volume, the asterisk (*) indicates a grouping of psalms in which the titles in that particular collection might not specifically indicate the predominant author in every case.

2. *Elohim*, the general name for God, prevails over *Yahweh*, the covenant name of God, throughout the bulk of Book II. *Yahweh* occurs 32 times in Book II, while *Elohim* occurs 198 times. In clearest contrast, *Yahweh* appears 278 times and *Elohim* 48 times in Book I.

summons first to the nations of the world and then to God's people (Pss. 49–50), the second collection of Davidic psalms is presented (Pss. 51–71*).[3] This second collection of psalms attributed to David manifests a different attitude toward the nations and peoples of the world from the prevailing perspective in Book I. Even though they continue as David's deadly enemies, the psalmist repeatedly expresses himself to the nations in a manner that indicates a desire to *communicate* more directly with them. Within this second Davidic collection is found a special grouping of psalms that specify seven different enemies of God's anointed one (Pss. 54–60). Then a "dialogue between the kings" is reported (Pss. 61–68), including four psalms representing the cry of the messianic king (Pss. 61–64), followed by four psalms that respond by affirming the undisturbed reign of the Divine King (Pss. 65–68). Three psalms follow this kingship dialogue and describe the ongoing struggles of the messianic king even into David's old age (Pss. 69–71). Included in these final psalms of Book II is a distinctive psalm (Ps. 69), separate portions of which are quoted by three different authors of the New Testament. Book II concludes with a description of the glorious extension of Messiah's kingdom both geographically and temporally (Ps. 72). With this basic outline of the materials of Book II in mind, the structural and theological substance of the book may now be considered.

Seven Psalms of the Sons of Korah (Psalms 42/43–49*)

Seven psalms attributed to the "Sons of Korah," including a single psalm without title, serve as a special collection that opens Book II. The

---

To enhance the reader's awareness of this significant factor in Book II in its contrast with Book I, the term *Elohim* will be frequently employed when this general name for God appears in Book II. The reader may then become aware, among other things, of several places where it might have been assumed that *Yahweh* would be employed because of the close connection of context with the covenant, and yet *Elohim*, the general name for God, is used. For a further exploration of the use of *Yahweh* and *Elohim* across the Psalter, see Bruce K. Waltke and James M. Houston, *The Psalms as Christian Worship* (Grand Rapids: Eerdmans, 2010), 101n58.

3. Three of the psalms in this collection do not have the *leDavid* phrase in their title (Pss. 66, 67, 71). But these psalms very likely were also "by David."

introduction of a different author at the beginning of a new book in the Psalter suggests intentional arrangement by the editor. The absence of designation of author in a psalm's title following immediately after a previous psalm that does include an indication of authorship in the title often means that the two psalms should be considered together, most likely composed by the same author.[4] This principle is most clearly illustrated in Psalms 42 and 43, the opening psalms of Book II, in which a refrain binds the two consecutive psalms together:

> Why are you downcast, O my soul?
> Why so disturbed within me?
>> Put your hope in Elohim,
>>> for I will yet praise him,
>>> my Savior and my Elohim. (Ps. 42:5, 11; Ps. 43:5)

Introductory Psalms of Hope despite Distress (Psalms 42/43–44)

Book II opens with psalms of individual and corporate expressions of hope despite a deep sense of distress. In the first two psalms, which should be taken as one, the writer struggles with sadness in his soul because of his feeling of rejection by Elohim due to his forced inability to lead God's people in procession to the "house of Elohim" with "shouts of joy and thanksgiving among the festive throng" (Ps. 42:4). This external exclusion from the established dwellingplace of his Elohim leads the psalmist to a state of internal mourning. As the refrain indicates:

> Why have you forgotten me?
> Why must I go about mourning,
>> oppressed by the enemy? (Ps. 42:9)

> Why have you rejected me?
> Why must I go about mourning,
>> oppressed by the enemy? (Ps. 43:2)

---

4. See Gerald Henry Wilson, *The Editing of the Hebrew Psalter* (Chico, CA: Scholars Press, 1985), 173–77. Wilson's most convincing cases of this phenomenon are Psalms 9 and 10; 32 and 33; 42 and 43; and 70 and 71.

These two opening psalms (or psalm) of Book II provide a realistic picture of a significant consequence of the perpetual struggle with the enemy of God's people that every believer must face. The struggle will go on, not only without but also within. In this sense, the traditional reading of the Psalms from a personalized perspective is altogether appropriate.

Yet these opening psalms of Book II demand more. The psalmist is excluded from the house of God. He is being abused by a nation, a *goy* (גּוֹי), and pleads for deliverance "from a nation that shows no mercy" (מִגּוֹי לֹא־חָסִיד—Ps. 43:1). The reference could be to the apostate nation of northern Israel that on one occasion "took hostages [from the South] and returned to Samaria" (2 Kings 14:14c).[5] This oppressive nation, whichever it might be, refuses to allow its Judean captives to participate in the annual festivals held in Jerusalem. The enemy introduced in this second book of the Psalms is not an individual adversary but a national foe.

Despite the ongoing struggle within and without, the psalmist "talks to himself," counsels himself that he must sustain his hope in God with the threefold repetition of a refrain:

> Why are you depressed,
>   O my soul?
> and so violently agitated
>   within me?
> Put your hope in Elohim,
>   for in due time I shall praise him,
>   my Savior and my God. (Ps. 42:5; cf. v. 11; Ps. 43:5)

A further point of hope despite distress finds expression in Psalm 44, but this time in a corporate context. God has rejected and humbled his people. He has scattered them "among the nations" (Ps. 44:11; cf. v. 14). Yet he remains as their King "who decrees victories for Jacob" (Ps. 44:4). The closing words of this psalm anticipate God's rising up and redeeming them because of his unfailing love (Ps. 44:26). So these introductory psalms express hope in the context of an ongoing struggle

---

5. The same term *goy* (גּוֹי) is disparagingly applied to the kingdom of Judah in Isaiah 1:4.

to establish Messiah's kingdom of righteousness and peace in response to the opposition of other nations as well as deeply personal struggles.

The Kingship of Elohim and His Messiah (Psalms 45–48)

Following these three psalms introducing personal and national dilemma, four psalms celebrate the kingship of Elohim and his Messiah over the nations (Pss. 45–48). In a most startling and dramatic fashion, a royal wedding song addresses the messianic king as God himself on his throne, riding forth victoriously in behalf of truth, humility, and righteousness:

> Your throne, O Elohim,
>> will last for ever and ever.
> A scepter of justice
>> will be the scepter of your kingdom.
> You love righteousness
>> and hate wickedness.
> Therefore Elohim, your Elohim,
>>> has set you above your companions
>>> by anointing you with the oil of joy. (Ps. 45:6–7)[6]

6. For an overview of the various treatments of this startling passage, see, among others, John Goldingay, *Psalms, Volume 2: Psalms 42–89* (Grand Rapids: Baker, 2007), 53n6. Peter C. Craigie, *Psalms 1–50*, Word Biblical Commentary 19 (Waco, TX: Word Books, 1983), 336, rejects several popular proposals (such as "your divine throne" and "your throne is God's") for syntactical reasons, and then settles for Mitchell Dahood's unique "God has enthroned you," though acknowledging that this rendition is "not without difficulty." The one rendering that has no grammatical difficulty finds ancient support in the Septuagint, which properly treats *Elohim* as a vocative, and clearly identifies the messianic king as *Elohim*: "Your throne, O Elohim, is forever and ever." Hans-Joachim Kraus, *Theology of the Psalms* (Minneapolis: Augsburg, 1986), 183, forthrightly affirms that Psalm 45:7 should be understood as "a reference to the deity of the ruler . . . . As 'Son of God' he is truly God. His kingdom is ultimately identical with the kingdom of God." Contrariwise, Brevard S. Childs, *Biblical Theology of the Old and New Testaments: Theological Reflection on the Christian Bible* (London: SCM Press, 1992), 193f., speaks of the "mythopoetic language of Pss. 45 and 72." Yet the persistence of this concept of the universal reign of a divine Messiah is never diminished even into its new covenant manifestations. Hebrews 1:8–9 speaks of Jesus as the Son who is the God-Messiah of Psalm 45. This "Son" is the "heir of all things" through whom God made the universe (Heb. 1:2). He is "the radiance of God's glory and the exact representation of his being" and is currently "sustaining all things by his powerful word" (Heb. 1:3). He is specifically identified in Hebrews as Jesus

How could it be that Messiah is suddenly presented as God in this psalm! What precedent has prepared for this startling announcement, particularly in view of the unshakable commitment to monotheism in the Old Testament faith?

The precedent quite naturally arises from the focal point of God's covenant with David, which serves as a foundational factor for the book of Psalms in its role in redemptive history. God's covenant with David specifically indicated regarding the expected Messiah, "I shall be his Father, and he shall be my Son" (2 Sam. 7:14). As previously indicated, Psalm 2 with its declaration regarding Messiah as God's Son seated at the right hand of the Almighty serves as one of two major pillars providing entrance into the temple of the Psalter (Ps. 2:7). From this perspective, the identification of Messiah as God may be viewed as a natural extension of the promise to David regarding his messianic successor as Son of God.[7] Despite the many efforts to tone down the straightforward designation of the messianic king as *Elohim*, the phrase is quite specific. The immediately succeeding reference to "Elohim, your Elohim" (Ps. 45:6) strongly supports this understanding. The phrase "Elohim, your Elohim" clearly distinguishes the *Elohim* (i.e., God) who anoints the messianic king (v. 7c) from the *Elohim* (i.e., the "you" who is being anointed) whose throne will "endure forever" (v. 6). From a redemptive-historical perspective, David's bringing up the ark to Mount Zion indicated his intent to have God's throne merge with

the historic person (Heb. 4:14; 5:8). Clearly, these words are intended to be regarded as more than a mythologically poetic way of speaking. Says Kidner: "The Hebrew resists any softening here, and it is the New Testament, not the new versions, which does it justice when it uses it to prove the superiority of God's Son to the very angels (Heb. 1:8f). This paradox is consistent with the incarnation, but mystifying in any other context." Derek Kidner, *Psalms 1–72: An Introduction and Commentary on Books I and II of the Psalms* (London: Inter-Varsity Press, 1973), 172. The NIV (2011 version) rightly renders the biblical text of Psalm 45:6 in its address to Messiah as follows: "Your throne, O God, will last forever and ever." But the explanation in the footnote (not in previous versions of the NIV) presents an unnecessary modification of the clear affirmation of the deity of the coming Messiah as confirmed by the comments of Hebrews 1:8–9. The note reads: "Here the king is addressed as God's representative."

7. Note the conclusion reached by Jesus' adversaries in response to his designating God as "My Father." They tried all the harder to kill him because he was calling God his own Father, "making himself equal with God" (John 5:17–18).

his own messianic throne. God's rule would be united with the rule of himself and his son-successors.

In this context, the exaltation of the COVENANT LORD Almighty above the nations in the three psalms following Psalm 45 is fully understandable. Elohim dwells in his holy place, in the city of Elohim, himself serving as the fortress of his people (Ps. 46:4–5). From this exalted vantage point, he lifts his voice, kingdoms fall, and the earth melts (Ps. 46:6). Elohim will be exalted among the nations and throughout the earth (Ps. 46:10). This Great King over all the earth subdues nations under the feet of his people, for he reigns over the nations, seated on his holy throne (Ps. 47:2–3, 8). The nobles of the nations assemble as the people of the God of Abraham, for the kings of the earth belong to Elohim (Ps. 47:9). Mount Zion serves as the city of the Great King, and so the next generation must hear of her majestic towers, ramparts, and citadels (Ps. 48:12–13).

Quite obviously, these three psalms have been grouped to celebrate the sovereignty of the COVENANT LORD as the Great King over the nations. Clearly, a progression may be seen in the movement from the personal struggle of David with his various enemies to establish his kingship in Book I (Pss. 3–41). Now the people of Elohim struggle with corporate enemies, which must conclude in victory because Elohim and his Messiah jointly reign from Mount Zion (Pss. 45–48).

Two Psalms with a Summons (Psalms 49–50)

After establishing God and his Messiah as King (Pss. 45–48), two psalms intervene (Pss. 49–50) before a second extended collection of the psalms of David is presented (Pss. 51–71*). How do these two psalms contribute to a progressive unfolding of the message of the book?

Both these psalms (Pss. 49–50) open with a formal "summons" to their intended recipients. Psalm 49 begins with an extended introduction that directs "all you peoples" and "all who live in this world" to "hear this" (Ps. 49:1). Fittingly after the previous three psalms that establish Elohim as King over the nations, this psalm now addresses the peoples of the world with "words of wisdom" that will "give understanding" by means of a "proverb" and a "riddle" (Ps. 49:3–4). More specifically, the psalmist addresses "both low and high, rich and poor," setting a proper context for God's impartial judgment (Ps. 49:2).

So what is the counsel that this instructed man of wisdom offers to the people of this world? In a style and content similar to the wisdom of the book of Ecclesiastes, the psalmist instructs them concerning the utter frustration of pursuing riches and even wisdom itself:

> For all can see that wise men die;
> the foolish and the senseless alike perish
> and leave their wealth to others.
> . . . .
> And death will feed on them . . . .
> Their forms will decay in the grave,
>   far from their princely mansions. (Ps. 49:10, 14;
>   cf. Eccl. 2:13–16)

Again, in a form similar to the book of Ecclesiastes, the psalmist makes no appeal to the sacred name of *Yahweh*, the COVENANT LORD of Israel. Instead, using *Elohim* as a broader designation for the deity, he declares:

> Elohim will redeem my life from the grave;
> he will surely receive me. (Ps. 49:15)

But in sharpest contrast:

> A man who has riches without understanding
> is like the beasts that perish. (Ps. 49:20)

> [For] this is the fate of those who trust in themselves. (Ps. 49:13)

Psalm 50 is directly connected with Psalm 49 in that it also formally issues a summons. But this time it is not the psalmist who issues a call directed to the peoples of the world in general, as in Psalm 49. This time the Mighty One, God the COVENANT LORD himself, speaks and summons the heavens above as well as the whole earth

(Ps. 50:1, 4). After the fashion anticipated by Moses long centuries earlier, God calls heaven and earth as his witnesses (cf. Deut. 4:26; 30:19; 31:28). They must bear their testimony, "that he may judge *his people*" (Ps. 50:4). In Psalm 49, the nations were assembled for judgment. But now the King of Nations in exercising his rightful prerogative as Judge summons his own people before himself (Ps. 50:6). These people have "cut a covenant" with him by sacrifice (Ps. 50:5). Their Elohim has no need of bulls, goats, cattle, and birds. He would not tell them if he were hungry (Ps. 50:9–13). He only instructs them: "sacrifice thank offerings," "fulfill your vows," and "call upon me in the day of trouble; I will deliver you, and you will honor me" (Ps. 50:14–15). All the troubles faced by his people as described in the previous psalms—troubles both individual and national—will be rightly resolved by their faithful Covenant Lord.

But still remaining among God's covenant people are the wicked who "recite my laws" and "take my covenant on [their] lips" (Ps. 50:16). They hate God's instruction, they join the thief, they partner with adulterers, they slander their own mother's son (Ps. 50:17–20). Though they abide within the community of the covenant, God himself will accuse them to their face. Unless they change their ways, he will tear them to pieces with none to rescue (Ps. 50:21–22).

So these two psalms (Pss. 49–50), coming after the establishment of God as King in Zion over the nations (Pss. 45–48), issue two broad-based summonses. The first summons is directed to the peoples of all the nations of the world in expressions that they can easily understand (Ps. 49). Then a second summons follows, directed to the people of the Covenant Lord in familiar words that they can properly comprehend (Ps. 50). Having offered these admonitions, the psalmist then turns to the second collection of the psalms of David.[8]

8. Wilson, *Editing*, 163, places a major emphasis on the role of the psalm titles in explaining the structural elements of this particular section. Having noted the principal role of the change in authorship at the transition points between the first four books, he then must deal with a quick-change sequence within Book II from "sons of Korah" to "Asaph" to "David" in three consecutive psalms (Pss. 49–51). At this point, he introduces the role of genre-notations in the headings, so that the term *psalm* in all three of these psalms "softens the transition and binds the collections together." A far stronger interlocking connection may be established by considering the substance of these psalms. By their common reference

The Second Collection of Davidic Psalms (Psalms 51–71*)

This second collection constitutes two-thirds of Book II and consists of eighteen psalms attributed to David by the title, with an additional three psalms that do not include this identification. As previously mentioned, the three psalms without Davidic identification in their titles are most likely also "by David."

Respondents to the Summons (Psalms 51–52)

The first two psalms of this collection relate chiastically to the two summonses just issued in Psalms 49 and 50. This placement of complete psalms in chiastic arrangement may be depicted as shown in figure 6.1.[9]

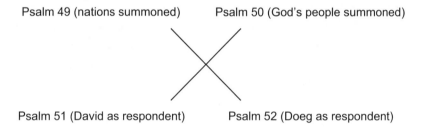

Fig. 6.1. Respondents to the Summons (Psalms 51–52)

Psalm 50 summoned God's own people, and correspondingly in Psalm 51 David the king is the first individual to respond to this summons. Psalm 49 summoned the nations, and correspondingly in

---

to a "summons," first to the peoples of the world (Ps. 49) and then to the people of God (Ps. 50), these two psalms are joined together. Then David the king is called to account (Ps. 51) as an application of the summons of Psalm 50. Next Doeg the Edomite is called to account (Ps. 52) as an application of the summons of Psalm 49. The structural result is a chiastic arrangement of general summons followed by corresponding respondents.

In this case, substance of the psalms proves to be a more reliable criterion for determining structure than titles. The Psalter editor had no problem moving through three different authors in three (or four) consecutive psalms, since the content of these psalms bound them together. Here the deliberate work of a later editor seems apparent.

9. The Greek letter *chi* (written as X) is used to specify a literary arrangement in which thoughts or words crisscross each other to form a parallelism. In this case, Psalm 49 corresponds to Psalm 52 and Psalm 50 corresponds to Psalm 51 in an *a-b-b-a* chiastic parallelism.

Psalm 52 Doeg the Edomite is presented as the first defendant to respond to this summons.

This proposed relationship between summons and respondents may appear to be concocted rather than inherent in the arrangement of these psalms, particularly in view of the fact that the titles of these four successive psalms relate to three different persons: the Sons of Korah (Ps. 49), Asaph (Ps. 50), and David (Pss. 51–52). The connections in substance between summons and respondents, however, strongly support the authenticity of the proposed connections:

Psalm 51 presents the familiar rehearsal of David's confession that he had committed adultery with Bathsheba. God had declared that he himself would judge his people (Ps. 50:4). More specifically, he had noted one particular violation of his law among others: "You throw in your lot with adulterers" (Ps. 50:18b). Now, most appropriately, the king himself must be the first to undergo the scrutiny of divine judgment (Ps. 51).[10] The two psalms are further connected by common substance. Both Psalms 50 and 51 officially recognize that God does not delight in sacrifices and burnt offerings (Ps. 50:8–13; 51:16). In addition, both psalms indicate that Elohim will accept thank offerings and a broken spirit (Pss. 50:14, 23; 51:17).

Psalm 52 designates Doeg the Edomite as the first to answer the summons of the nations in Psalm 49. Again, similar phrasings connect the two psalms. Psalm 49:6 has defined the wicked as those who "boast" and "trust in their great wealth," and Psalm 52:1, 7 describes Doeg as one who "boasts" and who has "trusted in his great wealth." The Psalter is replete with this type of connection by common phraseology.

Who among peoples from other nations could be more despicable than Doeg the Edomite? Spying on God's consecrated priests as they

---

10. Jamie A. Grant, *The King as Exemplar: The Function of Deuteronomy's Kingship Law in the Shaping of the Book of Psalms* (Atlanta: Society of Biblical Literature, 2004), 205f., underscores the accountability of the king in the context of Deuteronomy 17:14–20. The king must not acquire a great number of horses, thus manifesting his trust in military power rather than in Yahweh. He must not marry many foreign wives, which would imply "one law for the king and another for the people." He must not gather huge amounts of silver and gold, for massive wealth would "set the king apart from his fellows." The king has an obligation to observe the Torah of Yahweh just as all other Israelites have. He is "subject to the stipulations of the covenant in the same way that all other Israelites are subject to them." So in Psalm 51, the king is the first to give account for his errant behavior.

confer with David, he accuses them before King Saul of aiding David (1 Sam. 21:7; 22:9–10). When Saul then orders the slaughter of the priests, the king's personal bodyguards commit a flagrant act of military insubordination by refusing to obey their sovereign (1 Sam. 22:17). Yet Doeg the Edomite not only splatters the blood of eighty-five priests on their unstained white robes, but also then enforces the *cherem*-ban on their city of Nob, mercilessly murdering with his sword their men, women, children, infants, cattle, donkeys, and sheep (1 Sam. 22:18–19). By the extremity of these acts of desecration, he takes on the form of the ultimate enemy of God's people. He represents Satan himself in his zeal to destroy God's sacred seed. How appropriate, then, that he would be the first to answer the summons of God to the nations, that he might give account for all his actions.

The Substitution of *Elohim* for *Yahweh* in Book II

Before looking further into this second collection of Davidic psalms, it may be advantageous to consider more closely the distinctive use of the principal designation for God in Book II. Quite striking is the substitution in Book II of the general name of God (*Elohim*) for the covenant name of God (*Yahweh*), which is the more prominent name for God in Book I. Several instances in which a specific comparison is possible establish the likelihood of a deliberate substitution of the divine names.

Four Specific Comparisons of the Use of the Two Names

1. The psalm of confession in Book II (Ps. 51) uses *Elohim* to the exclusion of *Yahweh*, while the companion psalm of confession in Book I (Ps. 32) uses *Yahweh* exclusively.

2. The two psalms describing the "atheistic fool" are virtually identical in their wording. Yet Psalm 53 of Book II replaces *Yahweh* in Psalm 14 of Book I with *Elohim* four times.

3. Psalm 70 of Book II, consisting of only five verses, is virtually identical to Psalm 40:13–17 of Book I. Yet Psalm 70 uses *Elohim* three

times, two of which are located in places where *Yahweh* appears in the phrasing of Psalm 40.[11]

4. Psalm 71 of Book II is basically identical to Psalm 31:1–4 of Book I. Both psalms begin with *Yahweh* (Ps. 71:1; 31:1). But in the remainder of the two psalms, Psalm 71 uses *Elohim* nine times and *Yahweh of Hosts* two times, while Psalm 31 uses *Yahweh* nine times and *Elohim* two times.

These specific points of comparison make it quite plain that the editor/organizer of Book II favored the use of the general name of God over the revealed name of the COVENANT LORD of Israel. This preference does not mean that the editor of Book II had any aversion to the covenant name of God, as is seen in his frequent use of *Yahweh*. But the pattern of usage indicates that there was a preference for *Elohim* over *Yahweh* in many cases. A general comparison of the uses of these two names for God in Books I and II makes the same point.

A General Comparison of the Use of the Two Names

In addition to these four instances in which specific comparisons may be made regarding the relative use of *Yahweh* and *Elohim* in the first two books of the Psalter, a more general comparison makes it quite evident that while Book I (Pss. 1–41) strongly favors *Yahweh* (278 uses of *Yahweh* to 48 uses of *Elohim*), Book II (Pss. 42–72) with equal strength favors *Elohim* (197 uses of *Elohim* to 32 uses of *Yahweh*).[12] But what is the reason for this distinction?

11. In a quite distinctive alteration, Psalm 40, which favors *Yahweh*, switches to *Elohim* in its final phrase: "O my Elohim, do not delay" (Ps. 40:17c). At the same time, Psalm 70, which favors *Elohim*, switches to *Yahweh* in its otherwise identical final phrase: "O Yahweh, do not delay" (Ps. 70:5c).

12. These data are taken from Leslie McFall, "The Evidence for a Logical Arrangement of the Psalter," *Westminster Theological Journal* 62, 2 (2000): 229. Quite remarkable is the fact that Book I favors *Yahweh* over *Elohim* by 85 to 15 percent, while Book II favors *Elohim* over *Yahweh* by 86 to 14 percent. Data for the use of these two major divine names in the remaining books of the Psalter are as follows: Book IIIA (Pss. 73–83), *Yahweh* 13, *Elohim* 45; Book IIIB (Pss. 84–89), *Yahweh* 31, *Elohim* 16; totals in Book III (Pss. 73–89), *Yahweh* 44, *Elohim* 61; Book IV (Pss. 90–106), *Yahweh* 105, *Elohim* 19; Book V (Pss. 107–150), *Yahweh* 236, *Elohim* 28. Uses of *Elohim* for a god other than Israel's God are excluded from these tallies.

The Reason for This Distinction: Interaction with Foreign Nations

It might be proposed that two collections of Davidic psalms may have circulated independently for a time before they were merged. It could be suggested that a version of the Psalms went to the northern kingdom of Israel at the time of the division of Solomon's empire. A reluctance to use the name *Yahweh* in the north might be proposed as an explanation for its relative absence. But the obvious concentration on David and Zion throughout the bulk of Book II belies this proposal.

Or it might be suggested that a hesitation to pronounce the sacred name of *Yahweh* in later Judaism explains the phenomenon. But the covenantal name *Yahweh* strongly prevails in the final two books of the Psalter, Books IV and V. Chronology cannot in itself explain the sequential order of the five books of the Psalms. Yet it is fairly clear that most exilic and postexilic psalms appear in Books IV and V.[13]

A much more likely explanation for the difference in the use of the names *Yahweh* and *Elohim* has to do with the differing perspective of the two books. The most striking thing about the content of this second collection of Davidic psalms within Book II is the number of psalms that refer to the "peoples," the "nations," the "foreigners," or "all mankind."[14] Twelve of the twenty-one psalms in this collection (Pss. 51–71*) refer specifically to non-Israelite

---

13. Frank-Lothar Hossfeld and Eric Zenger, *Psalms 2: A Commentary on Psalms 51–100* (Minneapolis: Fortress Press, 2005), 5, propose that the preference for *Elohim* "presumes a gravitation to monotheism in which the generic name can become a proper name." This preference is explained in that the use of *Elohim* "emphasizes God's distance and transcendence; the remote, dark, mysterious God is accentuated." Apart from the highly questionable idea that the faith of Israel had evolved only to the point of a "gravitation to monotheism" in its preexilic period, the portrayal of Elohim in these psalms as "remote, dark, mysterious" hardly fits the presentation of God in the very psalms in question. A random selection of phrases expressing the deepest sentiments of the psalmist depict a rather intimate relation to Elohim: "My soul thirsts for Elohim, for the living Elohim" (Ps. 42:2); "I am like an olive tree flourishing in the house of Elohim; I trust in the unfailing love of Elohim for ever and ever" (Ps. 52:8); "My soul finds rest in Elohim alone" (Ps. 62:1); "My soul thirsts for you, my body longs for you . . . . I sing in the shadow of your wings" (Ps. 63:1, 7); "We are filled with the good things of your house" (Ps. 65:4).

14. Hossfeld and Zenger, *Psalms 2*, 5, concur with this explanation in their final observation regarding the preference for *Elohim*: "Finally, there is a preference for speaking of *Elohim* when God's universality is to be underscored . . . . In the Psalms such language seems more suitable when the nations are to be included in prayer."

peoples. This proportion stands in significant contrast with the Davidic psalms of Book I (Pss. 3–41*). In this first collection, only six of thirty-nine psalms clearly refer to non-Israelite peoples (Pss. 7, 9, 10, 18, 22, 33).[15] A survey of the role of "the nations" in this second collection of Davidic psalms confirms the significance of this factor in Book II:

Psalm 52. The title refers to "Doeg the Edomite," a foreigner to God's people. The psalm describes this enemy of David as one who "trusted in his great wealth," which corresponds to the identity of the "peoples" who "live in this world" and "trust in their wealth" (Ps. 52:7; cf. Ps. 49:6).

Psalm 56. The title alludes to the time when the foreign Philistines had seized David. The psalmist pleads, "O God, bring down the nations" (Ps. 56:7).

Psalm 57. Though the title refers to a domestic situation in which David fled from Saul, the psalmist exclaims:

> I will praise you, O Lord,
>   among the nations;
> I will sing of you
>   among the peoples. (Ps. 57:9)

Undergirding this emphasis, the refrain of this psalm anticipates God's worldwide exaltation:

> Be exalted, O God,
>   above the heavens;
> let your glory
>   be over all the earth. (Ps. 57:5, 11)

Psalm 58. The opening question concerning righteous judgment is set before the "judges" of the "sons of men [adam]." The ultimate

---

15. Other psalms that could refer to non-Israelite peoples or nations are Psalm 11 by the mention of the "sons of men" (Ps. 11:4) and Psalm 17 with its use of the rather unusual phrase "males of duration" (Ps. 17:14).

answer at the conclusion of the psalm is: "Surely there is a God who judges throughout the earth" (Ps. 58:1, 11).

Psalm 59. The psalmist prays that the "God of Israel" will rouse himself to punish "all the nations" (Ps. 59:5). In clear parallelism of expression with the foundational statement of Psalm 2, it is declared that Yahweh "will laugh" at them, that he "will mock all the nations" (Ps. 59:8; cf. Ps. 2:4, in which the same two verbs are used).

The title of this psalm refers to a distinctive moment in the life of David when "Saul had sent men to watch David's house in order to kill him," which would seem to indicate that the psalm is dealing with domestic rather than foreign enemies. Yet the parallel of expressions with Psalm 2, in which the enemies are the "nations" and the "peoples," as well as the plea for God to punish "all the nations" (Ps. 59:5), makes it evident that the experience of David with Saul is set in a context that anticipates conflict with other peoples as well.

Psalm 60. The title refers to the time when David fought with Aram Naharaim and Aram Zobah as well as with the Edomites. Obviously, the title depicts conflict with foreigners. Confirmation is found in the body of the psalm, which refers to victory over Moab, Edom, and Philistia (Ps. 60:7–9).

Psalm 61. The psalmist declares that he calls to God "from the ends of the earth" (Ps. 61:2). The phrase suggests that he is in distant lands, far from the tent of God in which he longs to dwell (Ps. 61:4).

Psalm 64. Despite the threatening swords and arrows of the wicked, the psalmist is confident that "all humanity" will fear and proclaim the works of God (Ps. 64:9).

Psalm 65. God is "the hope of all the ends of the earth and of the far-thest seas" (Ps. 65:5). He has stilled the roaring of the seas, symbolic of "the turmoil of the nations" (Ps. 65:7). "Those living far away" will fear (Ps. 65:8). This depiction of the revolt of nations against God in terms of the roaring of waters finds consummate expression in the book of Revelation, where the "waters" are identified as "peoples, multitudes, nations and languages" (Rev. 17:15; cf. 17:1).

Psalms 66–67. These two interrelated psalms break out in a paean of universal praise. "All the earth" is summoned to shout with joy to God and bow down to him (Ps. 66:1, 4). For "he rules by his power forever" (מֹשֵׁל בִּגְבוּרָתוֹ עוֹלָם), and his eyes watch the nations (Ps. 66:7). So the peoples should praise our God (Ps. 66:8). The psalmist pronounces the Aaronic benediction (Ps. 67:1; cf. Num. 6:22–27), so that

> [God's] ways may be known on earth,
> [his] salvation among all nations. (Ps. 67:2)

The refrain of Psalm 67 underscores this universalism of God's praise:

> May the peoples praise you, O God,
> may all the peoples praise you. (Ps. 67:3, 5)

A major consequence of this universal praise is that "all the ends of the earth will fear him" (Ps. 67:7).

This expansive picture of universal praise in these two psalms (Pss. 66–67) anticipates the climactic psalm of Book II, in which Solomon describes the rule of Messiah's kingdom as stretching from the River to the ends of the earth (Ps. 72:8). These two psalms (Pss. 66–67) do not have the "By David" phrase in the title. Yet they fit quite appropriately in this Book II collection of Davidic psalms.

Psalm 68. This psalm opens by rehearsing the wording used by Moses each time the nation of Israel set out in its march across the desert: "May God arise, may his enemies be scattered; may his foes flee before him" (Ps. 68:1; cf. Num. 10:35). Clearly, it is non-Israelite nations that are to be opposed: "Kings and armies flee in haste; . . . the Almighty scattered the kings in the land" (Ps. 68:12, 14). Following a vivid portrayal of God's people crossing the desert and processing to Mount Zion, the psalmist declares:

> Because of your temple at Jerusalem
> kings will bring you gifts.

> Rebuke the beast
>> among the reeds,
> the herd of bulls
>> among the calves of the nations.
>
> . . . .
> Scatter the nations who delight in war. (Ps. 68:29–30)

The psalmist then notes specific nations that will submit to God's rule, including Egypt and Cush. As a consequence, the "kingdoms of the earth" are urged to sing praise to the Lord (Ps. 68:31–32).

This large proportion of references to "the peoples" and "the nations" in the Davidic collection of Book II stands in sharpest contrast with the much smaller proportion in Book I, where only six of thirty-nine psalms in the Davidic collection (Pss. 3–41*) clearly mention the peoples of other nations.[16] Suffice it to say that the evidence points to a deliberate choice of specific Davidic psalms to be included in Book II. The permeation of these psalms with references to "the peoples" corresponds closely to the cluster of "kingship" psalms at the beginning of Book II, in which God and his Messiah are established as King among the nations (Pss. 45–48). A comparison of the first collection of five kingship psalms in Book I (Pss. 20–24) reveals a significant difference with this second collection of kingship psalms in Book II (Pss. 45–48). In the first collection, struggle with opposition to Yahweh's and Messiah's kingship is much more apparent. King Messiah is in a position of prayer for victory over his enemies (Pss. 20–21). He is a Messiah suffering from the agony of divine and human rejection, struggling with the power of dogs, lions, and wild oxen (Ps. 22:1–21). Yahweh is the Shepherd-King of his flock, providing tender care (Ps. 23:1). He is indeed the One who made the earth and all that is in it. Yet as King of Glory, he is just now entering through the everlasting doors after returning from battle (Ps. 24:1–10). Significant advancement may be seen in this second collection of kingship psalms appearing in Book II (Pss. 45–48). King Messiah is now declared to be Elohim on his throne, with nations falling beneath his feet (Ps. 45:5–6). God is exalted among the nations

---

16. Again, these are Psalms 7, 9, 10, 18, 22, 33.

(Ps. 46:10). He is the "great King over all the earth," reigning among the nations (Ps. 47:2, 8). Mount Zion is the city of the Great King that causes the nations to tremble and flee in terror (Ps. 48:2, 5–6).

This use of the more general name for God in Book II may be compared to a similar use in the book of Ecclesiastes. The author of this book makes exclusive use of *Elohim* as the more general name for God. The total message of Ecclesiastes supports this concept of a word of wisdom from God designed to communicate with the nations and peoples of the world.[17]

Posture of the Psalmist in Relation to His "Enemies" in Book II

If in Book II the psalmist is making some attempt to communicate with "the nations," how does he address them? What precisely does he expect in terms of their responses? How does his perspective compare to the attitude expressed toward "enemies" in Book I?

In Book I, a "Them and Us" Relationship

In Book I, the "enemies" are almost altogether referred to in the third person.[18] It is essentially a "them and us" relationship between Israel or King David and their foes. The adversarial relationship comes out strongly as the psalmist unveils his deepest feelings in the fourteen psalms that record his prayers regarding his enemies:

> Strike all my enemies on the jaw;
> break the teeth of the wicked. (Ps. 3:7)

> Declare them guilty . . . !
> . . . .
> Banish them for their many sins. (Ps. 5:10)

17. Paul the apostle to the nations employs the same approach when speaking to people outside the covenant community. Cf. his total absence of any reference to Israel's redemptive history when addressing idol-worshipers both in Lystra of Asia and in Athens of Europe (Acts 14:11–18; 17:22–31).

18. Two apparent exceptions in which the enemy may be addressed in the second person are Psalms 4:2–5 and 6:8. Psalm 37:27 is a third possibility, but may be better understood as an exhortation to God's people so that they may "dwell in the land," as in Psalm 37:34.

Rule over them from on high;
let the LORD judge the peoples. (Ps. 7:7–8)

Strike them with terror, O LORD;
let the nations know they are but men. (Ps. 9:20)

Break the arm of the wicked and evil man;
call him to account for his wickedness. (Ps. 10:15)

Confront them, bring them down. (Ps. 17:13)

Repay them
    according to their deeds,
    according to their evil works,

. . . .
Repay them!
Bring back on them their just recompense. (Ps. 28:4)

Let the wicked be put to shame
and lie silent in the grave. (Ps. 31:17b)

Contend, O LORD, with those who contend with me;
fight against those who fight against me. (Ps. 35:1)

May all who seek to take my life
    be put to shame and confusion;
may all who desire my ruin
    be turned back in disgrace. (Ps. 40:14)

Many more passages might be cited from Book I to demonstrate the attitude and expectation of the psalmist with respect to his enemies, both individual and national.[19] It is difficult, if not impossible, to find a single passage in which some form of blessing might be extended toward an enemy.

19. Cf. Pss. 5:4, 6; 9:3, 5–6, 15; 11:6; 16:4; 18:26–27, 37–40, 42; 21:9–10; 25:3; 28:4–5; 31:17; 33:10; 34:16; 35:3–6, 8, 26; 36:12; 37:2, 9–10, 13, 17, 20, 22, 28, 34, 36, 38. Extended treatments are found in Psalms 18, 35, and 37.

In Book II, a Commitment to Communicate

In turning to Book II (Pss. 42–72), the tone of address by the psalmist to the "nations" that are his enemies is quite different. The content of his message to them, as well as his expectations from them, introduces a different tone from the all-pervasive attitude of the psalmist in Book I. It would be possible to consider first the non-Davidic portion of Book II (primarily Pss. 42–50) and then the Davidic psalms (essentially Pss. 51–71*). But the similarities of the two groupings are extensive to the point that the whole of Book II may be treated as a unity, which in itself is a matter of significance in observing the "flow" of the Psalter. The editor had no difficulty in finding psalms of the Sons of Korah and psalms of David that were quite compatible with one another to constitute the substance of Book II.

Despite the ongoing life-and-death struggle with ungodly enemies, several features of this interaction with national enemies characterize this new commitment to communicate.

The Psalmist Communicates Directly with His "Enemies"

The psalmist in Book II regularly communicates directly with his "enemies" by employing the second-person *you,* which is a form of address only rarely used of enemies in Book I:

Clap your hands, all you nations;
shout to God with cries of joy. (Ps. 47:1; cf. v. 6)

Hear this, all you peoples;
listen, all who live in this world. (Ps. 49:1)

Why do you boast of evil, you mighty man?
Why do you boast all day long . . . ?
  Your tongue plots destruction;
  it is like a sharpened razor,
you who practice deceit. (Ps. 52:1–2)

Do you rulers indeed speak justly?
Do you judge uprightly among men?

No, in your heart you devise injustice,
and your hands mete out violence on the earth. (Ps. 58:1–2)

In Book II, both warning admonition and encouraging invitation pointedly and personally address the enemies of the psalmist. This distinctive mode of address is all the more striking in that it speaks to nations and their rulers, and not merely to individuals.

The Psalmist Commits Himself to Sing the Praises of Elohim to the Nations

The psalmist in Book II declares the steadfastness, the determination of his heart and soul:

I will praise you, O Lord, among the nations;
I will sing of you among the peoples.
For great is your love, reaching to the heavens. (Ps. 57:9–10)

The psalmist is under compulsion. This thing he must do. He must praise Elohim among the nations. All peoples must hear of the greatness of Elohim's love that reaches to the heavens. Yet in the same psalm he fully recognizes that he is "in the midst of lions, among ravenous beasts, men whose teeth are spears and arrows, whose tongues are sharp" (Ps. 57:4). These people have spread a net for his feet and dug a pit in his path (Ps. 57:6). But his prayer is that Elohim's glory will be "over all the earth" (Ps. 57:11). He clearly manifests his zeal for Elohim's glory to be spread across the entire world.

The Psalmist Reminds the Nations That Elohim Will Defeat Them Again as He Has Done in the Past

Without a single instance in which the psalmist addresses Elohim by his covenant name *Yahweh*, Psalm 44 declares that Israel's fathers have told them about the way Elohim drove out the nations and planted them. He affirms that he does not trust his bow or sword. Instead, it is Elohim who gives the people the victory over their enemies. Currently they have suffered defeat. But the psalmist pleads with Elohim: "Rise

105

up and help us; redeem us because of your unfailing love" (Ps. 44:1–2, 6–7, 9, 26). Might it be that by using the more general name for God (*Elohim*), the psalmist seeks to communicate this message of the past and future defeat of their enemies simultaneously to the enemies as well as to his own people?

Throughout Psalms 45–48, the psalmist declares that Elohim and his Messiah triumph over the nations. Therefore, the nations will praise Elohim forever (Ps. 45:17). He will make wars cease to the ends of the earth, and will be exalted among the nations (Ps. 46:9–10). The nations should clap their hands and shout to Elohim with cries of joy, since the great King over all the earth has subdued nations under their feet (Ps. 47:1–3). Trembling seized the nations when the kings dared to join forces to assault Mount Zion. So his praise should reach to the ends of the earth (Ps. 48:6, 4, 10).

In the Davidic collection of this section, the psalmist calls on Elohim to "bring down the nations" in his anger (Ps. 56:7). He is confident that when Elohim avenges the righteous, "humanity" (אָדָם) will say, "Surely there is an Elohim who judges the earth" (Ps. 58:11). In what appears to be a deliberate echo of Yahweh's attitude to the rebellious nations as expressed in programmatic Psalm 2, the psalmist indicates that Elohim will "punish all the nations," that he will "laugh at them" and will "scoff at all those nations" (Ps. 59:5, 8).[20] Elohim will consume them in his wrath, and "then it will be known to the ends of the earth that Elohim rules over Jacob" (Ps. 59:13). The conquering Elohim (not Yahweh) declares that Moab is his washbasin, and he tosses his sandal over Edom. So Elohim's people will gain the victory over their enemies (Ps. 60:8, 12). This message the nations would be wise to hear and understand.

Elohim Provides the Prospect of Redemption for All His Creation

All the peoples of the world would do well to hear this word. It is a good word for the nations to understand. No man can redeem the life of another, but Elohim will redeem from the grave the life of

---

20. The words for "laugh" and "scoff" (לָעַג, שָׂחַק) are identical to the expressions in Psalm 2:4.

those who trust him. All can see that wise men die and leave their wealth to others. For a man who has riches without understanding is like the beasts that perish (Ps. 49:1, 7, 15, 10, 20).

Elohim is "the hope of all the ends of the earth and of the farthest seas." He stills the turmoil of the nations. To those living far away he calls for songs of joy because of the way he cares for the land and waters it, enriching the soil abundantly (Ps. 65:5, 7–9). This word of hope for the nations, rooted in the common grace of Elohim's goodness, is a distinctive message found in Book II of the Psalms.

Kings of the Earth Will Bring Gifts to the Mountain of Elohim

The "beast among the reeds," the "herd of bulls among the calves of the nations," must be rebuked, humbled, and scattered. But then their kings will bring gifts, bars of silver, to the temple of Elohim at Jerusalem (Ps. 68:28–30; cf. Ps. 68:18). How amazing is this anticipation of the subjugation of nations throughout the world under King Messiah. Wise men still seek him.

Nations Will Gladly Respond to the Admonishment to Praise Elohim

According to the psalmist, the kings of the earth belong to Elohim. So they and their nations must spontaneously clap their hands and shout to Elohim with cries of joy (Ps. 47:9, 1). All humanity will fear and proclaim the works of Elohim (Ps. 64:9). The kingdoms of the earth will sing praises to the One who rides the ancient skies above and thunders with his mighty voice (Ps. 68:32–33).

In our review of these distinctive elements of Book II (Pss. 42–72), it becomes evident that the editor/organizer of the Psalter has moved beyond the stage of redemptive realization found in Book I (Pss. 3–41). In Book I, David struggles with many enemies as they attempt to derail his every effort to establish the messianic kingdom of righteousness, mercy, love, and peace. But now he is making every effort to *communicate* with them. Indeed, it cannot be said that in the presentations of Book II the worldwide kingdom of Elohim and his Messiah has been realized in its final form. The ongoing struggle is clearly seen in the number of psalms related to concrete moments in the life of David before the Lord had defeated all his enemies and Saul (cf. the Ps. 18 heading), including Psalms 51, 52, 54, 56, 57, 59, 60, and 63.[21] But the distinctive stance in Book II in relation to the nations must be given its proper recognition. To a significant degree, the King and his kingdom have come.

To this point in the analysis of Book II, the following elements have been noted:

- Psalms 42/43 and 44: Introductory Psalms of Hope despite Distress
- Psalms 45–48: The Kingship of Elohim and His Messiah
- Psalms 49–52: Two Psalms with a Summons and Their Respondents

The next grouping of Book II opens with atheism revisited (Ps. 53), which is followed by the identification of seven specified enemies (Pss. 54–60).

Atheism Revisited (Psalm 53)

This psalm may be perceived as the formal introduction to the next grouping of this second Davidic collection. It has been generally recognized that Psalm 53 is virtually an exact reproduction of Psalm 14. But why? What would be the reason for duplicating the same thought in such detail?

The different usage of the word for God provides the clue for answering this question. Both psalms begin: "The fool says in his

21. These several psalms that are related to specific incidents in the life of David appearing in Book II might indicate a fixed second collection of Davidic psalms that were joined to the Book I collection with little or no editorial rearrangement. Or they might indicate that the editor/collector was not interested primarily in a chronological arrangement, but placed these particular Davidic psalms in Book II because of their suitability as indicators of an intention to communicate more directly to the peoples of the world, as indicated in the previous discussion.

heart, 'There is no Elohim.' " But Psalm 53 retains the term *Elohim* throughout, never introducing the word *Yahweh*, the covenant name for God, as does Psalm 14. Even when speaking of "calling on God" and his restoring the fortunes of his people Israel, Psalm 53 continues with *Elohim* in contradistinction from Psalm 14. Why?

This distinctive use of *Elohim* reinforces the commitment of Book II to *communicate* with non-Israelite peoples. Psalm 53 is not merely a throwaway, a needless repetition of an earlier psalm. Instead, it serves as a heading for the next grouping of this second collection of Davidic psalms, addressing this world's atheists head-on. In language that the world can easily understand, it speaks to mankind even while simultaneously communicating with God's own people.

The most substantial difference between these twin addresses to the atheist appears in the contrasting judgment pronounced over them. Both groups of atheists will be "overwhelmed with dread" (Ps. 14:5a; 53:5a). But the "evildoers" of Psalm 14 are simply informed that Yahweh is the refuge of the poor (Ps. 14:6). Yet in Psalm 53, Elohim will "scatter the bones" and "put to shame" these atheists that he has "despised" (Ps. 53:5b).

Seven Specified Enemies (Psalms 54–60)

Having set out its formal introduction for this section with Psalm 53, the collection presents seven different enemies of David in seven successive psalms (Pss. 54–60). Each of these seven psalms concludes with a note of confident triumph:

Psalm 54. The Ziphites from David's own tribe of Judah traitorize him. But: "My eyes have looked in triumph on my foes" (Ps. 54:7).

Psalm 55. An unnamed closest friend betrays him (Ps. 55:12–14). But: "Bloodthirsty and deceitful men will not live out half their days. . . . As for me, I trust in you" (Ps. 55:23).

Psalm 56. The Philistines seize him in Gath. But: "You have delivered me from death and my feet from stumbling, that I may walk before God in the light of life" (Ps. 56:13).

Psalm 57. Saul forces David to flee into a cave. But: "Be exalted, O God, above the heavens; let your glory be over all the earth" (Ps. 57:11).

Psalm 58. Rulers judge unjustly. But: "Surely the righteous still are rewarded; surely there is a God who judges the earth" (Ps. 58:11).

Psalm 59. Saul's henchmen come to kill David in his own house. But: "O my Strength, I sing praise to you; you, O God, are my fortress, my loving God" (Ps. 59:17).

Psalm 60. Enemies come from distant countries. But: "With God we will gain the victory, and he will trample down our enemies" (Ps. 60:12).

Yet the question may be legitimately asked: Why does this second grouping of Davidic psalms include so many psalms that refer to specific circumstances that occurred before David was established as king? If Psalm 18 in Book I provided a transition point at which David was delivered from all his enemies and from Saul, why now in Book II has the Psalter taken us back again to the days before the defeat of all these enemies?

In response to these questions, it should first be recognized that the editor of these psalms obviously did not intend to arrange the Davidic psalms in a strictly chronological order. As will be seen later, two collections of Davidic psalms also occur in Book V, where the context is predominantly exilic and postexilic. Yet these later Davidic psalms are appropriate for the time of the nation's exile and restoration. The pattern that emerges in the Psalter is a placement of Davidic psalms appropriate to the specific purpose of the editor. The basic arrangement of the Psalter is clearly not chronological but developmental. This particular collection of Davidic psalms in Book II suits the point of progression in which a message can be communicated to the nations regarding the establishment of the Davidic kingship and the ultimate defeat of every enemy that this kingship might face. Relatives from his own tribe, a closest friend, neighboring Philistines, King Saul, rulers of the land, murderous henchmen, enemies from distant lands—a catalogue of enemies that few people have ever faced. But a lesson may be learned even by all the potential enemies of the messianic king: his God will defeat them all.[22]

Dialogue between the Two Kings (Psalms 61–68)

The next section of this second Davidic collection describes a "dialogue between the two kings." In the process of this dialogue, four psalms represent the cry of the messianic king (Pss. 61–64). Then four psalms respond by affirming the undisturbed reign of the Divine King (Pss. 65–68).

First, the messianic king cries out for God to intervene on his behalf as he struggles to establish God's kingdom of righteousness and peace (Pss. 61–64):

Psalm 61. A banished David cries to Elohim "from the ends of the earth" with his longing to dwell in God's tent (Ps. 61:2). He prays for the "increase [of] the days of the king's life" across many generations, asking that he be enthroned in Elohim's presence forever (Ps. 61:6–7). So his prayer focuses on both elements of the Davidic covenant: the *dynasty* (across generations) and the *dwellingplace* (in God's tent).

Psalm 62. Four times over, David in distress repeats the fact that his hope rests in Elohim alone. His opponents "fully intend to topple him from his lofty place" (Ps. 62:4). But God alone is the "Rock" of his salvation (Ps. 62:2, 6; cf. Ps. 62:7).

Psalm 63. Banished to the desert of Judah, David thirsts for Elohim. His whole being longs for him in a dry and parched land where there

---

22. Rather than seeing the titles of these psalms that include specific historical circumstances as authentic historical references, Brevard S. Childs, *Introduction to the Old Testament as Scripture* (London: SCM Press, 1979), 521, proposes that these psalms were first cultic but then later "historicized" by placing them within the specific history of David. His conclusion is that this process made these psalms readily applicable to the common man. But such a theory pays the price of losing the integrity that is essential for the effective communication of truth.

is no water. But he recalls that he has seen Elohim's power and glory in his sanctuary. So he can sing in the shadow of his wings. The king will rejoice in God (Ps. 63:11).

Psalm 64. David pleads for Elohim to hear his complaint, to protect his life from the threat of his enemies. For the enemies of David "sharpen their tongues like swords and aim their words like deadly arrows" (Ps. 64:3). But in a sovereign act of retributive justice, God will "shoot them with arrows . . . . He will turn their own tongues against them" (Ps. 64:7–8). A sweeping affirmation declares that all humanity (כָּל־אָדָם) will proclaim the works of Elohim. As a consequence, all the upright in heart will praise him (Ps. 64:9–10).

Then the dialogue between the two kings records a response that affirms the undisturbed reign of the Divine King (Pss. 65–68). As King of the world, he has the full capacity to meet the needs of the messianic king:

Psalm 65. This psalm declares the blessedness of those who have been chosen to live in the courts, house, and temple of Elohim (Ps. 65:4). Elohim is the "hope of all the ends of the earth" who has "stilled . . . the turmoil of the nations" (Ps. 65:5, 7). Even those living far away, where the morning dawns and the evening fades, fear his wonders and respond with songs of joy (Ps. 65:8).

Psalm 66. This psalm broadens the perspective of the domain of Israel's God, calling on "all the earth" to shout for joy to Elohim (Ps. 66:1). "All the earth" must bow down to him (Ps. 66:4). His eyes watch the nations (Ps. 66:7). All the peoples of the world are summoned to praise "our Elohim" (Ps. 66:8). Indeed, it is Israel's God that the nations will praise, though he is not identified by his covenant name *Yahweh*.

Psalm 67. This psalm introduces the magnificent "undulation" that anticipates the apostle Paul's redemptive history of Romans 11. The praises of God go forth from Israel toward the nations and turn back again from the nations to Israel. The psalmist begins by pronouncing the ancient priestly benediction of Israel:

> May Elohim be gracious to us
> > and bless us
> > and make his face shine upon us. (Ps. 67:1; cf. Num. 6:24)

But then he spells out the purpose for this blessing from Elohim on his people:

> That your ways may be known on earth,
> > your salvation among all nations. (Ps. 67:2)

Next he anticipates the expected consequences of this knowledge of God:

> May the peoples praise you, O Elohim;
> > may all the peoples praise you.

> May the nations be glad and sing for joy,
> > for you rule the peoples justly
> > and guide the nations of the earth.

> May the peoples praise you, O Elohim;
> > may all the peoples praise you (Ps. 67:3–5).

But in the end, the blessing comes "full-round" to Israel once more:

> Then the land will yield its harvest,
> > and Elohim, our Elohim, will bless us.
> > Elohim will bless us,
> and all the ends of the earth will fear him. (Ps. 67:6–7)

Quite remarkable indeed is the injection of *Elohim*, the general name for God, into the ancient Aaronic benediction. For the original priestly blessing involved the threefold repetition of the covenant name of *Yahweh*. "In this way," says Yahweh, "I will *set my name* on the Israelites, and I will bless them" (Num. 6:27). How, then, can this unique blessing settle on the people when the name pronounced over them as the source of their blessing is *Elohim* rather than *Yahweh*? Certainly it is inconceivable that the God of Israel would surrender any aspect of his distinctiveness into a communal sea of god-concepts. But it is quite conceivable that the one and only God of creation and redemption may expand the object of his blessing to embrace peoples from all the nations.

Psalm 68. After the recapitulation of the priestly benediction on God's people that traces its origin back to the time of Israel's desert wanderings (Ps. 67:1; cf. Num. 6:22–27), this next psalm reenacts the procession of God's people across the desert to the Land of Promise as they are led in triumph by their God and King.[23] The earth shook before the God of Sinai (Ps. 68:8). Kings and armies fled in haste before him (Ps. 68:12). The tens of thousands of the chariots of Elohim came from Sinai to Mount Zion, where he has chosen to reign (Ps. 68:16–17). With the singers parading before and the musicians following after, "my God the King" processes into his sanctuary (Ps. 68:24–25). Kings of nations will bring him gifts; the "bulls" of the nations will stand rebuked (Ps. 68:29–30). The kingdoms of the earth will sing praise to Elohim (Ps. 68:32). Elohim is awesome in his sanctuary; Elohim of Israel gives power and strength to his people (Ps. 68:35).

This grouping of four psalms affirming undisturbed divine kingship with their strongly universalistic dimension underscores the broadened perspective of Book II when compared with Book I. Clearly, *communication* on a different level is taking place. It is not that the two books have messages in conflict with each other. But the universalistic emphasis of Book II represents a communication with the nations of the world beyond the perspective found in Book I. In much of the phrasing in Book II, the use of the covenant name *Yahweh* would have been totally appropriate, even begging to be used. Yet with a forceful consistency, this collection insists

---

23. That actual processions were regularly enacted with the ark of the covenant leading the way to the temple remains unproved for lack of evidence. The greater likelihood is that Psalm 68 is "actualizing" the ancient historical moment rather than describing a regular cultic event. For a full discussion supporting the concept of a cultic procession, see Craig C. Broyles, "The Psalms and Cult Symbolism: The Case of the Cherubim-Ark," in *Interpreting the Psalms: Issues and Approaches*, ed. Philip S. Johnston and David G. Firth (Downers Grove, IL: InterVarsity Press, 2005), 139–56.

on using the general name *Elohim*. The most likely reason for this usage of the more general name of God is the advanced concern of the psalmist to *communicate* with the nations of the world even as he strengthens the faith of his own people.

Ongoing Struggles (Psalms 69–71)

Three psalms follow the kingship dialogue and describe the ongoing struggles of the messianic king even into his old age (Pss. 69–71). Even though God has processed ahead of his people out of Egypt, over to Sinai, across the desert, through the conquest, and up to the glories of Mount Zion, the representative spokesman for God's people must endure severe humiliations before his final exaltation. So Psalms 69–71 recount the troubles of Israel's representative man, the people's messianic king.[24] Even to his old age, the struggle continues:

> Do not cast me away
> > when I am old;
> do not forsake me
> > when my strength is gone. (Ps. 71:9)

> Since my youth, O God,
> > you have taught me,
> and to this day
> > I declare your marvelous deeds.
> Even when I am old and gray,
> > do not forsake me, O God, until I declare
> > > your power to the next generation,
> > > your might to all who are to come. (Ps. 71:17–18)

In this triad of psalms anticipating the triumphant conclusion of Book II, Psalm 69 stands out as a "focal messianic psalm" that depicts the sufferings of God's Messiah. Three different authors of the New Testament

24. Psalms 69 and 70 of this triad of psalms are specifically attributed to David. Psalm 71 quotes an extensive section from Psalm 31, an earlier Davidic psalm, which strongly suggests that David also originated Psalm 71.

quote four different passages from this single psalm. First, John in his Gospel turns to this psalm to explain Jesus' zeal in cleansing the temple:

> I am a stranger to my brothers,
> an alien to my own mother's sons;
> > for zeal for your house consumes me,
> > and the insults of those who insult you fall on me. (Ps. 69:8–9;
> > > cf. John 2:17)

Then at the end of Jesus' life, John appeals to this same psalm to vivify the prophetic anticipation of the sufferings of the messianic king:

> Scorn has broken my heart
> and has left me helpless;
>
> I looked for sympathy,
> > but there was none,
> for comforters,
> > but I found none.
>
> They put poison
> > in my food
> and gave me vinegar
> > for my thirst. (Ps. 69:20–21; cf. John 19:28–30)

In explaining the righteous judgment of God that has fallen on betraying Judas as well as on unbelieving Israel, both Luke and Paul quote sections from Psalm 69. According to Luke, the apostle Peter found the explanation for the tragic death of Judas prophetically anticipated in the judgment pronounced over the persecutors of the Lord's Messiah in Psalm 69:

> May their place
> > be deserted;
> let there be no one
> > to dwell in their tents,
> for they persecute
> > those you wound

and talk about the pain
of those you hurt. (Ps. 69:25–26; cf. Acts 1:20)

According to the apostle Paul's analysis in Romans 11, as in the days of the Old Testament so also "at the present time" there is "a remnant according to the election of grace." But the "rest" were judicially hardened in their sinful unbelief, "as it is written":

May the table set before them
become a snare;
may it
become retribution and a trap.
May their eyes be darkened
so they cannot see,
and their backs bent
forever. (Ps. 69:22–23; cf. Rom. 11:9–10)

It might be asked: What led John, Luke, and Paul to this same psalm in support of four different aspects of redemptive history, which include the cleansing of the temple, the crucifixion of Jesus, the judgment on Judas, and the hardening of Israel?

The answer to this question might be in part the specific role of Psalm 69 in the arrangement of the Psalter. In Book II, the messianic king continues to struggle with his adversaries to establish God's kingdom of righteousness and peace despite the progress that has been made. Coming immediately after the "dialogue between the kings," Psalm 69 vividly describes the adversaries of the Messiah, but concludes with the confident assertions that Yahweh "hears the needy" so that heaven and earth may praise him (Ps. 69:33–34). The position of this psalm immediately after the "dialogue" between the cry for help of the messianic king and the affirmation of God's undisturbed reign (Pss. 61–68) could provide a partial answer to the prominence of this psalm in the purview of the writers of the New Testament.

Other descriptions of the humiliations recorded in these three psalms of ongoing struggle concluding Book II anticipate the agonies of Jesus as recorded by the Gospel writers of the New Testament:

117

> Hasten, O God, to save me;
> O LORD, come quickly to help me.
>
> May those who seek my life
>   be put to shame and confusion;
> may all who desire my ruin
>   be turned back in disgrace. (Ps. 70:1–2)
>
> My enemies speak against me;
> those who wait to kill me conspire together.
> They say, "God has forsaken him;
>   pursue him and seize him,
>   for no one will rescue him." (Ps. 71:10–11; cf. Matt. 27:43)

From these psalms situated virtually at the end of Book II, it becomes quite obvious that the struggle for the establishment of the messianic king and his kingdom is not altogether over. A situation that may be described in terms of the *already* and the *not yet* prevails. Yes, the Lord has established his Messiah in a position of rule over the nations. Yet the challenges to his position continue.

Triumphant Images of Messiah's Rule (Psalm 72)

Having described these sufferings as necessary for the ultimate establishment of Messiah's reign, the psalmist concludes Book II with a psalm of Solomon celebrating the triumphs of Messiah's kingly rule (Ps. 72).[25] This "focal messianic psalm" marks the end of Book II with an unprecedented representation of the extension of Messiah's kingdom across all space and time. Elohim endows the king, the royal son, with his justice (Ps. 72:1). This messianic king will save the children of the needy (Ps. 72:4). He will endure as long as the sun and moon

25. Hossfeld and Zenger, *Psalms 2*, 2n2, interpret the *leSolomon* phrase in the title of Psalm 72 to mean "For Solomon" rather than "By Solomon," proposing that David composed this psalm "for" his son. This proposal would fit in with the attributing of the immediately preceding grouping of Psalms 51–70 to David as author. But if *leDavid* is taken to mean "By David" in these previous instances, it would seem most likely that *leSolomon* would mean "By Solomon," as it does in the case of Psalm 127.

(Ps. 72:5). He will rule from sea to sea and from the River to the ends of the earth (Ps. 72:8). All kings will bow to him, and all nations serve him (Ps. 72:11). His name will endure forever, and continue as long as the sun (Ps. 72:17).

The past two thousand years of history since the time of Jesus the Christ make it plain that these exalted words should not be analyzed as "mythopoetic" in nature. Each continent of this world in which we live has had its unique opportunity to hear and believe the gospel. This spread of the good news about the Christ has never ceased, so that today every continent has received the gospel of the Savior. How sad it is to see some countries and even continents that once possessed the priceless treasure of Messiah and his kingdom now despising the light of the gospel that once made them great. How it makes a person shudder when he considers the inevitable judgment that will be greater than that which fell on Sodom and Gomorrah. At the same time, how glorious it is to see new nations, peoples, tribes, and continents rushing to claim for themselves the inheritance in Christ's kingdom that others have scorned.

This glorious psalm of Messiah's universal and eternal rule concludes with an echo of the opening benedictions of the book of Psalms: "Blessed is the man who delights in the law of the LORD" (Ps. 1:2), and "Blessed are all who trust in Yahweh's Messiah" (Ps. 2:12). Fittingly, Book II of the Psalms concludes with similar benedictions:

> All nations will be blessed through him,
> and they will call him blessed. (Ps. 72:17)

With this climactic benediction, Book II echoes the original blessing spoken over Abraham the lone patriarch. In him all the people of the earth were to be blessed, and those nations who blessed him God would bless (Gen. 12:2–3). By this conclusion to Psalm 72, the psalmist indicates that God has been true to his covenantal promises. Abraham has become the father of many nations. Through his royal seed, all the peoples of the earth receive God's fullest blessing as covenanted with David.

The editor/arranger of the Psalms has left intact the statement that once concluded an early collection of David's psalms now assembled in Books I and II: "The prayers of David the son of Jesse are ended" (Ps. 72:20). This phrase may be clearly seen as an indicator of ancient tradition in view of the facts that (1) this particular psalm is attributed by its title specifically to Solomon rather than to David even though the subscript of this psalm declares that the "prayers of David the son of Jesse are ended"; and (2) the collection of prayers by David is by no means ended, as the third and fourth purposeful collections of Davidic psalms in Book V make quite clear. Yet the ancient tradition of Davidic psalms remains intact.

Conclusion to Book II: Ongoing Significance of David's Experiences

A canonical role for David's psalms in the life of the Christian currently living under the new covenant must be based on the principle that David's experiences properly serve as prototypes for the experiences of every believer in the Christ. The apostle Paul has shown us the way to see our connection with the sweet psalmist of Israel. Quoting from the law as well as the former and latter prophets, he underscores the consummative truth that "we" are "the temple of the living God" that David desired to build. God has built us into a house of his own where he forever dwells (2 Cor. 6:16–18; cf. Lev. 26:12; 2 Sam. 7:14; Isa. 52:11; Jer. 32:38; Ezek. 37:27). As a consequence of the merger of God's throne with Messiah's throne, a perpetual dynasty for God's kingdom has been established. By the expansive wonders of new covenant realization, every believer in Jesus the Christ-Messiah participates in the ultimate blessing of sonship to God. In Paul's enlightened understanding of God's climactic covenant with David, his new covenant application reads as follows: "I will be a Father to *you* [plural], and *you* [plural] will be my sons *and daughters* [!], says the LORD Almighty" (2 Cor. 6:18; cf. 2 Sam. 7:14). By boldly modifying the key text of this climactic covenant, Paul applies David's promise to each new generation. All persons who trust in King Messiah Jesus are declared by God's eternal covenant to be his sons and daughters.

120

Based on Paul's perspective, God's Word has explicitly told us that we are completely justified in applying the various truths of the Psalms to the experiences of all new covenant believers. Indeed, not every believer might undergo the intensity of trial and triumph as did David. In fact, it is almost certain that no single person since David, with one exception, has undergone the depths of agonies and the heights of exhilaration of that particular man. For he was a unique individual raised up specifically as the "man after God's own heart" to display in all its fullness the glorious life of the person who is one with Almighty God. In a similar way, Jesus the Christ as great David's greater Son experienced in his turn the realities described in the Psalms in a unique and heightened manner.

So the assumption underlying the celebration of these psalms by numerous individuals and worshiping communities across the past three thousand years is that this one man's experience of God is for us all. The history of the worshiping community has proved it to be true. Whether it be in times of joyful celebration or doleful agonizings, by God's appointment David's experience is our experience. Both individually and corporately, the record of his experience is for us. Still further, if a proper transference is to occur, every new generation must think covenantally. We must tell it to the next generation, that they in their turn may convey to their children this wondrous witness to the works of God.

7

BOOK III (PSALMS 73–89): DEVASTATION

Book III, composed of seventeen psalms, introduces a quite different perspective on the life of God's redeemed people. No longer is the focus on the person of David and his constant struggle as he seeks to establish his throne despite the incessant attacks of his foes. In significant contrast with Book I and Book II, only a few psalms in Book III are individualistic in form.[1] This book deals much more extensively with the corporate community of the people of God and its *devastation* by international forces.

Most striking in Book III is this theme of the defeat of God's people at the hands of invading international enemies. Though victory is sometimes registered, the predominant message is the stunning defeat of God's people as they face these powerful forces of foreign nations. The book concludes dramatically with the throne and crown of the Davidic king cast into the dust (Ps. 89:38–39, 44).

This book is divided into two parts of unequal length according to the attribution of authorship in the titles. Psalms 73–83 are ascribed to Asaph, and Psalms 84–89*[2] are largely attributed to the Sons of Korah. This division in Book III of basically the first two-thirds ascribed to Asaph followed by one-third ascribed to the Sons of Korah reverses the propor-

---

1. The *I*-perspective in Book III occurs only in Psalms 73, 77, 84, 86 (the only psalm indicated in the title as being "by David" in this book), and 88 (an individual facing death). Eleven of the remaining twelve psalms are essentially corporate in their mode of expression. Psalm 89 speaks extensively of the Messiah in the third-person singular. Only at the conclusion is the plaint of the psalmist expressed in the first-person singular (Ps. 89:46–51).

2. As elsewhere, the asterisk (*) attached to a listing of psalms indicates that the psalms of that collection might not all specifically refer to the same author in their titles.

tions of Book II, which ascribe roughly the first one-third to the Sons of Korah (Pss. 42–49*), followed by two-thirds to David (Pss. 51–71*).

A distinction in the dominant use of the names for God reinforces this division within Book III. In the "Asaph" segment (Pss. 73–83), *Elohim* prevails over *Yahweh* at a ratio of 3 to 1 (*Elohim* 47, *Yahweh* 13). In the "Sons of Korah" segment (Pss. 84–89*), *Yahweh* prevails over *Elohim* at a ratio of 2 to 1 (*Yahweh* 31, *Elohim* 16). The favoring of *Yahweh* over *Elohim* in this collection of the "Sons of Korah" psalms contrasts with the dominant usage of *Elohim* in the earlier "Sons of Korah" grouping in Book II (Pss. 42–49*). It is difficult to determine the reason for this shift in the proportionate use of the names for God in the two "Sons of Korah" collections, except to note the special concern of Book II to *communicate* with non-Israelite peoples by using the more general name for God. The *devastation* depicted in Book III concludes with the dramatic casting to the dust of both the crown and throne of the Davidic line, and by noting that it is none other than Yahweh, the God of the Davidic covenant, who has brought this devastation (Ps. 89:18, 39, 44–46).

The precise identity of "Asaph" and the "Sons of Korah" cannot be finally determined, though their names appear in Chronicles among the generational grouping of people responsible for the sacred music of tabernacle and temple.[3] These people mentioned in the titles of Book III cannot be identified with contemporaries of David and Solomon, since the bulk of these psalms are related to the time of the invasion of Israel by foreign nations, occurring some three to four hundred years after David. The statement that the "Sons of Korah" were a "hereditary guild of temple officials" is an appropriate assumption.[4]

The substance of Book III may be summarized as follows: (1) two psalms introduce the focus of the book on the distress and devastation of God's people, one viewing the problem from an individual's perspective

---

3. According to Chronicles, Asaph was one of David's three chief musicians, along with Heman and Jeduthun. Sons of these three men were officially appointed as temple musicians by David. The sons remained under the supervision of their fathers, while the three fathers were directly under the supervision of David (1 Chron. 25:1, 6). This original arrangement of generational responsibility for the music of the temple explains the appearance of these same names in connection with psalms originating decades, even centuries, after David. The "Sons of Korah" were a part of the generational grouping responsible for the sacred music of tabernacle and temple (1 Chron. 6:22, 31–32).

4. Derek Kidner, *Psalms 1–72: An Introduction and Commentary on Books I and II of the Psalms* (London: Inter-Varsity Press, 1973), 6.

(Ps. 73), and one from a corporate perspective (Ps. 74); (2) two psalms affirm the kingship of God over earthly kings despite the devastation they can bring (Pss. 75–76); (3) seven psalms report the devastation and deliverance of both the southern and the northern kingdoms of Israel, with a centralized focus on the "Son" of Psalm 80 (Pss. 77–83); (4) the initial psalms of the Sons of Korah in this book offer a striking change of tone with a positive perspective (Pss. 84–87*); (5) the book concludes with individual and corporate distress over devastation, offering little hope of deliverance (Pss. 88–89).

Introductory Psalms to Book III (Psalms 73–74)

As previously indicated, the first two psalms of Book III introduce the distress and devastation of God's people. In a manner quite similar to the introductory psalms of Book II, the first psalm in Book III views the problem from an individual's perspective (Ps. 73; cf. Pss. 42/43), while the second psalm presents the problem from a corporate perspective (Ps. 74; cf. Ps. 44).

Psalm 73 opens Book III with an individualistic psalm that wrestles with the *shalom*, the peaceful, flourishing life of the wicked. In the initial verses of this psalm, the "boastful" (הוֹלְלִים) and the "wicked" (רְשָׁעִים) stand in parallelism over against "Israel" and those who are "pure in heart" (Ps. 73:3, 1). It could be that these descriptions contrast two groups within the nation of Israel itself. Yet the same parallelism involving the "boastful" and the "wicked" recurs in Psalm 75:4, where they are more precisely identified as international enemies who "lift up [their] horns" against heaven. Considering the predominant theme in Book III of the invasion of foreign forces into the land of the Lord's people, these enemies of Psalm 73 could be proud world conquerors who "set their mouths against the heavens, and their tongue struts through the earth" (Ps. 73:9). These boastful proud ones of Psalm 73 might be identified with occupying troops of a nation that has conquered Israel. Having settled into the land, they enjoy every advantage that is denied the resident people.

But God will destroy them in his good time. As the psalmist says, "As a dream when one awakes, so when you arise, O Lord, you will despise them as fantasies" (Ps. 73:20).

124

Psalm 74, the second introductory psalm of Book III, speaks more pointedly of international invaders who have come with devastation into the land. Grouping by titles as previously indicated obviously has some significance in the structure of Book III. But far more significant for understanding the structure of this portion of the Psalter is the permeating role of international invaders. Quite alarming is the record of the crushing defeat of both the kingdom of Judah in the south and the kingdom of Israel to the north, even though occasional victories are also registered. The entire nation is being carried into exile.

This second psalm of Book III vividly describes the *devastation* of Zion's sanctuary by an invading army. Images of men wielding axes, smashing carved paneling, casting fire into God's sanctuary, defiling his dwellingplace intensify the impact of the poetic description (Ps. 74:5–7).

When did this destruction occur? To which invasion does the psalm refer? Obviously, the psalmist writes well beyond the circumstances of David's lifetime, which would have been the principal time frame of most of the psalms in Books I and II. Apparently this psalm refers to the invasion of Babylon in the sixth century B.C., which would have jumped across time to a period some four hundred years after David. Though generally connected with the final destruction of Jerusalem by Nebuchadnezzar in 586 B.C., Psalm 74 might be responding to the Babylonian invasion ten years earlier, in 596 B.C. The biblical narrative reports that during the brief three-month reign of eighteen-year-old Jehoiachin, grandson of Josiah, Nebuchadnezzar's officers set siege to Jerusalem. When the dreaded Babylonian king himself arrived, Jehoiachin surrendered the city. Then Nebuchadnezzar removed "all the treasures from the temple of the LORD . . . and took away all the gold articles that Solomon king of Israel had made for the temple of the LORD" (2 Kings 24:10, 12–13). Since the young Judean king capitulated willingly, the likelihood is that the city's major buildings were left intact, though the temple was ransacked. Nothing in the narrative of Kings suggests the destruction of Jerusalem at the time of this occupation of the city. This narrative perspective in the book of Kings conforms to the picture of Psalm 74, in which concentration centers on the chaos brought into God's temple. The substance of the psalm presents a picture of something less than the total devastation connected with the 586 B.C. invasion that occurred ten years later. The prayer of the psalmist depicts continuing residence of prominent Israelite people even after the invasion:

> Do not hand over the life of your dove
>   to wild beasts;
> do not forget the lives of your afflicted people
>   forever. (Ps. 74:19)

The more finalizing destruction of the city of Jerusalem along with the temple is vividly reported in Psalm 79. This latter psalm connects the defiling of the temple with the reducing of Jerusalem to rubble (Ps. 79:1). The image of a total destruction of the city in Psalm 79 conforms to the record in the book of Kings. Because King Zedekiah did not surrender to Nebuchadnezzar, the siege continued for eighteen months. Very likely in revenge for this stubborn resistance and all the inconvenience it caused his army, Nebuchadnezzar burned the temple, the royal palace, "and all the houses of Jerusalem. Every important building he burned down" (2 Kings 25:1–2, 9). This description suits well the picture of the destruction that included the city of Jerusalem in Psalm 79.[5]

5. The choice for the historical setting of Psalms 74 and 79 has been primarily between the 586 B.C. destruction of Jerusalem by Babylon and the defilement of the temple by Antiochus IV in 168 B.C. Quite interestingly, John Calvin expresses openness to either option: "There is some plausibility in both these opinions." John Calvin, *Commentary on the Book of Psalms* (Grand Rapids: Baker, 1993), 2:159. Cf. also his treatment of Psalm 79. Ibid., 2:281. Little or no discussion has considered the 596 B.C. destruction of Jerusalem as an option for the setting of Psalm 74. Hans-Joachim Kraus, *Psalms 60–150: A Commentary* (Minneapolis: Augsburg, 1989), 97, rejects the dating in the days of Antiochus for Psalm 74 and cautiously favors the sixth-century B.C. setting over the second-century B.C. scenario. In favor of dating Psalm 74 in connection with the 596 B.C. invasion are (1) the absence of any reference to the destruction of the city alongside the temple's devastation in Psalm 74, which conforms to the report of 2 Kings 24:12 regarding the early surrender of the city by young King Jehoiachin; and (2) the much more thorough destruction described in Psalm 79 in which the city itself is devastated, which would favor a 586 B.C. dating for Psalm 79. Psalm 79:1, 3 and 2 Kings 25:9 agree in depicting this devastation of the city rather than simply the temple as reported in Psalm 74 and implied in 2 Kings 24:12–13. Note the repeated anticipations of the burning of the *city* in Jeremiah's prophecies during the final days of King Zedekiah's reign (Jer. 37:8, 10; 38:18). On balance, it seems more likely that Psalms 74 and 79 are responding to two different events than that they are reacting to the same historical circumstance.

God's Kingship over Earthly Kings (Psalms 75–76)

Psalm 75 serves as a response to the pleading outcry for deliverance from the oppression of the invading forces as described in Psalm 74.[6] God alone chooses the "appointed time" to bring judgment on the wicked (Ps. 74:2). In his time, the evil people of the earth will drink the dregs of God's cup of judgment (Ps. 74:8). The wicked nations of the world are warned not to "lift up" their horns, symbolic of the assertion of military, economic, and political power:

> To the arrogant I say,
> "Boast no more,"
> and to the wicked,
> "Do not lift up your horns.
> "Do not lift up your horns against heaven;
> "do not speak with outstretched neck." (Ps. 75:4–5)

The lifted-up horns of the arrogant will be cut off, for none but God has the authority to exalt a man (Ps. 75:10, 6; cf. Zech. 1:18–21).

Psalm 76 almost certainly describes the humiliation of Sennacherib king of Assyria as a consequence of the visitation by the angel of the Lord outside the gates of Jerusalem in 701 B.C. (cf. Isa. 36–37). This understanding of the historical setting for Psalm 76 is at least as old as the Septuagint translation, which adds to the psalm's title the phrase "Concerning the Assyrian" (πρὸς τὸν Ἀσσύριον).[7] The description of the defeated army is quite vivid:

> Valiant men lie plundered, they sleep their last sleep;
> not one of the warriors can lift his hands.
> At your rebuke, O God of Jacob,
> both horse and chariot lie still. (Ps. 76:5–6)

The psalm ends with the declaration that God "breaks the spirit of rulers; he is feared by the kings of the earth" (Ps. 76:12).

---

6. The reference to Asaph in the title is a generic term that would include Asaph's descendants.

7. Derek Kidner, *Psalms 73–150: A Commentary on Books III–V of the Psalms* (London: Inter-Varsity Press, 1975), 274, says that "no event could be more strongly suggested than the elimination of Sennacherib's Assyrian army by the angel of the LORD (Isa. 37:36)."

127

So the psalmist will not surrender the supremacy of God's king-ship over the nations. Despite the trying times that have come because of invasion by foreign nations, God remains as the ultimate Ruler of this world.

Seven Psalms of Devastation and Deliverance with a Centralized Focus on the "Son" of Psalm 80 (Psalms 77–83)

This special collection of seven psalms underscores the theme of the nation's devastation by reporting the destruction of the south-ern kingdom by Babylon in 586 B.C. (Ps. 79) and the destruction of the northern kingdom by Assyria in 722 B.C. (Ps. 80). At the same time, two messianic figures emerge as potential deliverers of these two national entities of God's people. A son of David and a son of Joseph will serve as Israel's deliverer (Ps. 78:65–66, 70–72; cf. Pss. 89:35–37; 80:1–2, 15, 17).

Psalm 77 opens with an *I*, referring to an individual in distress. Yet this individual's disturbance arises from the peril created by international enemies. As he indicates, "You display your power among the peoples" (Ps. 77:14). Then in dramatic fashion he recalls the miraculous interven-tion of God at the exodus when he delivered Israel from the tyranny of Egypt (Ps. 77:16–20), providing further indication that the psalmist is troubled over a situation much larger than his own personal problems. Instead, he faces a challenge to national security. So this psalm fits into the flow of international enemies previously depicted in Psalms 74–76.

Psalm 77 introduces references to the tribe of Joseph and his descendants that run throughout this grouping of psalms that form the central focus of Book III (Pss. 77–83). The psalmist indicates that by his mighty arm God redeemed his people, "the descendants of Jacob and Joseph" (Ps. 77:15). In this middle section of Book III, the northern and southern tribal groups of Israel experience devastation and deliverance.

The final phrase of Psalm 77 introduces an image of pastoral ten-derness in the midst of international turmoil: "You led your people like a flock by the hand of Moses and Aaron" (Ps. 77:20). Once introduced, this touching imagery recurs in the next three psalms as a means of mol-lifying national traumas. God led the people like sheep through the desert

(Ps. 78:52); David shepherded them as God's chosen king (Ps. 78:72); we are "the sheep of your pasture" (Ps. 79:13); you as the "Shepherd of Israel" will "lead Joseph like a flock" (Ps. 80:1). This extension of a common phrasing across several psalms represents a typical technique of organizational arrangement that reappears throughout the Psalter.

Psalm 78, after a thorough review of God's faithfulness in redemption despite the nation's repeated failures, focuses on the climactic nature of God's covenant with David. This concentration on the Davidic covenant is fully understandable. For the Lord's oath to David serves as the ultimate covenant enacted under the provisions of the Old Testament. Quite illuminating in terms of the broader biblical-theological context of the Psalms as a whole is the fact that four to five hundred years after David's life, the Psalms continue their interaction with the Lord under the auspices of God's covenant with David. Jerusalem as the Lord's permanent dwellingplace and David's descendants' ruling in union with God's dominion continue as the grand themes that unite the Psalter. No indicator may be found suggesting an end to the Davidic promises even after his kingdom is devastated. No advances develop in God's redemptive purposes beyond the provisions of the Davidic covenant, other than the predictive promises of the new covenant.

After extensive introductory observations (Ps. 78:1–8), the psalmist surprises the reader with his sudden depiction of the failure of the men of Ephraim, who "turned back in the day of battle" (Ps. 78:9; cf. Hos. 7:1, 11, 16). At the climax of a lengthy rehearsal of God's deliverances from Egypt, across the desert, through the conquest, and then through their oppression under the merciless regime of the Philistines, the psalmist recalls how the COVENANT LORD "rejected the tents of Joseph" and "did not choose the tribe of Ephraim." Instead, he "chose the tribe of Judah, Mount Zion, which he loved" (Ps. 78:67–68). He "chose David his servant . . . to be the shepherd of his people Jacob, of Israel his inheritance" (Ps. 78:70–71). So David shepherded them "with the integrity of his heart and the skillfulness of his hands" (Ps. 78:72). In the broader context of Book III, this psalm underscores the fact that in spite of all the setbacks caused through the series of invasions by conquering international armies, the dynasty of David and God's dwellingplace in Zion remain secure as a consequence of the COVENANT LORD's personal interventions.

Psalm 79 returns to the theme of international invasions of the COVENANT LORD's land. This time, going a significant step beyond the devastations described in Psalm 74, the nations "have invaded your inheritance; . . . have defiled your holy temple, . . . have reduced Jerusalem to rubble" (Ps. 79:1). In literal fulfillment of the curses of the Abrahamic covenant, these merciless invaders have "given the dead bodies of your servants as food to the birds of the air" and have "poured out blood like water all around Jerusalem, and there is no one to bury the dead" (Ps. 79:2–3; cf. Gen. 15:10–11; Jer. 14:16; 34:20). By these sobering images the psalmist vivifies the final destruction of Jerusalem by the Babylonians in 586 B.C.

Thus far in Book III, international assailants have included an earlier invasion of Jerusalem by Babylon in 596 B.C. (Ps. 74), the invasion of Judah by Assyria in 701 B.C. (Ps. 76), the conquest of Israel by the Philistines in about 1060 B.C. (Ps. 78:60–64), and the destruction of Jerusalem by Babylon in 586 B.C. (Ps. 79). Interspersed among these devastating judgments have been regular accounts of God's faithfulness in delivering his people from these chastening afflictions. Clearly, this collection of devastations by international forces goes beyond any conflict with "enemies" described in Books I and II. A deliberate arrangement of the Psalter seems quite apparent.

At the heart of this framework of psalms reporting national devastations in Book III is a special collection of psalms alluding to destruction and deliverance for the northern tribes, designated as "Joseph" and his descendants. As the central psalm of this collection of seven psalms, Psalm 80 interacts with the destruction of the northern kingdom of Israel by Assyria in 722 B.C.[8] This psalm functions as the central psalm of this special collection that frequently alludes to the role of "Joseph" or "Ephraim" as the figurative embodiment of the descendants of Rachel the beloved wife of Jacob.[9] In addition, Psalm 80 is strategically located at the midpoint of

8. As previously noted, the Septuagint explicitly recognizes this historical setting for Psalm 80 by inserting in its title "Concerning the Assyrian." Kidner, *Psalms 73–150*, 289, notes that this indicator of circumstance "seems a valid inference from the psalm."

9. The arrangement of a special collection of psalms around a central psalm occurs more than once in the Psalter. Psalms 20–24 represent a collection of five "kingship" psalms, featuring two psalms about the messianic king (Pss. 20–21) and two psalms about the Divine King (Pss. 23–24) with a central psalm that combines a presentation of both kingships (Ps. 22). Psalms 111–117 are the first collection of *Hallelu-YAH* psalms in Book V, with three psalms before and three psalms after central Psalm 114. An even larger collection may be seen in the Songs of Ascents, numbering fifteen psalms (Pss. 120–134), with seven psalms preceding and seven psalms following Psalm 127, attributed to Solomon. Cf. the excursus at the end of chapter 9 regarding the possibility of "poetic pyramid" groupings in the Psalter.

Book III. Even further, according to the reckoning of the Jewish scribes, a careful count of letters places this psalm at the central point of the entire Psalter.[10] At first the psalm seems to stand alone in its distinctive dealing with the fall of Samaria, the capital city of the northern kingdom of Israel, as indicated by its opening references to "Joseph" and "Ephraim." This psalm appears to be isolated by a sea of references to Judea, Jerusalem, Zion, the temple of Jerusalem, and the dynasty of David. But the reappearance of the key words "Joseph" and "Ephraim" in closely adjoining psalms unveils one more deliberate grouping in the Psalter. Except for a single reference to the historical experience of the person of Joseph in Book V (Ps. 105:16-22), all other mentions of "Joseph" in the Psalter refer to the tribal community, and are clustered about Psalm 80 at the midpoint of Book III (Pss. 77:15; 78:67; 80:1; 81:5). In a similar way, three references to "Ephraim" appear in this same grouping of psalms (Pss. 78:9, 67; 80:2). The only other mentions of "Ephraim" in the Psalter occur as the psalmist delineates the territorial claims of the Lord (Ps. 60:7, echoed in Ps. 108:8).

This grouping of references in the psalms to the tribal descendants of Jacob's beloved wife Rachel (Joseph and Benjamin along with Joseph's sons Ephraim and Manasseh) opens with a combined allusion to God's redemption of "the descendants of Jacob and Joseph," which sets the stage for a tracing of the experiences of the two groups (Ps. 77:15). This reminder of the earlier redemption from Egypt for both "Jacob" and "Joseph" provides encouragement in the current time of distress when the Lord appears to have rejected his people forever (Ps. 77:2, 9–10).

"Joseph" and his descendants reappear in the psalm that immediately follows (Ps. 78), which emphasizes God's rejecting Joseph and selecting David's line instead. God did not choose the tents of Joseph or the tribe of Ephraim, but chose the tribe of Judah, "Mount Zion, which he loved" (Ps. 78:9, 67–68). Instead of Saul from the tribe of Benjamin from the Rachel tribes, God chose David of the tribe of Judah from the Leah tribes to be his messianic king. This psalm climaxes with a picture of David as the kingly messianic figure who "shepherded" God's people with integrity of heart and skillfulness of hands (Ps. 78:72).

---

10. Psalm 80 is in fact the center of the Psalter by measurement of bulk lettering. Christian D. Ginsburg, *Introduction to the Masoretico-Critical Edition of the Hebrew Bible* (London: Trinitarian Bible Society, 1897), 69, notes that according to the Talmud, the ancients were called "Scribes [i.e., *Sopherim* or Counters] because they counted all the letters in Holy Writ." The traditional Hebrew text raises the *ayin* of מִיַּעַר in Psalm 80:14 to indicate that it is "the middle letter in the Psalter."

131

The following two psalms (Pss. 79–80) describe in turn the dev-astation of Jerusalem by the Babylonians (Ps. 79) and the devastation of Samaria by the Assyrians (Ps. 80). In response to the destruction of the northern kingdom, hope focuses on a single individual, a "son" that God has raised up for himself (Ps. 80:15). This "son" functions in a way that parallels the role of the messianic "son" promised to David (2 Sam. 7:14). This unique son is called the "man of [God's] right hand" (*ish yemino*), the "son of man" (**ben adam**) that God has raised up for himself (Ps. 80:17). The dual phrasing involves a play on the name *Ben-yamin*, the favored youngest son from among the Rachel tribes, whose name means "Son of the Right Hand" (cf. Ps. 80:2, 17). The northern kingdom's only hope resides in this strongly empowered figure, the "man of [God's] right hand," the "son of man" that God has raised up for himself as their deliverer (Ps. 80:15, 17).

This "son of man," this "man of God's right hand" as deliverer of the descendants of Joseph embodies the leadership role assigned for Joseph of Rachel alongside Judah of Leah. This position of prominence for a descendant of Joseph can be understood only in the context of the ancient prophetic blessings of Moses on the various tribes of Israel. Jacob had declared that the scepter, the rulership over God's people, would never depart from Judah "until he should come to whom it prop-erly belongs" (Gen. 49:10). Yet in Moses' later prophetic benediction over the various tribes, Joseph is designated as "the prince among his brothers . . . like a firstborn bull; his horns are the horns of a wild ox. With them he will gore the nations, even those at the ends of the earth" (Deut. 33:16–17). Subsequently the book of 1 Chronicles confirms this priority of position for Joseph and his descendants by declaring that Reuben's rights as firstborn "were given to the sons of Joseph son of Israel; . . . and though Judah was the strongest of his brothers and a ruler came from him, the rights of the firstborn belonged to Joseph" (1 Chron. 5:1–2).

The book of Psalms never completely resolves this tension created by two tribes with descendants in the leadership position among God's people. The Lord rejects Shiloh, Ephraim, and Saul the descendant of Benjamin from the Rachel tribes in favor of Jerusalem, Judah, and David of the Leah tribes (Ps. 78:9, 67). Yet a position of priority remains for the Joseph tribe as well. From Joseph, Ephraim, Benjamin, and Manasseh, the Lord God

Almighty will raise up for himself a "man of the right hand," a "son of man" (Ps. 80:1–2, 15, 17). The phrasing describing this "savior" is clearly based on the name "Ben-jamin," which means "son" "of the right hand."

The focal point of this psalm appears in the multiple plays on words found in Psalm 80:15 and 17. Three different phrases are employed as equivalent to the "vine," which refers to the nation of Israel that God brought out of Egypt in verse 14: (1) the "son" (*ben*) you have made strong for yourself (Ps. 80:15b); (2) the "man of your right hand" (*ish yemino*—Ps. 80:17a); and (3) the "son of man" (*ben adam*) you have made strong for yourself (Ps. 80:17b). Several observations may be made regarding these phrases. First, as previously indicated, the words clearly involve a play on the name *Benjamin* (*ben-yamin*, "son of the right hand"). This name is introduced in the opening of the psalm (Ps. 80:2), and both elements of the name ("son" and "right hand") reappear in these concluding verses. In addition, the phrase "you have made strong" captures the significance of the "right hand," which is the position of strength. Second, the person described in these phrases represents both a single individual and the corporate community of Israel. He embodies in himself the community in that the defining phrases substitute for the "vine" of verse 14, which refers to Israel as a community. At the same time, he is an individual in that the passage points to a particular person who functions as savior to Israel, and devastated Israel cannot be its own savior. Third, the play on the name *Benjamin* in these key verses militates against the concept of a Davidic Messiah. The entire context of the psalm speaks of the descendants of Rachel (Joseph, Ephraim, Benjamin, and Manasseh), not the descendants of Leah (Judah and David). Fourth, this individual is a messianic figure from the tribe of Joseph and his son Ephraim, a "Messiah ben Joseph" or "ben Ephraim." This singular saving hero, descended from Joseph/Ephraim, is the one who will restore his devastated people. He will provide the means by which God's face will shine in blessing them once more (Ps. 80:3, 7, 19). He will be their savior (Ps. 80:19). He is the source of the ancient tradition in Judaism of a "Messiah ben Joseph" or "ben Ephraim."[11]

11. The Aramaic Targum explains the term "son" in Psalm 80:16 [Eng. v. 15] as "anointed king." Cf. David M. Stec, *The Targum of Psalms* (Collegeville, MN: Liturgical Press, 2004), 157. Franz Delitzsch, *Biblical Commentary on the Psalms* (Grand Rapids: Eerdmans, 1959), 2:388, notes that the Targum renders verse 16b as "King Messiah." For basic information about this "Messiah ben Joseph" or "Ephraim," see Moses Buttenwieser, "Messiah," in *The Jewish*

From a new covenant perspective, this tradition of two "saviors" from two different tribal lines finds its resolution in a single Savior who combines in himself the major elements of both traditions. Because the ultimate Redeemer of God's people is so rich in significance, no one figure could encompass all the facets of his person and work. On the one hand, the royal image of a king with Davidic lineage depicts the perpetual sovereignty of the God-appointed Redeemer. On the other hand, the descent of a Joseph-figure who goes down into the pit, down into Egypt, and down into a dungeon followed by an ascent up to the right hand of the pharaoh and up to the position of lordship over the nations enriches the imagery of the Redeemer. So Jesus is the son of David, seated on his eternal throne. But in addition, Jesus deliberately chooses for himself the "son of man" title, and fills the phrase with imagery of both suffering through rejection and glory when returning in the clouds (Matt. 17:22–23; 24:30–31).

This grouping of psalms at the midpoint of Book III, having begun with a remembrance of the deliverance from Egypt for the descendants of both "Jacob and Joseph" (Ps. 77:15), returns to a celebration of the ancient deliverance from Egypt for both "Jacob and Joseph":

> This is a decree
> for Israel,
> an ordinance
> of the God of Jacob.
> He established it
> as a statute for Joseph
> when he went out against Egypt. (Ps. 81:4–5)

Encyclopedia (New York: Funk and Wagnalls, 1906), 8:511–12. The article refers to "a messianic figure peculiar to the rabbinical apocalyptic literature—that of Messiah ben Joseph." In the midrash literature, "Messiah b. Joseph will appear prior to the coming of Messiah b. David; he will gather the children of Israel around him, march to Jerusalem, and there, after overcoming the hostile powers, reestablish the Temple-worship and set up his own dominion." But then certain hosts will wage war against Messiah b. Joseph and slay him. According to one group, his corpse will be hidden by the angels until Messiah b. David comes and resurrects him. Cf. also Gerald J. Blidstein, "Messiah," in *Encyclopedia Judaica* (Jerusalem: Keter Publishing House, 1972), 11:1410–12, who comments on Jewish tradition regarding a Messiah son of Joseph "whose coming precedes that of the Messiah, son of David, and who will die in combat with the enemies of God and Israel." It is quite clear that in the traditions of Judaism a second messianic figure from the line of Joseph paralleled, and was not the same as, the Messiah coming from the line of David. For additional discussion of a Messiah ben Joseph, see D. C. Mitchell, "The Fourth Deliverer: A Josephite Messiah in 4QTestimonia," *Biblica* 86, 4 (2005): 545–53.

Obviously, temporal sequence does not function as the organizing principle of the psalmist in Book III. He has hopped and skipped from 596 B.C. to 701 B.C. to 1060 B.C. to 586 B.C. to 722 B.C. Yet all these various references to invading, conquering international armies unite this section of the Psalter. The "how long" of the psalmist that occurs repeatedly throughout this section (Pss. 74:9–10; 79:5; 80:4; 82:2; 89:46) is intensified when contrasted with the perspective of one of the primary "pillars" of the book of Psalms with its depiction of Messiah's subduing ungodly nations such as these with a rod of iron (Ps. 2:9).

Psalm 81 offers the prospect of an enhanced recapitulation of the nation's deliverances from Egypt and in the wilderness by a similar deliverance from the Israelites' contemporary enemies and foes. After his rehearsal of devastations in Psalms 74, 77, 79, and 80, the psalmist boldly declares that his people can be saved from all these oppressive armies. "If my people would but listen to me, . . . how quickly would I subdue their enemies" (Ps. 81:13–14; cf. vv. 8b, 11). Instead of water in the desert, they would enjoy "honey from the rock" (Ps. 81:16; cf. the promise of Deut. 32:13c), and so experience a greater deliverance than ancient Israel's exodus from Egypt.

According to Psalm 82, God the Judge judges the judges of the nations. In their capacity as rulers or princes who exercise judgment over their people, these human judges may even be designated as "gods" (Ps. 82:1, 6). But the Most High God will rise to judge the entire earth, for all the nations are his possession (Ps. 82:8).

Quite fascinating is the application by Jesus of this psalm to the controversy regarding his self-identity. His enemies were prepared to kill him because he claimed to be the Son of God. Instead of appealing to any one of the messianic Scriptures available to him, Jesus cites this passage from Psalm 82 in a classic "argument from minor to major" (*argumentum a minori ad maiorus*). Scripture designates "judges" as "gods" and "sons of the Most High" because they fulfill a Godlike function when they render a judgment (Ps. 82:1, 6). Jesus bases his self-identity as the Son of God on this passage from the Psalms:

Is it not written in your Law, "I have said, you are gods" [Ps. 82:6]? If he called them "gods," to whom the word of God came—and the Scripture cannot be broken—what about the one whom the Father set apart as his very own and sent into the world? Why then do you

135

> accuse me of blasphemy because I said, "I am God's Son"? Do not
> believe me unless I do what my Father does. But if I do it, even though
> you do not believe me, believe the miracles, that you may know and
> understand that the Father is in me, and I in the Father. (John 10:34–38)

Jesus refers to the "Scripture," using a singular form to underscore its
unity, as "*your* Law." As a result, his opponents cannot easily disparage
his words. Scripture designates judges as "gods" and "sons of the Most
High" (Ps. 82:6). Why, then, should they object when he represents
himself as the Son of God even as he performs works of God much more
dramatic than the rendering of a judicial decision by earthly judges?
He might have appealed to Psalm 45, where the Messiah is specifically
called "God." He might have referred to the prophecy of Isaiah regarding the Branch of Jesse, who is designated as "Mighty God" (Isa. 9:7).
But instead, he deals gently with his adversaries, seeking to lead them
to faith in himself by appealing to a Scripture that might cause them to
think and to follow his conclusion "from the minor to the major." Belief
in the lesser truth should clear the way for belief in the larger truth.

It has been rightly proposed that the quotations from the Old Testament found in the New Testament should be properly understood in the
larger context of the quotations' origins. The "servant of the LORD" passages in Isaiah when quoted in the New Testament should be understood
in the fuller context of the total message of Isaiah's "servant songs."[12] Until
more recent developments in psalm studies, the effort was rarely made to
interpret a particular psalm in its broader context because of the assumption
that each psalm stood on its own apart from connections with adjacent
psalms. But in view of the surfacing of broader contextual connections in
more recent Psalter studies, might it be that this quotation of Jesus from
Psalm 82 should be understood in the context of this collection of seven
psalms with its focus on Psalm 80? In Psalm 82, the judges of the earth are
designated as "gods" and even "sons of God" (Ps. 82:1, 6). In Psalm 80,
the suffering Messiah ben Joseph is called "son," referring to his position
as Son of God. So when Jesus quotes Psalm 82 in the face of his enemies
who intend to kill him because he has declared himself to be the Son of
God, could he be appealing not only to the sonship of judges according

---

12. Cf. the epical application of this approach in C. H. Dodd, *According to the Scriptures:
The Sub-structure of New Testament Theology* (London: Nisbet & Co., 1952), 88–96.

to Psalm 82, but also to the unique sonship of Messiah ben Joseph in Psalm 80? Perhaps Jesus intends to appeal to one of the most outstanding messianic passages of the Old Testament, a passage that presents Messiah as God's "Son" who suffers, deliberately identifying himself as the "son" of Psalm 80:15, 17, the suffering but ultimately exalted Messiah ben Joseph.[13]

Psalm 83, the last of the psalms of Asaph in this collection, depicts an aggressive coalition of no fewer than ten enemies encircling God's people. These nations are intent on annihilation, so that the name of Israel will be remembered no more (Ps. 83:4). Obviously, the "enemy" in this instance is not an individual, and the enemy's ire is not directed against a single person, as is commonly the case in Book I. Instead, whole nations band together against the whole nation of God's people. The long list of conspirators includes the Philistines and Tyre to the west, alongside Edom, Moab, and Assyria to the near and distant east and north, as well as Amalek to the south. This impressive array of enemies suggests an imagery of "the perennial aggression of the world against God and His people."[14] Yet climaxing this list is "Assyria," which has the effect of connecting Psalm 83 more specifically with central Psalm 80 and the devastation of Samaria by Assyria. In addition, the appeal to previous deliverances from Midian, Sisera, Jabin, Oreb

13. Cf. the discussion of the messianic interpretation of Psalm 80 in the Talmud by Samson H. Levey, *The Messiah: An Aramaic Interpretation: The Messianic Exegesis of the Targum* (Cincinnati, OH: Hebrew Union College-Jewish Institute of Religion, 1974), 119–20, 142–44. Levey notes that the Targum interprets "Son" in Psalm 80:16 [Eng. v. 15] directly as "King Messiah." He comments: "At first glance this may appear to be an incongruity, not only for the Targum, but for Jewish Messianism generally, since it would appear that the Targum takes the Messiah to be the son of God," which he regards as *"much too anthropomorphic and Christological to be acceptable in Jewish exegesis."* Ibid., 119. He continues: "Although *it sounds Christological, almost as though it had been injected by a Christian exegete*, it is probably Jewish to the core." Ibid., 120 (emphasis added). Levey explains: "The present passage in the Targum represents . . . a case of Messianic interpretation which seems out of place, both theologically and exegetically, and yet has been preserved intact, without modification or deletion." Ibid. He proposes that the official targumim "stem from Maccabean times when hope for a restoration of the Davidic kingship would constitute treason to the Hasmonean dynasty." Ibid., 142. His comments speak volumes about the inescapable character of the witness of Scripture to the true identity of the Lord's Messiah, who is eventually proved to be Jesus. In his conclusion regarding Messiah in the targumim, Levey states: "He will be of the Davidic lineage, though he may have a non-Davidic predecessor, the Ephraimite Messiah, who will die in battle." Ibid. Indeed, Jesus as the "Ephraimite Messiah" died in battle with satanic powers. But being of the "Davidic lineage," he continues to rule as the resurrected Messiah.

14. Kidner, *Psalms 73–150*, 300.

and Zeeb, and Zebah and Zalmunna by Israel's judges (Ps. 83:9–12) also locates this psalm in the northern kingdom, including the territory of the half-tribe of Manasseh in Transjordan. The ultimate end envisioned in this deliverance is not merely the destruction of all these national and international enemies, but "that they will seek your name, O COVENANT LORD," which clearly manifests God's grace toward rebellious nations (Ps. 83:16).

So the editor/collector of the book of Psalms appears to have deliberately grouped seven psalms at the midpoint of Book III about the redemptive experiences of Joseph alongside "Jacob" (Pss. 77–83). These two patriarchal figures represent the northern kingdom of Israel and the southern kingdom of Judah. This grouping of psalms interweaves the life experience of the two kingdoms: their original deliverance from Egypt, their devastation by foreign nations, the raising up of a singular messianic figure for each, and their hope of a second, consummate deliverance. This collection represents one more element of structure within the Psalter, an element not quite so apparent as other structures. But the seven psalms (Pss. 77–83) contain substantial evidence of having been grouped by an editor with the specific intent of relating the devastation of both kingdoms as well as their deliverance by their respective messianic figures.

A Change of Tone in the Psalms of the Sons of Korah (Psalms 84–87*)

After a rehearsal of the assaults of various enemies across the ages, this collection of psalms attributed to the "Sons of Korah" introduces a significant change of tone. Now the return of Yahweh's blessings is underscored. The renewed prominence of *Yahweh* as the preferred name for God provides a foundational focus for these psalms of encouragement.

Peace and Blessing in the Midst of Perpetual Warfare (Psalms 84–85)

In this context of perpetual warfare with international enemies, the psalmist seeks the promise of peace in the only place where it may be found: in the intimacy of immediate presence before Yahweh himself. In Yahweh's dwellingplace, in the courts of Yahweh, peace may be found. Reaching the peak of poetic diction, Psalm 84 declares:

> How lovely are your dwellings,
>   O Yahweh God of Hosts!
> My soul longs, even faints,
>   for the courts of Yahweh.
> My heart and my flesh cry out
>   for the Living God.
>
> Even the sparrow has found her a home,
> And the swallow a nest
>   where she may lay her young,
>   even your altars,
>   O Yahweh of Hosts,
>   my King and my God. (Ps. 84:1–3)

What a picturesque image of peace in the midst of mortal conflict. At no other place than the altar of God, the mother bird finds a peaceful locale to build a nest for her young. For this psalmist, life consists of nothing more than setting your heart on pilgrimage until you appear before God in Zion. For there God will look with favor on your Savior, your Anointed One (Ps. 84:7, 9). Once more, the key to a full appreciation of the passage resides in its relation to the Davidic covenant. Only as Yahweh looks on the face of their Anointed One can the people experience the peace they seek, which will be found at Yahweh's permanent dwellingplace in the temple of Jerusalem.

This prospect of enjoying promised peace in the midst of international conflict sets the tone of Psalm 85 as well. Yahweh has restored the fortunes of Jacob in the past by forgiving the people's iniquity, covering all their sins, and turning from his fierce anger (Ps. 85:1–3). Now the psalmist pleads that by his grace the Lord will restore them again. Covenant love and faithfulness, righteousness and peace will kiss each other. Yahweh will indeed give what is good (Ps. 85:12).

An Individualistic Psalm of David (Psalm 86)

In this extended context of corporate psalms characterizing virtually the whole of Book III, Psalm 86 stands out because of its individualistic

139

character. Psalm 86 alone of the seventeen psalms of Book III is designated as a prayer "of David." This psalm closely resembles the many individualistic psalms in the extended collection of Davidic psalms found in Books I and II. Yet its specific content suits perfectly the overall message of Book III. This particular psalm (Ps. 86) is among only eight of the seventy-three psalms attributed to David that speak of the Lord's conquest of the nations. In this psalm, David triumphantly declares, "All the nations you have made will come and worship before you, O Lord; they will bring glory to your name" (Ps. 86:9). So Psalm 86 fits well into the context of Book III, where so many of the other psalms in this book specifically refer to the threats of the invading nations of the world.

Distinctive Deliverance from International Enemies (Psalm 87)

In Psalm 87, this deliverance from international enemies takes a distinctive turn. For in this psalm, some of the identical enemies previously catalogued in Book III are overcome, not by force of arms but by conversion. Rahab, representing Egypt, alongside Babylon, Philistia, Tyre, and Cush, is "born in Zion." To make this startling point more emphatic, the same truth is repeated three times over in three consecutive verses: "born in Zion," "born in her," "born in Zion" (vv. 4, 5, 6). Can you believe it? Israel's perpetual enemies transformed into native-born citizens of Zion. What a way to conquer an adversary!

Concluding Psalms of Distress (Psalms 88–89)

Though never expressing the idea of utter abandonment by the Lord, Book III has regularly represented *devastation* as the current condition of God's people. They are in the process of going into exile. In this context, the final two psalms of Book III give expression to the distress brought about by this devastation, first from an individual's perspective (Ps. 88) and then from the viewpoint of the corporate community (Ps. 89).

Individual Distress, with Slight Hope (Psalm 88)

As one of the few individualistic psalms in Book III, Psalm 88 deals extensively with the specter of death. As perhaps the only psalm that expresses no explicit hope of overcoming the threatening enemy, Psalm 88 sounds a somber note:

Day and night I cry out to you. (Ps. 88:1)

My life draws near the grave. (Ps. 88:3)

I . . . go down to the pit. (Ps. 88:4)

I am set apart with the dead. (Ps. 88:5)

I am . . . like the slain who lie in the grave. (Ps. 88:5)

You have put me in the lowest pit, in the darkest depths. (Ps. 88:6)

Your wrath lies heavily upon me. (Ps. 88:7)

You have overwhelmed me with all your waves. (Ps. 88:7)

The psalmist anticipates his future as a confrontation with death, the grave, destruction, the place of darkness, the land of oblivion (Ps. 88:10–12). He has been close to death from his youth, he has suffered God's terrors, he is in despair, God's wrath has swept over him, God's terrors have destroyed him, his loved ones have been taken from him (Ps. 88:15–18a). Rather than ending with an upbeat note, the last phrase of the psalm declares that "darkness is my closest friend" (Ps. 88:18b). Quite naturally, a psalm dealing so specifically with death must be individualistic in its approach. For death is a specter that each person must face by himself alone.[15]

15. Walter Brueggemann, *The Message of the Psalms: A Theological Commentary* (Minneapolis: Augsburg, 1984), 80, offers a helpful note on the apparent hopelessness in this psalm: "this psalm is not a psalm of mute depression. It is still speech. . . . In the bottom of the Pit, Israel still knows it has to do with Yahweh. It cannot be otherwise." Brueggemann next refers to William Styron's *Sophie's Choice*. A character named Stingo travels his sad way on a bus from Washington to New York to bury his two close friends. A black woman next to him lines out Psalm 88. These words from the psalmist console when easy words could offer no comfort. Says Brueggemann: "Psalm 88 stands as a mark of realism for biblical faith. It has its pastoral use, because there are situations in which easy, cheap talk of resolution must be avoided. Here are words not to be used frequently, but for the limit[ed] experiences when words must be honest and not claim too much." Ibid., 81.

At the same time, Psalm 88 must be read in the context of its clear connection with Psalm 89. In the same tone in which Psalm 88 reflects on the fleeting character of life, Psalm 89 declares:

> Remember how fleeting is my life.
> For what futility you have created all men!
>
> What man can live and not see death,
> or save himself from the power of the grave? (Ps. 89:47–48)

Despite these troubling circumstances, the hope of a messianic King from the line of David still beats strongly in the heart of the psalmist. Though muffled by the historical context of the exile, Psalm 89 repeatedly gives a strong expression of hope based on the covenantal promise made to David.

Corporate Distress, with Muffled Hope (Psalm 89)

Psalm 89 as the final psalm of Book III appropriately sounds a hopeful though muffled messianic note despite exceedingly distressful circumstances. This psalm concludes Book III with reflections on the climactic covenant of the Old Testament that God swore to David, focusing on God's covenant promise regarding messianic David's ever-lasting *dynasty* and God's permanent *dwellingplace*. Three times over, this concluding psalm of Book III reaffirms that David's line will be established forever, and that his throne joined to God's throne will endure through all generations, as long as the sun, the moon, and the heavens endure (Ps. 89:4, 29, 36). As previously indicated, the word *house* in the original record of God's covenant with David underscores the two principal promises of the Davidic covenant. First, the COV-ENANT LORD will establish a "house" for David, referring to his per-petual dynasty (2 Sam. 7:11b). Simultaneously, David's son will build a permanent "house," a dwellingplace for God's Name (2 Sam. 7:13). For God himself will set up his permanent throne on earth, from which he will rule his people as well as all the nations of the world.

Yet at the present moment, God has been very angry with his Anointed One, renounced his covenant, defiled David's crown in the dust, and cast his throne to the ground (Ps. 89:38–45). The eighty-ninth psalm, and therefore Book III, concludes with a first-person cry to the Lord that he should remember how his Anointed One has been mocked at his every step by all the nations (Ps. 89:50–51).

But who is this particular Anointed One of the Lord, this *I* who claims for himself the covenant promises made generations earlier to David? Is he one of the last kings of Judah, or one of the sons or the grandson of Josiah? Could he be young King Jehoiachin, languishing as an exiled captive in Babylon? Or could the psalmist intend this singular *I* to represent the entire remnant of believers?

Most likely, this voice represents the cry of one of David's descendants who suffered the shame and deprivation of exile. From the new covenant perspective, Matthew in his Gospel traces the genealogy of Jesus from the time of Judah's exile through Jeconiah (Jehoiachin), Shealtiel, and Zerubbabel. This same Zerubbabel filled a leadership role for those returning from exile to the land. Zerubbabel's genealogy ultimately led to Joseph the husband of Mary, of whom was born Jesus who is called Christ (Matt. 1:12–16). So despite all the agonies and national setbacks described so vividly in Book III, God's covenantal promise to David ultimately finds its fulfillment in Jesus the Christ.

The Failure of Faith

But how is this ongoing tragedy of Book III to be understood? How could both the nations of Israel and Judah be carried into exile by foreign nations? How could the "house," the temple of the Lord, be so totally devastated, and the crown of the "house" of David be cast into the dust? How could both these focal elements of the Davidic covenant seem to end in utter failure?

The "negative space" of Book III answers these most difficult questions in terms of the failure of faith on the part of Yahweh's covenant people. Trust in Yahweh that might have functioned as the instrument of their deliverance appears at its weakest. This fact becomes evident when the use of the various terms for "faith" or "trust" as they appear in Book III are compared with their usage in the remainder of the Psalter. Of the five terms that express reliance on the Lord in the Psalms, very few instances in Book III indicate that God's people trusted him for their victory over these invaders. A summary of the usage of these terms for "trust" confirms this point:

1. The basic term for "trust" in the Lord (בָּטַח) occurs close to fifty times in the Psalms, with almost half these occasions appearing in Book I. The establishment of David's kingship over the incessant opposition of numerous enemies required his constant extension of trust in Yahweh alone. In contrast with Book I, the term occurs only three times in Book III, and only two of these instances speak positively of trust: "Blessed is the person who trusts in you" (Ps. 84:12); and "I am trusting in you" (Ps. 86:2). In the third case, the negative is affirmed: "They did not believe in God or trust in his salvation" (Ps. 78:22).

2. The word meaning "to hope for," "to wait for" the Lord (קָוָה) might have originated from the concept "twist, stretch, then of [the] tension of enduring."[16] In times of stress, a person's faith is stretched to the limit. He is at the breaking point. His hope of deliverance from distress is strained to its ultimate capacity like the extended thread of a spider's web. The term occurs seventeen times in the Psalter, and is found ten times in the second portion of Book I (Pss. 18–41). In one instance, the concept appears twice in a single verse: "*Wait for* the LORD; be strong and take heart and *wait for* the LORD" (Ps. 27:14). Only by this unbroken trust could the strong opposition to the establishment of the messianic kingdom be overcome. Yet the term never occurs a single time in Book III.

3. The "fear of the LORD" (יִרְאַת יְהוָה) "is a common expression in the Psalter (27 times)."[17] Yet the phrase appears only four times in Book III: "You alone are to be feared," and "bring gifts to the One to be feared" (Ps. 76:7, 11); "His salvation is near those who fear him" (Ps. 85:9); "give me an undivided heart, that I may fear your name" (Ps. 86:11).

4. The idea "to seek shelter" in the Lord (חָסָה) occurs twenty-five times in the Psalms, fifteen of these instances appearing in Book I. Psalm 2 concludes by declaring the blessedness of the person who "seeks shelter" in Yahweh's Messiah (Ps. 2:12), which underscores the foundational nature of this trust in the whole of the Psalter. A repeated imagery of seeking shelter "in the shadow" or "in the shelter of [Yahweh's] wings" communicates a sense of intimate relationship with the Almighty. In one passage, this comfort beneath Yahweh's wings appears in parallel to "dwelling in

16. Francis Brown, *The New Brown-Driver-Briggs-Gesenius Hebrew and English Lexicon* (Peabody, MA: Hendrickson, 1979), 875.

17. Gordon J. Wenham, *Psalms as Torah: Reading Biblical Song Ethically* (Grand Rapids: Baker Academic, 2012), 151.

[Yahweh's] tent," which indicates that the locale of this intimacy is to be found in the Holy of Holies where the wings of the cherubim overarch the ark, symbolizing the presence of God on his throne (Ps. 61:4). This immediacy of access to the Almighty is available to "both high and low" (Ps. 36:7; cf. Ps. 57:1). Yet despite the nation's desperate need for consolation and comfort in the presence of the Lord during a time of repeated invasion by international armies, this term is wholly absent from Book III.

5. To "believe" in the Lord (אָמַן) occurs in the form of multiple *Amens* that conclude each of the first four books of the Psalter. The term appears six times in the body of Book III, but never in a positive sense. Four times the term denounces the unbelief of the people: "Their spirit did not believe in God" (Ps. 78:8); "they did not believe in God" (Ps. 78:22); "Despite his wonders, they did not believe" (Ps. 78:32); "They were not steadfast in his covenant" (Ps. 78:37). In contrast, Yahweh is declared to be "steadfast" to David (Ps. 89:28), and his throne "steadfast" in the sky (Ps. 89:37).

These five words for "trust," all totaled in Book III, add up to six positive uses compared to five negative uses. Two of the five key terms for "trust" never appear in Book III, and a third never appears in a positive sense. As might be expected, the paucity of references to reliance on the Lord in Book III corresponds to the devastation that came on the nation as depicted in this book of the Psalter. If the people will not trust in the Lord, they cannot expect to be delivered from their enemies. Book III is distinctive for its presentation of these threatening international enemies as well as the paucity of references to the nation's response in faith. Each new generation would do well to remember this fact when troubled with its own challenges.

Conclusion to Book III

So Book III of the Psalms provides a totally different perspective on the ongoing significance of the two major elements of the Lord's covenant with David. Instead of anticipating the establishment of the Davidic dynasty that will come only through David's intense personal struggles (Book I), or presenting the rule of God and his Messiah as an accomplished fact, though constantly under attack (Book II), Book III of the Psalms raises the dark specter of international armies who devastate David's dynasty and the Lord's dwellingplace at the temple in Jerusalem. This third book of

145

the Psalter ends with the distressing circumstance in which the Lord's enemies have "mocked every step of your anointed one" (Ps. 89:51).

Yet it must not be concluded that the Davidic covenant has failed. This final psalm of Book III (Ps. 89) repeatedly recites the focal provisions of the Davidic covenant in anticipation of the coming King-Messiah, descendant of David. David's everlasting *dynasty* and the eternal *dwellingplace* of his throne are clearly underscored in this last poem of Book III:

> You said, "I have made a covenant
>   with my chosen one,
> I have sworn
>   to David my servant,
>   'I will establish your line
>   forever,
>   and make your throne firm
>   through all generations.'"
> (Ps. 89:3–4; cf. Ps. 89:17b–37)

Nevertheless, this final psalm of Book III concludes on a negative note. Yahweh has broken through all the walls of Jerusalem, and has defiled the king's crown in the dust (Ps. 89:39–40). He has put an end to his splendor and cast his throne to the ground (Ps. 89:44). Thus ends Book III. If any hope remains for the continuation of the people of the covenant, it must be found in the two final books of the Psalter.[18]

---

18. Gerald Henry Wilson, *The Editing of the Hebrew Psalter* (Chico, CA: Scholars Press, 1985), 213, overlooks the significance of the repetition of the promises to David throughout Psalm 89 when he states: "At the conclusion of the third book . . . the impression left is one of a covenant remembered, but a covenant failed. The Davidic covenant introduced in Psalm 2 has come to nothing and the combination of three books concludes with the anguished cry of the Davidic descendants." An anguished cry indeed it is, commensurate with the agonies of the exile. Yet the covenanting word of the Lord to David will ultimately be realized, as specifically affirmed in messianic Psalms 110, 118, and 132 as well as in all the psalms that celebrate the restoration of Zion in Books IV and V.

8

BOOK IV (PSALMS 90–106): MATURATION

The tone of Book IV in the Psalter is clearly different from the pre-ceding message of Book III. Instead of a repeated rehearsal of the nation's devastation at the hand of its international enemies, this book represents a more mature perspective on the "permanent dwelling-place" and the "perpetual dynasty" promised in the Davidic covenant. Book IV concentrates on the ancient reality that God himself is his people's dwellingplace and that Yahweh is their King. It is not that exile has destroyed all hope for a reinstatement of the promised mes-sianic kingdom of David, as numerous psalms and their groupings in Books IV and V clearly indicate. But a more mature perspective now arises—a perspective that has been fostered by stretching the people's faith through their experience of the exile.

It has been proposed that the intent of the last two books of the Psalms is "to redirect the hopes of the reader away from an earthly Davidic kingdom to the kingship of Yahweh."[1] While it may be affirmed that these last two books intend to underscore the kingship of Yahweh, this emphasis is never separated from a simultaneous intent to foster a resurgence of hope in the kingdom of the Davidic Messiah. Indeed, the faithful must be directed "to trust in Yahweh as king rather than in fragile and failing human princes,"[2] as Psalms 145 and 146 in Book V

1. Cf. Gerald Henry Wilson, "King, Messiah, and the Reign of God: Revisiting the Royal Psalms and the Shape of the Psalter," in *The Book of Psalms: Composition and Reception*, ed. Peter W. Flint and Patrick D. Miller Jr. (Leiden: Brill, 2005), 392.
2. Ibid., 393.

particularly indicate. But their faith must seriously embrace the promise of a human Messiah from the line of David to reign perpetually, as well as the certainty of a permanent dwellingplace for Yahweh in the midst of his people, as underscored in Psalms 101, 110, 118, and 132.[3]

Instead of surrendering all hope that the covenantal promise regarding the perpetuity of the Davidic dynasty will be realized, the faith of the psalmists has reached a higher level of maturity. Rather than destroying their faith, the nation's exile from Jerusalem and the vacuous state of the Davidic throne have produced a stronger grasp both of the certainty of the merger of God's throne with David's throne and at the same time of the pain, the unending struggle, that will be involved in the full realization of that merger.[4] Greater trust must be placed in the eternal kingship of Yahweh, who will be true to his covenantal promise to David.[5] Book III concluded with God's covenant people and their king suffering in the agonies of exile, with the dwellingplace of Yahweh utterly devastated. Yet in a way that cannot be humanly explained, the nation's exile at the hands of international enemies has become the "proving ground" of the people's faith in the certainty that Yahweh will do it. By deprivation of kingship, priesthood, temple, and sacrifice, the faith of God's people experienced maturation through "forced growth." Several distinctive elements underscore this emphasis in the psalms of Book IV, as the subsequent discussion will indicate.

3. Wilson's effort to disregard the assurances of the Davidic promise as recorded in Psalm 132 (ibid., 396–98) fails to reckon with the constant emphasis in the Psalms and elsewhere in Scripture on the merger of David's throne with God's throne. His disparaging treatment of the messianic promise in Psalm 110 (ibid., 398–400) involves him in a laborious effort to avoid the focal thrust of the text.

4. Cf. Jamie A. Grant, *The King as Exemplar: The Function of Deuteronomy's Kingship Law in the Shaping of the Book of Psalms* (Atlanta: Society of Biblical Literature, 2004), 34: "There is no need to posit trust in competing sovereignties of Yahweh and his 'anointed,' rather, according to the royal psalms, theirs is a joint reign."

5. This point is brought out strongly in the comments of M. A. Vincent, "The Shape of the Psalter: An Eschatological Dimension?," in *New Heaven and New Earth: Prophecy and the Millennium: Essays in Honour of Anthony Gelston*, ed. P. J. Harland and C. T. R. Hayward (Leiden: Brill, 1999), 77: "The human king may have been taken away because of the repeated sinfulness of both him and his people, but God remains enthroned in heaven. . . . Since God is king his promises will yet be fulfilled and either he himself, or his representative (the future messianic king) will come."

Book IV consists of the following basic groupings: (1) two introductory psalms presenting the prospect of prosperity and long life (Pss. 90–91); (2) a special collection of nine psalms declaring that "Yahweh is King" (Pss. 92–100); (3) three psalms reaffirming the ongoing significance of Davidic kingship (Pss. 101–103); and (4) the first triad of *Hallelu-YAH* psalms, including two concluding psalms of historical recollection (Pss. 104–106).

Two Introductory Psalms: The Prospect of Prosperity and Long Life (Psalms 90–91)

In sharpest contrast with the turmoils of Books I, II, and III, the fourth book of the Psalms anticipates a long life of prosperity for God's people. The opening psalms of this book underscore this theme. Psalm 90 records the prayer of the psalmist with his expectation regarding length of days and fullness of life:

> Satisfy us in the morning
>   with your unfailing love,
>   that we may sing for joy and be glad
>   all our days.
> Make us glad
>   for as many days as you have afflicted us,
>   for as many years as we have seen trouble.
> . . . .
> Establish the work of our hands for us—
> yes, establish the work of our hands. (Ps. 90:14–17)

Following this theme, the Lord declares regarding his servant, "With long life will I satisfy him and show him my salvation" (Ps. 91:16). This promise of blessing in long life also concludes the third successive psalm that opens Book IV:

> The righteous will flourish like a palm tree,
> . . . .
>   planted in the house of the LORD . . . .
> They will still bear fruit in old age,
>   they will stay fresh and green. (Ps. 92:12–14)

149

This picture of prosperity and long life depicts a circumstance radically different from the unending struggle for survival as presented in Book I. By this point in the Psalter, the perspective on life for God's people has significantly matured. Even in exile they anticipate God's ongoing blessings.

The Distinctive Role of Psalm 90

Psalm 90, the first psalm of Book IV, has been described as the "heart or centre of the whole collection" of the book of Psalms.[6] Indeed, in considering its position in relation to Book I, Book II, and Book III, this psalm plays a pivotal role. In Book I (Pss. 1–41), David the anointed king of Israel struggles against his enemies to establish the beneficent rule of God on earth. Book II (Pss. 42–72) testifies to the establishment of this messianic kingdom by its anointed king, but always in a context of continuing struggle against enemies. Book III (Pss. 73–89) gives witness to the defeat of this messianic kingdom at the hands of international enemies, concluding with the dragging into exile of Israel's anointed king.

But now Book IV, beginning dramatically with Psalm 90, celebrates the Lord himself as the eternal dwellingplace of his people (Ps. 90:1). Even back to the time of Moses the man of God, identified in this psalm's title as its author, God has continued to be his people's secure dwellingplace:[7]

> Lord, you have been our dwellingplace
> throughout all generations.
> Before the mountains were born
> or you brought forth the earth and the world,
> from everlasting to everlasting you are God. (Ps. 90:1–2)

6. Joseph Addison Alexander, *The Psalms: Translated and Explained* (Grand Rapids: Zondervan, 1864; repr., n.d.), 378.

7. The term for "dwellingplace" (*maon*, מָעוֹן) is regularly used for the dwellingplace of Yahweh. It first appears in the prayer of Moses in anticipation of the people's bringing the third-year tithe after entering the land. The Israelite is to pray in this manner: "Look down from heaven, your holy dwellingplace, and bless your people Israel and the land." For heaven as the dwellingplace of Yahweh, see also 2 Chron. 30:27; Ps. 68:5; Jer. 25:30; Zech. 2:13. For the temple in Jerusalem as Yahweh's dwellingplace, see 1 Sam. 2:29; 2 Chron. 36:15; Ps. 26:8. For Yahweh himself as the dwellingplace of his people, see Pss. 71:3; 90:1; 91:9.

According to the analysis of one author, "The focus of the Psalter up to this point has been the kingship of David and David's descendants. Moses represents a different time in the history of ancient Israel. The ascription of the psalm to Moses focuses the attention of the reader/hearer back to a time before the judges, before the settlement in Palestine."[8] At that time Yahweh himself was declared to be King among his people (Deut. 33:5). This same author proceeds to explore the many connections between Psalm 90 and the Song of Moses as recorded in Deuteronomy 32 as well as in Moses' poetic blessing on the tribes of Israel in Deuteronomy 33 just before his death:[9]

(1) Only in the heading of Psalm 90 and the heading of Deuteronomy 33 is Moses described as the "man of God."
(2) Psalm 90:2 describes the creative work of Yahweh as "begetting" and "giving birth," while Deuteronomy 32:18 describes the creative work of God in "begetting" and "giving birth" to Israel with the same two words.
(3) Psalm 90:13 asks Yahweh to "have compassion" on his "servants"; and Deuteronomy 32:36 says that Yahweh will "have compassion" on his "servants."

A further connection between Psalm 90 and the person of Moses may be seen in a rather startling connection to another circumstance in the life of Moses. In Exodus 32, Moses intercedes for the people by asking that the Lord would spare them despite their sinful corruption associated with the incident of the golden calf. Moses pleads with Yahweh that he would "turn" (*shuv*, שׁוּב) from the heat of his anger and "relent" (*hinaham*, הִנָּחֵם) (Ex. 32:12b). The earnest pleas embedded in these verbs are repeated in the identical verbs of Psalm 90, but this time with the more emphatic form of the imperative: "Turn now [*shuvah*, שׁוּבָה], O Yahweh, . . . and relent [*hinaham*, הִנָּחֵם] because of your servants" (Ps. 90:13).

8. Nancy L. deClaisse-Walford, *Reading from the Beginning: The Shaping of the Hebrew Psalter* (Ann Arbor, MI: UMI Dissertation Services, 1996), 147f.
9. Ibid., 148–53.

Only in these two passages in Scripture and no others is Yahweh urged to "turn" and "relent."[10]

These parallels of expression between Psalm 90 and critical moments in the life of Moses support the Mosaic origin of Psalm 90. The connections also underscore the deliberateness of the placement of Psalm 90 as the opening psalm of Book IV, just after Psalm 89 had concluded with the banishment of the nation from the Land of Promise. Now the people have been exiled from their land once more, just as they were compelled to exist outside the land during their sojourn in Egypt and their wandering in the wilderness under Moses' leadership. Quite significantly, after this opening allusion to Moses in Psalm 90, all references in the Psalter to Moses are grouped in Book IV, with a single exception.[11]

Despite the Israelites' exile from the Land of Promise, the Lord has been and continues to be their place of permanent dwelling, their "Rock" of stability throughout all generations. Even earlier than the time of Moses, even before the mountains were born, the COVENANT LORD has always been—God! Death might sweep away each new generation. People might finish their years with a moan as they are consumed by God's anger. Even the whole of the nation might be carried into captivity. Yet in the mercy of the Lord, they may find complete satisfaction in God's unfailing love, they may sing for joy all their days, and the work of their hands may be permanently established (Ps. 90:14–17). So this psalm functions as a transition between the awesome devastations of God's people at the hands of a series of

---

10. David Noel Freedman, "Who Asks (or Tells) God to Repent?," *Bible Review* 1, 4 (1985): 56–59.

11. Book III mentions Moses once in a psalm of historical recollection (Ps. 77:20). In this psalm, an individual in distress cries out to Elohim. This person determines that he will remember the wondrous works of Yahweh. He then recalls the miraculous interventions of the exodus (Ps. 77:16–19). He concludes by reviewing the way in which God led his people like a flock "by the hand of Moses and Aaron" (Ps. 77:20). References to Moses in Book IV are found in Psalms 90:1 [Eng. heading]; 99:6; 103:7; 105:26; 106:16, 23, 32. Gerald Henry Wilson, *The Editing of the Hebrew Psalter* (Chico, CA: Scholars Press, 1985), 187–88, notes the reference to Moses in Psalm 90 as the first psalm of Book IV and the threefold reference to Moses in Psalm 106 as the final psalm in Book IV. He suggests that thematic parallels along with certain praise groupings strongly support "purposeful editing" of this section.

international enemies and the perpetual expectation of living out their lives in the intimacy of fellowship with the Lord.

The next psalm (Ps. 91) displays the same tone: "In the shelter of the Most High," "in the shadow of the Almighty," covered "with his feathers," and abiding "under his wings," the person who trusts in the one true God finds his refuge in the intimate presence of the Lord himself in the Most Holy Place of his sanctuary (Ps. 91:1–4).

Yahweh Malak ("The LORD Is King"): A Special Collection of Book IV (Psalms 92–100)

A distinctive phrase in a special collection of psalms in Book IV reinforces Yahweh's ongoing kingship: *Yahweh Malak* ("The LORD is King") (Pss. 93:1; 96:10; 97:1; 99:1).[12] This specific wording occurs as

12. This particular phrase has been the subject of intense discussion and debate. Hans-Joachim Kraus, *Theology of the Psalms* (Minneapolis: Augsburg, 1986), 86–91, provides an extensive overview of the various understandings of this key phrase, including historical, eschatological, and cultic perspectives. Kraus offers an effective critique of Sigmund Mowinckel's theory of an annual "enthronement festival" in which it is proposed that Yahweh "became" King through Israel's cultic ceremony. He notes (1) that the syntax of the phrase does not support the idea that Yahweh "has become" King; (2) that, contrary to Babylonian traditions, Israel had no representation of God as an idol that could be made to participate in an "enthronement" procedure; (3) that, contrary to the experience of "nature-gods" such as Baal, Yahweh never lost his throne, and so never needed to be reinstated as King year by year; (4) that no rival gods existed in Israel's theology over which Yahweh had to establish his kingship. Ibid., 88. In his commentary on the Psalms, Kraus elaborates further on the grammar of the phrase. He looks first at the word order, noting that an inverted order (*Malak Yahweh*) would in fact describe a "lively and stirring event," in which a person is made king (cf. 1 Kings 1:11). But the order of words in these psalms is *Yahweh Malak*, describing "an [unchangeable] state of being" (1 Kings 1:18). Hans-Joachim Kraus, *Psalms 60–150: A Commentary* (Minneapolis: Augsburg, 1989), 233. Says Kraus regarding the statement of Psalm 93:2, "Firm stands your throne from of old, from eternity you are, O God": "The unchanging, eternal state of Yahweh's being King is here emphatically stressed." Kraus, *Psalms 60–150*, 234. This unchanging, eternal state of Yahweh's kingship is supported by the immediately following phrase in the first two *Yahweh Malak* psalms:
> The world is firmly established,
>   it cannot be moved. (Pss. 93:1; 96:10)

This repeated phrase underscores the fact that Yahweh has been King since creation, and that as King he has sustained the world in its immovable state. In commenting on this phrase, one author notes: "The declaration thus does imply an answer to the question of when Yhwh's assertion of authority took place. It was an aspect of Yhwh's activity in

an independent, self-contained phrase only in Book IV of the Psalms—and also in a psalm celebrating the historical moment of David's bringing up the ark of God to Mount Zion as recorded in the book of Chronicles. At that critical moment when the Lord's throne is first situated on Mount Zion in Jerusalem, this psalm exclaims:

> Let the heavens rejoice,
> Let the earth be glad;
> Let them say among the nations,
>   "*Yahweh Malak!*" (1 Chron. 16:31)

So it appears that this dramatic declaration of the Lord's kingship had its origin at the moment when David brought up the ark of the covenant to Jerusalem. That redemptive-historical moment held a profound significance for all subsequent history. For at that point, Yahweh's throne was effectively joined to David's throne. It was, as a matter

---

bringing the world into being." John Goldingay, *Psalms, Volume 3: Psalms 90–150* (Grand Rapids: Baker, 2008), 68.

Yet after his thorough discrediting of Mowinckel's proposal, Kraus proceeds to offer the possibility that because of Israel's later dependence on Assyria, "immediately prior to the exile there was introduced in Judah a cultic celebration of the enthronement of God, which . . . was then applied to Yahweh." Kraus, *Psalms 60–150*, 90. Kraus also proposes the theory that a "cultic entrance of Yahweh" into the temple might have existed associated with the procession of the ark into the temple. Ibid., 89. It may be noted that Psalm 47 declares, "God has ascended amid shouts of joy, the LORD amid the sounding of trumpets" (Ps. 47:5). But this exclamation of the psalmist is hardly sufficient to establish a ritual in which the ark of the covenant was first removed from the Most Holy Place and then returned again in annual procession.

In the end, the redemptive-historical perspective is quite sufficient to satisfy all the evidence of Scripture. In a most dramatic moment of redemptive history, David brought the ark to Jerusalem that his throne might be united with God's throne. This event needed to occur only once in the nation's history, just as the coronation of each successive king in Israel occurred only once. From a consummative perspective, the shadowy image of the ascension of the ark anticipates a single climactic event in redemptive history, in which the resurrected Christ-King ascends to the right hand of the Father and sits to rule forever. This grand event needs to occur only once in the history of God's redemptive program. From the point of his ascension, the exalted Christ reigns without interruption. For further discussion of the phrase *Yahweh Malak*, see Hans-Joachim Kraus, *Psalms 1–59: A Commentary* (Minneapolis: Augsburg, 1988), 86–89, and the thorough discussion of Craig C. Broyles, "The Psalms and Cult Symbolism: The Case of the Cherubim-Ark," in *Interpreting the Psalms: Issues and Approaches*, ed. Philip S. Johnston and David G. Firth (Downers Grove, IL: InterVarsity Press, 2005), 139–56.

of fact, as significant as the moment of the Israelites' exodus from Egypt and their triumph at the Red Sea. For then Moses anticipated this meaningful moment in David's life when he declared at the conclusion of his song of triumph at the sea: "Yahweh will rule as King forever and ever" (יְהוָה יִמְלֹךְ לְעֹלָם וָעֶד)—Ex. 15:18). At the time the ark was brought up to Mount Zion, Yahweh's rule as King was affirmed once and for all.

Bringing Up the Ark: A Critical Moment in Redemptive History for Book IV (Psalms 96, 105–106)

Introduction: Chronicles, Psalms, and Bringing Up the Ark

A special relationship between the Psalms and the books of Chronicles undergirds this focalization on the bringing up of the ark.[13] The close relationship between these two books is understandable, since the composition of Chronicles and the final composition/shaping of the Psalter may well have occurred in approximately the same time frame. References in Chronicles to worship with music and song that are absent from the books of Kings connect it directly with the use of the book of Psalms in worship. No fewer than ten passages in Chronicles record incidents involving worship that compare closely to the book of Psalms, as indicated in the excursus appended to this chapter. This extensive interaction helps to explain the total integration into the Psalter of the psalm recorded in Chronicles that celebrated the bringing up of the ark to Jerusalem. Four matters arising out of this relationship between Chronicles and Psalms deserve further exploration.

The Dispersal of the Total Psalm of 1 Chronicles 16 across Book IV

Of particular significance for Book IV is the dispersal in its totality of this historic psalm as recorded in 1 Chronicles 16 celebrating the momentous event of David's bringing up the ark to Jerusalem. The full

---

13. For further elaboration on the relationship between Chronicles and Psalms, see the excursus at the end of this chapter.

155

impact of this event in the Psalter will be appreciated only when it is recognized that three different psalms of Book IV combine to mirror the entirety of this celebratory psalm:

- Psalm 96:1–13 mirrors 1 Chronicles 16:23–33 (11 verses)
- Psalm 105:1–15 mirrors 1 Chronicles 16:8–22 (15 verses)
- Psalm 106:1, 47–48 mirrors 1 Chronicles 16:34–36 (3 verses)

The dispersal of the totality of this psalm celebrating the establishment of Yahweh as King alongside David in Mount Zion underscores the merger of God's kingship with Messiah's rule. From the perspective of Book IV, Yahweh's kingship is not to be regarded as yet to be realized at some time in the future. Instead, God must now be worshiped as King, not only among his people but also throughout the nations of the world. Clearly, the last two books of the Psalter, related primarily to the time of exile and restoration when God's people had no king, intend to underscore the fact that Yahweh is King among his people.[14]

Yahweh Malak as the Focus of Psalms 92–100

The distinctive declaration of "*Yahweh Malak*" provides the focus for this special collection of nine psalms in Book IV (Pss. 92–100). Positioned as the central hub of these nine psalms is Psalm 96, which, very significantly, parallels in its totality the second half of the psalm celebrating David's bringing up the ark to Jerusalem (Ps. 96:1–13; cf. 1 Chron. 16:23–33).[15] Not only does this special collection in Book IV of the Psalter contain the only other appearances of the

---

14. Quite interesting is the fact that "king" is never applied directly to David or his descendants in Books IV and V of the Psalter, although reference is made twice to David's descendant as the "anointed one," which is essentially the equivalent of "king" (Ps. 132:10, 17).

15. David M. Howard Jr., *The Structure of Psalms 93–100*, ed. William Henry Propp, Biblical and Judaic Studies 5 (Winona Lake, IN: Eisenbrauns, 1997), 141–55, deals extensively with the interconnectivity of Psalm 96 with the other psalms of this grouping. But he does not note that Psalm 96 altogether mirrors the psalm celebrating the bringing up of the ark to Jerusalem in 1 Chronicles 16. Yet the basic reason that these psalms focus on the *Yahweh Malak* theme is the redemptive-historical significance of the bringing up of

156

Yahweh Malak phrase in Scripture outside 1 Chronicles 16, but it also contains a second distinctive phrase that appears only in the three central psalms of this special collection as well as in the Chronicler's psalm (Pss. 95–97; 1 Chron. 16). The phrase *"over all gods"* (עַל־כָּל־אֱלֹהִים) might appear to be a commonplace phrase in Scripture. But insofar as the present author has been able to determine, these precise words occur only in the poem celebrating the bringing up of the ark along with the three psalms centrally placed in this special collection:

- Yahweh is to be feared *"over all gods"* (1 Chron. 16:25).
- Yahweh is the great King *"over all gods"* (Ps. 95:3).
- Yahweh is to be feared *"over all gods"* (Ps. 96:4).
- Yahweh is greatly exalted *"over all gods"* (Ps. 97:9).

As a consequence of this distinctive repetition, Psalms 95, 96, and 97 form a centered triad in this collection of nine psalms, with Psalm 96 positioned as its "epicenter."

The Inclusion of Psalms 92 and 100 in This Collection

The presence of a deliberate grouping of *Yahweh Malak* psalms in Book IV is made apparent by the appearance of this phrase first in Psalm 93, then again in Psalms 96 and 97, and finally in Psalm 99. The phrase appears nowhere else in the Psalter, a fact clearly indicating that this special collection extends at least from Psalm 93 through Psalm 99. Yet a comparison of Psalms 92 and 100 with Psalms 90 and 91 that open Book IV verifies the intention of the final organizer/editor of the Psalter to include Psalms 92 and 100 at the extremities of this grouping of *Yahweh Malak* psalms. Even though the key phrase does not appear in these two psalms, their focus on praise and worship binds them together with the *Yahweh Malak* collection. Psalm 92's title stands out in distinction from Psalms 90 and 91, the two introductory psalms of the book. Psalm 90 simply says, "A prayer of Moses the

---

the ark. Yahweh's kingship in this special Psalter collection can be fully understood only in terms of the ascent of the ark to Mount Zion.

man of God." Psalm 91 has no title. In substance, this psalm expresses a calmness arising from the intimacy of one person's relationship to *Elyon*, the *Most High*.

In contrast with the title of the opening psalm of Book IV, Psalm 92's title provides distinctive directions for the employment of this psalm in a context of corporate praise and worship. It is a *mizmor*, a "praise-song," a term that occurs in the heading of fifty-seven psalms. *Shir*, the next term in this title, means simply "song," a term primarily employed to express communal rather than individual piety.

The third portion of the title of Psalm 92 strongly confirms its praise-and-worship context. A unique phrase declares this particular psalm to be "For the Sabbath day." When this phrase is considered in the context of Israel's weekly worship practices, it is clear that the editor/author of this psalm envisioned its use on a regular basis, perhaps even during the nation's weekly assembly for worship.

The worship context for Psalm 92 as reflected in its title is strongly confirmed by the substance of its opening verses:

> It is good to praise the LORD,
> and make music to your name, O Most High;
>> to proclaim your love
>>> in the morning,
>> and your faithfulness
>>> every night,
>> to the music
>>> of the ten-stringed lyre,
>> and the melody
>>> of the harp.
> For you make me glad
>> by your deeds, O LORD.
> I sing for joy
>> at the work of your hands. (Ps. 92:1–4)

These opening verses include numerous elements directly associated with worship: praising the Lord, making music, proclaiming his love and faithfulness, employing musical instruments, rejoicing over the Lord's works, and singing for joy. These indicators place

Psalm 92 specifically in the context of Israel's regular offerings of praise and worship, which serve as the overriding context of the *Yahweh Malak* grouping. In contrast, Psalms 90 and 91 do not have these same specific indicators of a worship context. Psalm 100, with its pointed focus on praise and worship, appropriately rounds out this special collection.

These clear worship pointers strongly link Psalms 92 and 100 with Psalms 93–99, where the same worship elements listed in Psalm 92 are repeatedly mentioned. In the context of the distinctive affirmation that "the LORD is King" (*Yahweh Malak*—Pss. 93:1; 96:10; 97:1; 99:1), the psalmist summons the Lord's people as well as the entire inhabited earth to sing for joy, to come with thanksgiving, to extol him with music and song (Pss. 95:1–2; 96:12–13; 98:4–6, 8–9; 100:2, 4); to sing to the Lord a new song (Pss. 96:1; 98:1); to worship the Lord (Pss. 95:6; 96:9; 97:7; 99:5, 9; 100:2); to declare his glory and praise him (Pss. 96:3, 7–8; 99:3; 100:4); and to rejoice before him (Pss. 96:11–12; 97:1, 8, 12; 100:1). Possibly no other grouping of psalms so directly and so consistently summons God's people to worship, to praise and to thank him as their Sovereign King.[16]

16. The declaration of Yahweh's kingship over the nations throughout this collection is made directly in the face of the domination over God's people by conquering Assyrian and Babylonian empires. Psalms 93 and 94 deal with the challenge to Yahweh's sovereignty posed by these powerful foes. These foreign powers are the "seas/rivers" that have lifted up their voice, their pounding waves (Ps. 93:3), in accord with the regular employment of "raging sea" as an image of revolting nations in Scripture (Ps. 46:1–4, 7; Isa. 8:5–8; 17:12–13; Jer. 6:23; 46:7–8; Rev. 17:1, 15). But Yahweh on high is mighty, mightier than the thunder of the great waters and breakers of the sea (Ps. 93:4). His might is displayed in his "statutes" that stand firm, governing his "house" in holiness for endless days (Ps. 93:5). Says Ernst Wilhelm Hengstenberg, *Commentary on the Psalms* (Edinburgh: T&T Clark, 1854), 3:151: "There can be no doubt that the sea comes into notice here [in Ps. 93:3–4] as the symbol of worldly power." Mowinckel's application of this psalm to an annual (cultic) enthronement of Yahweh is strongly rejected by Kraus, *Psalms 60–150*, 234. Kraus notes that this idea "is rejected in the context of Psalm 93 with the statement: 'Firm stands your throne from of old, from eternity you are, O God!' The unchanging, eternal state of Yahweh's being king is here emphatically stressed." The conclusion of Kraus regarding the relation of Psalm 93 to the ancient mythological struggle with chaos is not clear. On the one hand, he affirms, "Mythological events of this kind [as in the Ras Shamra texts of Ugarit in ancient Syria] are in the background of the conceptions that turn up in Psalm 93." Ibid., 235. On the other hand, he declares on the same page: "The mythical descriptions of the struggle with chaos are fully cast off. In this lies the peculiarity of Psalm 93."

This uniting theme across Psalms 92–100 with its key *Yahweh Malak* phrase sets apart these psalms as a distinctive grouping.[17] Psalm 96 serves as the central hub of the collection, being constituted entirely of an extended parallel with the historical record of Israel's celebration as the people brought the ark to Jerusalem and so confirmed the union of Yahweh's throne with David's throne (1 Chron. 16:23–33). The Lord's position as King to be worshiped therefore serves as the uniting factor of this special collection. As previously noted, Psalms 95 and 97 flank Psalm 96, having the distinction of being the only other passages in Scripture along with Psalm 96 and 1 Chronicles 16 that contain the particular phrase "over all gods" (Pss. 95:3; 96:4; 97:9). At the outer extremities of this collection are Psalms 92 and 100, neither of which contains the *Yahweh Malak* formula, but both of which are called "A psalm" and focus on praising, thanking, and worshiping the Lord.

The Relation of 1 Chronicles 16 to Psalms 105–106

The two psalms in addition to Psalm 96 that complete the mirroring of the poem in 1 Chronicles 16 are Psalms 105 and 106. Reconstructing the history of the relationship of these three psalms in Book IV to 1 Chronicles 16 is indeed challenging. To a certain extent, the question is beyond the reach of current certainty. Yet several observations are worth considering.

First, the psalm found in 1 Chronicles 16 celebrating the bringing up of the ark to Jerusalem gives every evidence of being a unified construction.[18] The psalm naturally moves from a general summons to thanksgiving (1 Chron. 16:8–13), to a rehearsal of the Lord's faithful-

---

17. Howard, *Structure of Psalms 93–100*, 170, notes the many connections between Psalm 92 and Psalms 90 and 91. At the same time, he observes that Psalm 92 "nevertheless functions well in anticipating the predominant motif of the following psalms. . . . Psalm 92 casts an eye back to Psalms 90–91, but it also looks ahead to the following psalms." Ibid., 171. In all these observations he is correct. Yet structurally he groups Psalm 92 with the opening psalms of Book IV rather than with the *Yahweh Malak* collection.

18. Gary N. Knoppers, *I Chronicles 10–29: A New Translation with Introduction and Commentary*, Anchor Bible (New York: Doubleday, 2004), 644, cites several recent authors who in his judgment have shown that the poetry of 1 Chronicles 16:8–36 "is not a collage of disconnected pieces, but a skillful and artfully arranged composition."

ness in his covenant (1 Chron. 16:14–22), to a summons to all peoples and then the whole cosmic creation to praise the Lord, climaxing with a doxological conclusion (1 Chron. 16:23–36).

Second, Israelite tradition, communicated either orally or otherwise, has proved its capacity to retain poetic materials in their integrity across many centuries, as seen in the preservation of the Song of Moses and the Song of Deborah, both of which display indicators of authentic antiquity. This observation could be applied equally to the Song of the Bringing Up of the Ark, whether or not this psalm is attributed specifically to David.[19]

Third, the later authors/editor(s) of the Psalms frequently recast psalms into different settings suitable to later circumstances, as in Psalm 53's use of Psalm 14, Psalm 70's use of Psalm 40, Psalm 71's use of Psalm 31, Psalm 108's use of Psalms 57 and 60, and Psalm 135's use of Psalms 113 and 115. In the case of the psalm celebrating the bringing up of the ark in 1 Chronicles 16, it might at first seem strange that the order of sections as they appear in the Psalter does not correspond to the order found in the psalm itself. Psalm 96:1–13

---

19. The words introducing the poem of 1 Chronicles 16 might or might not justify the conclusion that David composed the psalm on the occasion of the bringing up of the ark. The NIV translates the words: "That day David first committed to Asaph and his associates this psalm of thanks to the LORD" (1 Chron. 16:7). The ESV provides a more accurate translation: "Then on that day David first appointed that thanksgiving be sung to the LORD by Asaph and his brothers." Kidner, *Psalms 73–150*, 347, states that the phrase "does not claim that these were necessarily the very words that were sung on that occasion." But in his appended note he judiciously adds: "They may have been." The older proposal of Hengstenberg, *Psalms*, 3:270, that the psalm of 1 Chronicles 16 intends to provide only a sampler of the type of psalms performed in Israel's worship services, ignores the unity of the poetic piece as well as the meaningful breakdown of the entirety of the 1 Chronicles psalm into three coherent units in Psalms 96, 105, and 106. It is far easier to imagine these three Psalter psalms as being derived from one master psalm than that three different Psalter units have been reconstituted into one coherent Chronicler psalm. In addition, the response of the people at the conclusion of the psalm as reported in 1 Chronicles represents a reaction to a fixed piece of poetry rather than a liturgical response to a disunified sampler: "Then all the people said 'Amen' and 'Praise the LORD'" (1 Chron. 16:36b). Both Knoppers, *1 Chronicles 10–29*, 651, and Ralph W. Klein, *1 Chronicles: A Commentary*, Hermeneia (Minneapolis: Augsburg Fortress, 2006), 368, agree that the intent of the Chronicler's report is to describe the response of the people to the psalm just presented. But they also agree that the Chronicler has modified the liturgical conclusion of Psalm 106 to make it fit the historical report of 1 Chronicles, rather than vice versa. Though debatable, it seems more likely that the historical would become liturgical than that the liturgical would be made into the historical.

corresponds to the second section of 1 Chronicles 16 (vv. 23–31); Psalm 105:1–15 corresponds to the first section of 1 Chronicles 16 (vv. 8–22); and the opening and concluding verses of Psalm 106 (vv. 1, 47–48) correspond to the concluding verses of the poem in 1 Chronicles 16 (vv. 34–36). Yet the content of these three psalms makes the reason for their placement quite plain. Psalm 96 focuses on the "*Yahweh Malak*" declaration, with the parallel section of 1 Chronicles containing the critical phrase. Psalm 105 as a psalm of historical recollection naturally gravitated to the rehearsal of Israel's history as found in the earlier portion of 1 Chronicles 16. Psalm 106 concludes Book IV with a doxology paralleling the conclusion of 1 Chronicles 16, which focuses on the critical phrase "*Gather* us from the nations" (1 Chron. 16:35; Ps. 106:47). This concluding phrase of Psalm 106 provides a major literary link across the "seam" of Book IV into the opening of Book V, with its reference to "those he has *gathered* from the lands" (Ps. 107:3). Taking these considerations into view, we see that the precise position of the three diverse portions of 1 Chronicles in three nonconsecutive psalms of Book IV indicates careful editorial arrangement.

Fourth, one further consideration of the relationship of 1 Chronicles 16 to these psalms deserves notice. According to 1 Chronicles 15, this bringing up of the ark was a most significant moment in Israel's history, requiring extensive preparations. After establishing buildings for himself in Jerusalem, David prepared a place to receive the ark, including the pitching of an appropriate tent (1 Chron. 15:1). David's "engineering team" very likely would have been involved in determining the precise location of the tent, which might have included a leveling of the site that would eventually be the place where David's proposed temple would be constructed. Then the king made it clear to the public that only the Levites would bear the ark (1 Chron. 15:2). He assembled the whole nation in Jerusalem (1 Chron. 15:3), which would have involved sending out runners some weeks or possibly months ahead of the scheduled event. This great occasion would be remembered for generations to come. The event could be compared to the coronation of a new king representing a new dynasty in Israel. Large "media coverage" would be involved. Additionally, David gathered 962 descendants of Israel's priesthood from six different clans along with their specified leaders (1 Chron. 15:4–10). He appointed priestly leaders to oversee the consecration of all these people for the specific task of bringing up the ark (1 Chron. 15:11–15). He designated Levitical leaders to appoint singers and instrumental accompanists to perform uplifting songs of joy (1 Chron. 15:16–24). One particular Levite with specialized musical skills was selected as choirmaster over the multiplicity of choirs (1 Chron. 15:22).

After this extensive preparation, the ark was finally brought up to Jerusalem. David, the elders, and the commanders of thousands traveled to the house of Obed-Edom in Kiriath-Jearim to lead the procession with rejoicing and sacrifices. A round trip of fifteen to twenty miles would have involved taking the whole day for the celebration (1 Chron. 15:25–26). Various choirs followed the procession along the way (1 Chron. 15:27). Special robes of fine linen had been prepared for David, the Levites carrying the ark, and all the singers (1 Chron. 15:27).

Quite obviously, this extensive preparation was not made overnight. Months of planning, practice, and preparation could easily have been involved. Numerous rehearsals by choirs and instrumentalists would have to take place.

This elaborate preparation for the bringing up of the ark would have provided ample time for David as well as other Israelite musicians to compose psalms appropriate for this dramatic occasion. It is almost unthinkable that David would not have composed a psalm suitable for this great celebration. The psalm recorded in 1 Chronicles 16 quite believably was his own.[20]

In any case, it seems very likely that the psalm of 1 Chronicles 16 would have been readily recognized across subsequent generations as

20. Though regularly rejected, the proposal of Peter R. Ackroyd, *I & II Chronicles, Ezra, Nehemiah*, Torch Bible Paperbacks (London: SCM Press, 1973), should be given further consideration. Ackroyd notes that the psalm in 1 Chronicles 16 "provides us with an additional psalm comparable to others found outside the Psalter (e.g., Ex. 15:1–18; Judg. 5; 1 Sam. 2:1–10)." Ibid., 64–65. The implication of his remark is that the psalm in 1 Chronicles 16 may also be regarded as a psalm that circulated, perhaps altogether independently, of the Psalter as we now know it.

the poem associated with the bringing up of the ark to Mount Zion. This psalm would then provide the meaningful redemptive-historical framework for the *Yahweh Malak* collection of psalms. Not only the appearance of this distinctive phrase that occurs in these Scriptures alone, but the larger historical framework of the psalm would regularly remind the people of the Lord's kingship. From Psalm 92 through Psalm 100 the nation is encouraged to sing and celebrate for one great reason: the Lord is King. He has always been King, he is currently King, he will always be King.

In light of these various factors, it becomes apparent that the great focus of Book IV centers on the well-established kingship of Yahweh over Israel and the nations. God's people have clearly reached a matured perspective on Yahweh's lordship over all the peoples of the world. His sovereignty should be celebrated in worship, for he has been King since creation, he is currently King, and he will continue as King until the consummation.

Additional Phrases Describing the Lord's Kingship in the *Yahweh Malak* Collection of Book IV

In addition to the repetition of this dramatic declaration of "*Yahweh Malak*" in Book IV, the Lord is described by several regal phrases in this specific collection of psalms as "the great King" (Ps. 95:3), "the LORD, the King" (Ps. 98:6b), "the King [who] is mighty" (Ps. 99:4). A new confidence in the Lord's abiding kingship has been established. God's people can sing for joy to the Lord, who is the great King above all gods, for he holds in his hand the depths of the earth, the mountain peaks, the sea, and the dry land (Ps. 95:1–5). All the earth can shout for joy before the Lord, the King (Ps. 98:4–6). The Lord sits enthroned; he is exalted over all the nations, for as King he is mighty and has established justice throughout the earth (Ps. 99:1–4). Indeed, enemies remain opposed to God and his people. The wicked pour out arrogant words. They crush God's people and murder the widow and the fatherless. Yet the psalmist's confidence remains unshaken in the Lord as his fortress and his Rock. He will repay them for their sins and destroy them for their wickedness (Ps. 94:4–6, 22–23).

Summary Regarding Collections of Psalms Celebrating God's Kingship throughout the Psalter

As has been noted, collections of psalms celebrating God's kingship appear in the earlier books of the Psalter. As a matter of fact, as many as five different groupings of psalms may be seen as presenting God as King, with at least one collection occurring in each of the first four books of the Psalter. In these special collections, the Lord's kingship is regularly joined with Messiah's kingship. In Book I, the grouping is found in Psalms 20–24. As previously indicated, two psalms present David as king (Pss. 20–21), followed by two psalms presenting Yahweh as King (Pss. 23–24), with one mediating psalm developing both kingships (Ps. 22). In Book II, the kingship grouping appears in Psalms 45–48. In this instance, Messiah's kingship is first declared (Ps. 45), followed by three psalms presenting Elohim as King over the nations (Pss. 46–48). Psalms 65–68 represent another kingship grouping of psalms, this time in the second Davidic collection as found in Book II. Only one use of "king" is found in this collection. But the various psalms assert that God "stilled . . . the turmoil of the nations" (Ps. 65:7); he "rules forever by his power, his eyes watch the nations" (Ps. 66:7); he "rule[s] the peoples justly and guide[s] the nations of the earth" (Ps. 67:4). The final psalm in this collection climaxes with the procession of "my God and King" to "the mountain where God chooses to reign" (Ps. 68:24, 16). This psalm alludes to the messianic kingship by reference to the "little tribe of Benjamin, leading them" (most likely referring to the initial kingship of Saul) and the "great throng of Judah's princes" (possibly referring to the succession of Davidic monarchs) (Ps. 68:27).[21]

21. The reference to the "princes of Zebulun and Naphtali" could allude to the occasion in which these two tribes distinguished themselves under the leadership of Deborah and Barak: "The people of Zebulun risked their very lives; so did Naphtali on the heights of the field" (Judg. 5:18). For a stimulating discussion of this passage, see Ernst Wilhelm Hengstenberg, *Commentary on the Psalms* (Edinburgh: T&T Clark, 1855), 2:358–60.

In Book III, though not using "king," a couplet of psalms depict both God and Messiah in their regal roles (Pss. 75–76). Only God can exalt a man, and God's Messiah is committed to "cut off the horns of all the wicked" (Ps. 75:6, 10). From heaven, God who is over all pronounces judgment over the kings of the earth (Ps. 76:8, 12). Already in Book III, the psalmist has presented the nation of God's people as shattered by a foreign army (Ps. 74). But only after establishing this dual kingship of God and Messiah in Book III does the psalmist plunge both the northern and southern kingdoms into the darkness of defeat and exile at the hands of invading enemies (Pss. 79, 80, 89).

But now in Book IV, the *Yahweh Malak* psalms offer a different perspective on God's kingship. This fifth collection of kingship psalms depicts Yahweh as the permanently established sovereign over the nations. His perpetual kingship should cause heaven and earth, nature and the nations to rejoice.

Psalms 101–103*: A Triad of Psalms Reaffirming Davidic Kingship[22]

No specific mention of David or the messianic kingship occurs in the body of any psalm of Book IV. Authorship is attributed to David in the headings of Psalms 101 and 103, and he was also very likely the author of Psalm 102. But as the kingship has been smashed by invading armies, specific mention of Davidic kingship disappears.

This absence of specific reference to David or the promise of a messianic king in the body of Book IV has led some to conclude that the Psalter is now finished with the prospect of a fulfillment of the Davidic covenant.[23]

Among his observations he notes: "That even the *little* Benjamin should be ruler over the heathen, shows the greatness of the grace of God: compare 1 Sam. 9:21, where Saul, on his being appointed king, says with astonishment: 'Am not I a Benjamite of the smallest of the tribes of Israel?' " Ibid., 359.

22. As in previous chapters, the asterisk (*) indicates a grouping of psalms whose titles do not all attribute authorship to David or some other individual. Psalms 101 and 103 have the "By David" statement in their title, while Psalm 102, described in the title as the "prayer of an afflicted man," is most likely Davidic in view of its being a first-person psalm following immediately upon a first-person psalm that contains the "By David" statement in its title.

23. DeClaisse-Walford, *Reading*, 157, connects the acknowledgment of the Lord as sovereign in Psalm 90 of Book IV with Yahweh as King in Psalm 2, while at the same

But although he is not specifically mentioned in the body of the psalms of Book IV, the three psalms following immediately upon the *Yahweh Malak* collection of Psalms 92–100 reaffirm the ongoing significance of the Davidic kingship.

Psalm 101, attributed to David by its title, speaks in the first-person singular of the king's aspiration to adhere to the pattern of the Lord in his governance. According to one commentary, "Psalm 101, following the '*YHWH* is king' Psalms 93–100, is concerned with the translation of *YHWH'S* royal rule into that of the Jerusalem king."[24] In his "house" the king indicates his determination to walk "with blameless heart" (Ps. 101:2). Under his regal direction, not one "vile thing," no deeds of "faithless men," no "men of perverse heart," no one who "slanders his neighbor in secret" or has "haughty eyes and a proud heart" will he endure (Ps. 101:3–5). No one who "practices deceit" will dwell in his "house." He will "put to silence all the wicked in the land," and "every morning" he will cut off "every evildoer" from the "city of Yahweh" (Ps. 101:7–8). Only the "faithful in the land" will dwell with him. Only the people whose "walk is blameless" will serve as his administrators (Ps. 101:6). These characteristics of messianic rule are intended to mirror Yahweh's kingship in the rule of the messianic king. Torah and Messiah unite.

Psalm 102 expands on this portrayal of governance by the Davidic king. Yahweh rules in heaven but also in Zion, the designated place where Yahweh's kingship merges with David's (Ps. 102:13, 16, 19). This psalm underscores the importance of regal succession, one of the key features of the Davidic covenant. The psalmist aspires to the same extension "through all generations" of Yahweh's reign for the perpetual kingship of David's line. The common English translation of the final verse of this psalm by the word *children* obscures the concern of the psalmist. The text states:

---

time seeking to eliminate all hope for a Davidic kingship from the nation's expectations. In order to minimize the role of the anointed Son who rules alongside Yahweh in Psalm 2, the attempt is made to remove any worshipful reverence for the Son in Psalm 2 by opting for the textually unsupported suppositional reading "with trembling kiss his feet" (Ps. 2:11–12, according to the RSV of 1952) instead of the straightforward "Kiss the Son." J. Clinton McCann, *A Theological Introduction to the Book of Psalms: The Psalms as Torah* (Nashville: Abingdon Press, 1993), 156, also supports the idea that Book IV eliminates any prospect of a messianic kingship.

24. Frank-Lothar Hossfeld and Eric Zenger, *Psalms 3: A Commentary on Psalms 101–150* (Minneapolis: Fortress Press, 2011), 96.

The *sons* of your servants
    will live in your presence;
their seed
    will be established before you. (Ps. 102:28)

Psalm 103 underscores the forgiveness and covenant faithfulness of Yahweh toward his people. Even though they may be currently experiencing his chastening hand through exile because of their violation of the covenant, Yahweh graciously forgives. He is "compassionate and gracious, slow to anger, abounding in love." He "will not always accuse, nor will he harbor his anger forever." He "does not treat us as our sins deserve or repay us according to our iniquities." For "as far as the east is from the west, so far has he removed our transgressions from us" (Ps. 103:8–12).

> For from everlasting to everlasting Yahweh's covenantal faithfulness [his *hesed*] is with those who fear him, and his righteousness with their children's children—with those who keep his covenant and remember to obey his precepts. (Ps. 103:17–18)

This covenantal faithfulness of Yahweh, his *hesed*, provides hope for the continuation of the provisions of the Davidic covenant despite the current setbacks brought about by the exile.

Psalms 102 and 103 may be taken together as psalms in which the messianic king expresses repeated longing for his throne to be merged into the eternality of Yahweh's throne. These two psalms strongly express the eternality of Yahweh's dominion:

> But you, O Yahweh, sit enthroned forever,
>   and your remembrance from generation to generation.
> . . . .
> You are He,
>   and your years shall never end. (Ps. 102:12, 27)

> The covenant love of Yahweh is from eternity to eternity
>   to those who fear him,
> and his righteousness
>   to the sons of their sons. (Ps. 103:17)

168

At the same time, the psalmist, presumably David in his kingship, wrestles with the temporal limitations of his own life span:

> My days vanish like smoke,
> my bones burn up like hot coals.
> . . . .
> My days are like a lengthening shadow,
> I am like dried-up grass. (Ps. 102:3, 11)

> As for man,
>   his days are like grass;
>   he flourishes like the flower of the field.
> For the wind blows over it,
>   and it is gone;
> and his place
>   remembers him no more. (Ps. 103:15–16)

The resolution of this tension can be found only as Messiah's throne is taken up into Yahweh's throne, and Messiah is recognized in all his fullness as Son to God (2 Sam. 7:14). In terms of new covenant realization, the writer to the Hebrews makes this very connection when he applies the description of the eternality of Yahweh's throne to the rule of Yahweh's Son. Just after citing Psalm 45, in which Messiah is unequivocally identified as Elohim (Ps. 45:6–7; cf. Heb. 1:8–9), the author of Hebrews applies the statement of Psalm 102 to the Son:

> In the beginning, O Lord, you laid the foundations of the earth,
>   and the heavens are the work of your hands.
> They will perish, but you remain;
>   they will all wear out like a garment.
> You will roll them up like a robe;
>   like a garment they will be changed.
> But you remain the same,
>   and your years will never end. (Heb. 1:10–12; cf. Ps. 102:25–27)

David's longing for a permanent merger of his messianic throne with Yahweh's eternal throne finds its consummate realization in

169

the enthronement of Jesus the Christ. According to one commentator, "The God of Zion and of David never dies; David and Zion therefore can never die, for he has inseparably connected himself with them."[25]

The Lord's Regal Functions

As a further development of Yahweh's kingship, the psalms of Book IV underscore a number of the Lord's regal functions.

He Is the Creator (Pss. 90:2; 95:6; 100:3; 102:25; 104:5–9)

Though the idea of creation *ex nihilo* (out of nothing) might not be expressed in so many words, the concept is clearly present in the Psalms. "Before the mountains were brought forth, or ever you had formed the earth and world, from everlasting to everlasting you are God" (Ps. 90:2).

He Is the Rock (Pss. 92:15; 94:22; 95:1)

As previously indicated, this ancient expression goes back to the prophetic blessing of Jacob on the various tribal heads as recorded in Genesis 49. Of Joseph he said, "His bow remained steady . . . because of the Shepherd, the Rock of Israel" (Gen. 49:24). This prophetic utterance combines the image of shepherd/king along with rock/stability, and depicts the unshakable character of God's kingship.

He Is the Judge (Pss. 94:2; 96:13; cf. Pss. 7:6–17; 9:4–19)

Two psalms in Book I (Pss. 7, 9) and a cluster of psalms in Book IV (Pss. 94–99) provide the major development of the concept that the kingship of God establishes him as Judge. In both these groupings, the role of God as King over the nations plays a prominent part in his function as Judge. According to Psalm 7:

25. Hengstenberg, *Psalms*, 3:222.

Awake, my God; decree justice.
Let the assembled peoples
    gather around you.
Rule over them
    from on high;
        let the LORD judge the peoples.
Judge me, O LORD, according to my righteousness. (Ps. 7:6b–8a)

Clearly, God will judge his own people. In fact, the psalmist deliberately exposes himself to the Lord's righteous judgments. At the same time, God's rule over the nations can be equated with his exercise of judgment over them. As a righteous Judge, he searches minds and hearts and does not restrict himself to considering only a person's outward actions. A vital part of his royal function is bringing to an end the violence of the wicked and making the righteous secure (Ps. 7:9). He is "a righteous judge, a God who expresses his wrath every day" (Ps. 7:11).

Once again, the psalmist declares:

You have sat on your throne
    judging righteously.
You have rebuked the nations
    and destroyed the wicked.
. . . .
The LORD reigns forever;
    he has established his throne for judgment.
He will judge the world
    in righteousness;
he will govern the peoples
    with justice. (Ps. 9:4b–5a; 7–8)

So the function of God as a King who judges does not mean that he simply reaches a decision about the rightness or wrongness of people's behavior. Instead, he enforces his judgments by rewarding the righteous and destroying the wicked.

The later grouping of psalms that present God as Judge are closely connected to the *Yahweh Malak* psalms. In this case, not only do his people rejoice in his role as Judge, but the heavens, the earth, the sea, the fields, and all the trees of the forest sing for joy. So what is the occasion of this universal rejoicing? Two psalms of the *Yahweh Malak* collection conclude with almost identical wording:

> They will sing before the LORD,
>> for he comes,
>> he comes to judge the earth.
> He will judge the world
>> in righteousness
> and the peoples
>> in his truth. (Ps. 96:13; cf. Ps. 98:9)

In this case, the prospect of the Lord's coming to judge the world does not inspire a note of terror. Indeed, the wicked will receive their just deserts. But the overriding response of the earth will be joy in the Lord as he climaxes his great work of redeeming his people in righteousness.

He Is the Gracious Lord Who Forgives All His People's Sins (Pss. 90:13–14; 103:3, 8–10, 12; 106:6, 8, 30–31, 44–46)

Though as Sovereign Lord he consumes people for their sins, God hears their plea for the manifestation of his compassion. He forgives all sins, does not treat his people as their sins deserve, and removes their sins as far as the east is from the west. Although the people contemporary with the psalmist have sinned just as persistently as his nation rebelled throughout their wilderness wanderings, the Lord can be called on to deliver, remember his covenant, and save.

He Exercises His Providential Care over the Whole World (Ps. 104:10–30)

The beasts of the field, the birds of the air, the moon and the sun, along with all humanity, give glory to the Lord, who sustains the whole of his creation.

172

He Is the Sovereign LORD OF THE COVENANT Who Has Directed the Entire Life of His People (Pss. 105–106)

Through all their different experiences across the stage of redemptive history, the LORD OF THE COVENANT has been his people's guide and their support. He has never forsaken them utterly.

So God is indeed a great King over the whole of his earthly dominion. All the creatures of the world, all the nations of the world, all the history of the world remain subject to his gracious and righteous rule. Viewed from the perspective of a people suffering under the banishment of exile, these affirmations that Yahweh rules are calculated to instill great hope in the hearts of his people. The same application of these psalms may be made in every age.

The First Triad of *Hallelu-YAH* Psalms (Psalms 104–106)

It might be assumed that the exclamation "*Hallelu-YAH*" occurs quite regularly throughout the Old Testament. But that is simply not the case. As a matter of fact, the term occurs for the first time in these last three psalms of Book IV (Pss. 104–106), and otherwise only in Book V of the Psalter as well as very near the conclusion of the book of Revelation in the New Testament (Rev. 19:1, 3, 4, 6).

The appearance of this term is quite stylized in this triad of psalms. Psalm 104 ends with *Hallelu-YAH*, Psalm 105 ends with *Hallelu-YAH*, and Psalm 106 begins and ends with *Hallelu-YAH*. The next appearance of the term occurs in a triad of Book V. Psalm 111 begins with *Hallelu-YAH*, Psalm 112 begins with *Hallelu-YAH*, and Psalm 113 begins and ends with *Hallelu-YAH*. The third interconnected triad reverses this arrangement and follows the initial pattern set by Psalms 104–106: Psalm 115 ends with *Hallelu-YAH*, Psalm 116 ends with *Hallelu-YAH*, and Psalm 117 begins with *Hallelu Yahweh* and ends with *Hallelu-YAH*. Except for Psalm 135, which quotes portions of two previous *Hallelu-YAH* psalms (Pss. 113, 115), the only other place where this term occurs in the Psalms (as well as in the Old Testament) is in the "*Hallelu-YAH* finale" of Psalms 146–150. Quite obviously, this term serves as an instrument to bring the whole of the Psalter to its consummate conclusion. The special significance of this enthusiastic expression will be explored in the treatment of Book V in chapter 9.[26]

Contrasting Psalms of Historical Recollection (Psalms 105–106)

Two psalms of historical recollection recalling God's sovereign direction of the life of his covenant nation conclude Book IV (Pss. 105–106). These two psalms are linked together in several ways: (1) they both have an opening call for the people to "give thanks to Yahweh" (Pss. 105:1; 106:1b); (2) they both quote from David's psalm celebrating the bringing up of the ark to Jerusalem (Ps. 105:1–15, quoting 1 Chron. 16:8–22; Ps. 106:1, 47–48, quoting 1 Chron. 16:34–36); (3) they are both incorporated in the *Hallelu-YAH* triad that concludes Book IV, all three psalms ending with *Hallelu-YAH* (Ps. 104:35—ending verse; Ps. 105:45—ending verse; Ps. 106:48—ending verse).

Yet even though they review the same history of Yahweh's redemptive activity, Psalms 105 and 106 are quite different in their contrasting perspective on Israel's history of redemption. In the first instance (Ps. 105), the psalmist begins with a lengthy quotation from David's psalm celebrating the bringing up of the ark-throne of the Lord to Zion as a way of reviewing God's covenantal faithfulness to Abraham, Isaac, and Jacob (Ps. 105:1–15; cf. 1 Chron. 16:8–22). This review of redemptive history is followed by a rehearsal of God's covenantal faithfulness through the experiences of Joseph, Moses, and the days of the conquest under Joshua.

In the second instance (Ps. 106), the psalmist employs the record of Israel's unfaithfulness as a means of leading the current nation to confess its contemporary sinfulness (Ps. 106:6–46). Immediately after the introductory remarks of the psalmist (Ps. 106:1–5), the author abruptly connects the sin of his own day with the sin of ancient

---

26. A focus on the structural role of the *Hallelu-YAH* psalms in the Psalter may be found in the present author's forthcoming article entitled "The Strategic Placement of the 'Hallelu-*YAH*' Psalms within the Psalter," scheduled to appear in the June 2015 issue of the *Journal of the Evangelical Theological Society*.

Israel: "We have sinned, even as our fathers did" (Ps. 106:6). This psalm concludes Book IV with the final words of the song of King David as he celebrated the bringing up of the ark of the covenant to Jerusalem:

> Save us, O COVENANT LORD our God,
> and gather us from the nations,
>> that we may give thanks to your holy name
>> and glory in your praise.
> Praise be to LORD, the God of Israel
>> from everlasting to everlasting,
> Let all the people say, "Amen!"
> *Hallelu-YAH*. (Ps. 106:47–48; cf. 1 Chron. 16:35–36)

This thorough confession of sin joined to a plea for "gathering from the nations" concludes Book IV. By this conclusion, Psalm 106 prepares the way for themes of restoration from exile that will emerge in climactic Book V.

In this connection, it should be remembered that the ark of the covenant did not merely represent the throne of Yahweh from which he ruled on earth. The surface of the ark functioned as the atonement cover on which the blood was sprinkled by the high priest once a year for the forgiveness of the nation's sins (Lev. 16:14–17). Throughout this final psalm of Book IV, sin is repeatedly confessed:

> We have sinned, even as our fathers did;
> We have done wrong and acted wickedly. (Ps. 106:6)

> They soon forgot what he had done
> and did not wait for his counsel. (Ps. 106:13)

> In the camp they grew envious of Moses
> and of Aaron, who was consecrated to the LORD. (Ps. 106:16)

> They forgot the God who saved them,
> who had done great things in Egypt. (Ps. 106:21)

175

They did not believe his promise.
They grumbled in their tents
and did not obey the LORD. (Ps. 106:24–25)

They provoked the LORD to anger by their wicked deeds,
and a plague broke out among them. (Ps. 106:29)

By the waters of Meribah they angered the LORD,
. . . .
for they rebelled against the Spirit of God. (Ps. 106:32–33)

They sacrificed their sons and their daughters to demons.
(Ps. 106:37)

Many times he delivered them,
but they were bent on rebellion
and they wasted away in their sin. (Ps. 106:43)

After this repeated acknowledgment of guilt, the psalmist leads the worshiping people in the familiar chant that concluded the ancient psalm of David when he celebrated the bringing up of the ark to Jerusalem:

Praise be to the LORD, the God of Israel,
    from everlasting to everlasting.
Let all the people say, "Amen!"
Hallelu-YAH. (Ps. 106:48) [or: Praise to Yahweh.
    (1 Chron. 16:36)[27]]

For the ark symbolized potential for the atonement of their sins at the mercy seat of their Sovereign Lord and King.[28]

27. The final words of 1 Chronicles 16:36 do not precisely say *Hallelu-YAH*. Instead, they read הַלֵּל לַיהוָה, "Praise to Yahweh."

28. Some have proposed that the composition of Psalm 106 preceded the composition of 1 Chronicles 16:8–36, and that Chronicles is quoting the psalm rather than vice versa. Cf. the discussion of this option in Wilson, *Editing*, 77. Wilson concludes that the doxology of Psalm 106 is derived from the historical narrative of 1 Chronicles 16. Ibid., 185. For further discussion of this complex question, see the treatment of Psalm 96 above.

The two psalms of historical recollection (Pss. 105–106) climax the presentation of God's gracious and sovereign rule as King throughout Book IV. By quoting from David's ancient psalm celebrating the bringing up of the ark-throne of Yahweh that it might be joined to David's royal throne in Jerusalem in both these concluding psalms of historical recollection, the psalmist has effectively climaxed redemptive history with the union of God's throne with David's throne. God's great kingship merges with Messiah's kingship as guaranteed by the Lord's covenantal oath to David. As a consequence, the psalmist can recall that "many times he delivered them[;] . . . he took note of their distress . . . ; for their sake he remembered his covenant and out of his great love he relented" (Ps. 106:43–45).

So the covenantal blessing of salvation from all distresses continued throughout the course of old covenant redemptive history by the sovereign grace of King Yahweh. These blessings of redemption continue until today, as God's contemporary people pray in the words of David and the psalmist:

> Save us, O Covenant Lord our God,
> and gather us from the nations,
> > that we may give thanks to your holy name
> > and glory in your praise. (Ps. 106:47)

Conclusion to Book IV

A grouping of four psalms that conclude Book IV all begin and end with praise and thanksgiving to the Lord:

> Bless the Lord, O my soul;
> and all my inmost being, praise his holy name. "(Ps. 103:1;
> > cf. vv. 20–22)

> I will sing to the Lord all my life;
> I will sing praise to my God as long as I live.
> > (Ps. 104:33; cf. vv. 1, 35b–c)

Give thanks to the LORD, call on his name;
make known among the nations what he has done.
> (Ps. 105:1; cf. v. 45b)

Blessed be the LORD, the God of Israel,
> from everlasting to everlasting.
Let all the people say, "Amen!"
Hallelu-YAH! (Ps. 106:48; cf. v. 1)

This jubilant conclusion has been anticipated throughout Book IV by the numerous passages that summon God's covenant people, the nations of the world, and all nature to "sing," to "make music," and to "rejoice" before this glorious and gracious Lord:

It is good to praise the LORD
and make music to your name, O Most High,

. . . .
For you make me glad by your deeds, O LORD;
I sing for joy at the works of your hands. (Ps. 92:1, 4)

Come, let us sing for joy to the LORD

. . . .
and extol him with music and song. (Ps. 95:1a, 2b)

Sing to the LORD a new song;
sing to the LORD, all the earth.

Sing to the LORD, praise his name;
proclaim his salvation day after day.

. . . .
Let the heavens rejoice, let the earth be glad;
let the sea resound, and all that is in it;
let the fields be jubilant, and everything in them.

Then all the trees of the forest will sing for joy;
they will sing before the LORD, for he comes,
he comes to judge the earth.
He will judge the world in righteousness
and the peoples in his truth. (Ps. 96:1–2, 11–13)

178

Numerous other passages in various sections of the Psalms summon all creation to sing for joy to the Lord of heaven and earth.[29] But the uplifting context of Book IV in which the Lord is firmly established as King among the nations provides a special tone of jubilation to these many summonses to sing. May all of God's people in all ages break out in singing, for "*Yahweh Malak.*"[30]

So a distinctive perspective on God's sovereignty receives emphasis in Book IV. The principal thrust of kingship now centers on the eternal, unthreatened, universal dominion of Yahweh. He has ruled as King, he is ruling as King, he will rule as King. From eternity to eternity, and in all time between, "*Yahweh Malak.*"

This lordship is by no means restricted to God's rule in Israel. The nations, the peoples of the world, the families of the nations are summoned to ascribe glory to this One True God (Ps. 96:3, 7, 10). The distant shores should rejoice because he reigns (Ps. 97:1). He is the Most High over all the earth (Ps. 97:9). All the kings of the earth will revere his glory, and peoples and kingdoms will assemble to worship the LORD OF THE COVENANT (Ps. 102:15, 21). This matured recognition of Yahweh's kingship inspires the first breakthrough of unrestrained *Hallelu-YAHs* in the Psalter. The final three psalms of Book IV conclude with *Hallelu-YAH*, with the last of these psalms beginning and ending in this ecstatic expression of communal praise (Pss. 104:35; 105:45; 106:1, 48).[31]

29. Cf. Pss. 5:11; 7:17; 9:2, 11; 13:6; 18:49; 21:13; 27:6; 30:4, 12; 32:11; 33:1, 3 (Book I); Pss. 47:6–7; 51:14; 57:7, 9; 59:16–17; 61:8; 63:7; 65:13; 66:2, 4; 67:4; 68:4, 32; 71:22–23 (Book II); Pss. 75:9; 81:1; 87:7; 89:1, 12 (Book III); Pss. 90:14; 92:4; 95:1; 96:1–2, 12–13; 98:1, 8–9; 101:1; 104:12, 33; 105:2 (Book IV); Pss. 108:1, 3; 119:172; 132:9, 16; 135:3; 137:3–4; 138:1, 5; 144:9; 145:7; 146:2; 147:1, 7; 149:1, 5 (Book V). It may be noted that Book III, with its depiction of numerous conquering invaders, offers the least occasions for singing to the Lord.

30. Grant, *King as Exemplar*, 53, suggests that the placement of Psalm 1 with its emphasis on *Torah* as the introduction to the Psalter transformed the entire work so that it became a "book" instead of a "hymnbook." His proposal overlooks the repeated admonition to "sing" across all five books of the Psalter, as indicated in the previous note. No better way could be devised to effect transformation through Torah-teaching than by leading a people to sing the truth. Nothing simultaneously engages the whole person, body and soul, like singing. As the old saying of Judaism goes, "As a person sings, so is he."

31. The NIV blurs preciseness in expression by translating two distinctively different phrases in Psalm 103:1, 22 and 104:35 as "Praise the LORD," thereby obscuring the

Excursus 1: Ten References to Worship in Chronicles That Relate to the Book of Psalms

The following passages indicate the special interest in worship displayed in the books of Chronicles. These passages also demonstrate the closeness of relationship between Chronicles and the Psalms. It would not be difficult to imagine significant interaction between the authors/editors of these two portions of Scripture at some time during the postexilic period.

This excursus does not attempt to investigate the many literary-critical questions regarding the relation of Chronicles to Psalms. The materials of both sources are being treated simply as they present themselves. These comments only intend to stimulate further exploration of the relationship of these two books in terms of their mutual worship interests.

1. First Chronicles 6:31–32: The worship in song instituted by David after the ark settled in the tent in Jerusalem is related directly to subsequent worship in the temple under Solomon. People serving as worship leaders include Kohath and his sons Asaph, Heman, and Ethan (1 Chron. 6:33, 39, 42). The names of the three sons appear in headings of various psalms (Pss. 73–83, 88, 89).

2. First Chronicles 13:6–8: David leads singing and celebrating "with harps, lyres, tambourines, cymbals and trumpets" at the abortive attempt of bringing up the ark to Jerusalem. Four of the five instruments mentioned in Chronicles appear repeatedly in headings of various psalms.

3. First Chronicles 15:11–16: David orders the successful bringing up of the ark, which is accompanied with singing as well as with several of the same musical instruments mentioned in the headings of the psalms.

4. First Chronicles 16:7–36: The entirety of this song of David celebrating the arrival of the ark in Jerusalem is reproduced in three segments of three different psalms of Book IV (Pss. 96, 105, 106).

---

patterned use of *Hallelu-YAH*. Both the ESV and the KJV appropriately render one phrase as "Bless the LORD" and the other as "Praise [ye] the LORD" (i.e., *Hallelu-YAH*). But Scripture and its readers would have been served better by rendering *Hallelu-YAH* with a straightforward *Hallelu-YAH*.

5. Second Chronicles 5:11–14: When the ark is transferred from the tent to Solomon's completed temple, Asaph, Heman, Jeduthun, and their sons play the same musical instruments and sing the same words penned by David to celebrate the arrival of the ark in Jerusalem: "He is good; his covenant love endures forever." These identical words are reproduced in the opening verse of the final psalm of Book IV as well as the opening verse of Book V (Pss. 106:1; 107:1).

6. Second Chronicles 6:40–42: Solomon concludes his dedicatory prayer for the temple by specific reference to the words of Moses whenever the ark of the covenant led the people in their wilderness wanderings: "Rise up," until the traveling people of God should find a *place of rest* (Num. 10:33–36). These same words open Psalm 68, and find their echo in a psalm of ascents as it refers to the Lord's choice of Zion: "This is my *restingplace* for ever and ever; here I will sit enthroned" (Ps. 132:14). This psalm continues with a clear echo of Solomon's concluding words of dedication:

> May your priests, O LORD God,
>   be clothed with salvation,
> May your saints rejoice
>   in your goodness. (2 Chron. 6:41b)

> I will clothe her priests
>   with salvation,
> and her saints
>   will ever sing for joy. (Ps. 132:16)

7. Second Chronicles 7:1–4: When the glory of the Lord fills Solomon's temple at the time of its dedication, all the Israelites worship and give thanks to the Lord in the words chanted by David at the bringing up of the ark: "He is good; his covenant love endures forever" (2 Chron. 7:3; cf. Pss. 106:1b; 107:1, as noted above).

8. Second Chronicles 20:18–22: As Jehoshaphat's army marches out of Jerusalem in battle formation, the Kohathites and Korahites stand up and praise the Lord with a very loud voice. These Korahites are apparently generationally connected to the "Sons of Korah" mentioned in the titles of several psalms (Pss. 42–49; 84–88*).

181

9. Second Chronicles 29:25–30: At the restoration of proper temple worship, Hezekiah stations the Levites in the temple "with cymbals, harps and lyres in the way prescribed by David." As the offering begins, the singers sing and the trumpeters play "the instruments of David king of Israel," referring to the same instruments mentioned in the titles of several psalms.

10. Second Chronicles 30:21–22: At Hezekiah's renewed Passover celebration, the "priests [sing] to the LORD every day, accompanied by the LORD's instruments of praise."[32] It is highly likely that many of their songs and instruments were in accord with the psalms and directions provided by David and recorded in the Psalter.

---

32. Cf. also Ezra 3:10–11 at the laying of the foundation of the restored temple in the days of Ezra. Parallels in the books of Samuel and Kings have hardly any of these details. For additional discussion of these passages, see Gordon J. Wenham, *Psalms as Torah: Reading Biblical Song Ethically* (Grand Rapids: Baker Academic, 2012), 12–16.

9

BOOK V (PSALMS 107–150): CONSUMMATION

The book of Psalms begins with *confrontation* (Book I, Pss. 1–41). Though anointed by God to serve as messianic king of his people, David struggles with numerous enemies opposed to God's kingdom of righteousness and peace. Yet he is assured that the LORD OF THE COVENANT will establish his kingdom despite all opposition.

Though David still struggles with his enemies, the Psalter moves toward a position of *communication* with the peoples of other nations in Book II (Pss. 42–72). The nations should recognize that their defeat at the hands of God and his Anointed One is inevitable. They should join in the praise of God, and bring their offerings to his temple in Jerusalem. David's son Solomon expresses his confidence that the messianic kingdom will spread from sea to sea, and from the River to the ends of the earth. This kingdom will endure as long as the sun and moon.

Yet because of the sin of God's people and their lack of trust in him, the *devastation* of exile has come (Book III, Pss. 73–89). Invading forces of foreign nations have destroyed their temple and city. The crown and throne of their Messiah have been cast to the ground.

As painful as exile must have been, this experience serves as a catalyst to bring about *maturation* in the nation's perspective on the promises of the Davidic covenant (Book IV, Pss. 90–106). The covenantal promises regarding God's permanent dwellingplace and David's perpetual dynasty must focus on God himself. For he has been their dwellingplace through all generations. David's dynasty will eventually be realized only through its perfected union with God's rule.

So now the Psalter is prepared to present the climactic praises of the *consummation* of the kingdom (Book V, Pss. 107–150). By an elaborate structure, the psalmist presents the state of the people by an introductory psalm (Ps. 107); provides a brief but significant collection of Davidic psalms (Pss. 108–110); introduces an initial grouping of *Hallelu-YAH* psalms (Pss. 111–117); structures Book V by a positioning of the final coupling of a messianic psalm with a Torah psalm (Pss. 118–119); introduces fifteen counterbalanced Psalms of Ascents that draw a final focus on God's dwellingplace in Zion (Pss. 120–134); provides three transitional psalms of historical recollection (Pss. 135–137) and eight Davidic psalms suitable to an exilic setting (Pss. 138–145); and concludes with an appropriate *Hallelu-YAH* finale (Pss. 146–150) to climax the Psalter as a whole. With this framework in mind, we may consider the various segments of Book V.

An Introductory Psalm to Book V (Psalm 107)

Why, it may be asked, does Book V begin with a third consecutive psalm of historical recollection (Ps. 107)? Immediately after Book IV concludes with two extensive psalms recalling the major events of God's redemptive acts across Israel's history, why now should a third psalm of the same essential nature open the fifth and final book of the Psalms?

First of all, Psalm 107 is *not* a psalm that recalls the mighty events of Israel's redemptive history. Nothing is said of the exodus, Sinai, the wilderness wanderings, the conquest, or the establishment of the kingship in Israel. Indeed, mention is made of the distresses of wandering in desert wastelands and sitting as prisoners suffering in iron chains (Ps. 107:4, 10). But because specific indicators are absent, these hardships fit the circumstances of Israel's exile just as well as the people's Egyptian bondage and deliverance. Still further, the additional references to those who go down to the sea in ships and who reel and stagger like drunk men (Ps. 107:23, 27) hardly comply with a rehearsal of the historical circumstance of Israel's stay in Egypt. The same conclusion may be reached regarding God's turning rivers into a desert and flow-ing springs into thirsty ground, depicting a complete reversal of Israel's experience in the wilderness (Ps. 107:33). So first impressions must not be embraced too hastily in concluding that Psalm 107 is simply one more rehearsal of Israel's historical experience of redemption.

Second, Psalm 107 serves as an introduction to the final phase of the Psalter, which focuses on the climactic restoration of worship for God's people at Yahweh's permanent dwellingplace in Jerusalem. Psalm 107 begins by reiterating a thematic phrase from the ark-procession to Jerusalem, which had the effect of uniting Yahweh's throne with David's throne (1 Chron. 16:34, 36b; Ps. 107:1). This thematic phrase also links the final psalm of Book IV (Ps. 106) with the opening psalm of Book V (Ps. 107) in that both these psalms begin with the same refrain:

> Give thanks to the LORD, for he is good; his covenant love endures
> forever. (Pss. 106:1; 107:1)[1]

It might be assumed that this phrase is a commonplace in Scripture, having the sound of the simple and the memorable. It would be easy to imagine the "average Israelite" repeating this refrain regularly. But the phrase actually has a clearly defined pattern of usage in Scripture. It appears numerous times in Chronicles and Book V of the Psalms, but otherwise only once in Ezra, once in Jeremiah, and twice in Book IV of the Psalms (Ezra 3:11; Jer. 33:11; Pss. 100:5; 106:1). In all instances in the book of Chronicles, the phrase is exclusively related to progress in the establishment of the temple in Jerusalem, and to worship in that locale, with a single exception.[2]

According to the Chronicler, the phrase had its origin in the psalm celebrating the bringing up of the ark to Jerusalem:

---

1. The term *hesed* (חֶסֶד) embraces such a broad spectrum of Yahweh's gracious dealings with his people that one term in the English language cannot fully represent its significance. It includes the Lord's love, his mercy, his grace, his covenantal faithfulness. The phrase "covenant love" is being used as approximately representing this all-embracive characteristic of the Lord's dealings with his people, particularly as it relates to God's covenant.

2. Second Chronicles 20:21 records the dramatic moment when King Jehoshaphat appointed musicians preceding his army into battle to sing in these very words: "Give thanks to the LORD, for his covenant love endures forever."

Then on that day David first appointed that thanksgiving be sung
to the LORD by Asaph and his brothers. . . .

Oh give thanks to the LORD, for he is good;
    for his steadfast love endures forever! . . .

Then all the people said, "Amen!" and praised the LORD.
(1 Chron. 16:7, 34, 36b ESV)[3]

With the same wording, the Chronicler records Israel's song at
the time of the transfer of the ark by Solomon from David's tent to
his newly constructed temple, as well as when fire came down from
heaven at the conclusion of Solomon's dedicatory prayer for the temple:

He is good; his covenant love endures forever. (2 Chron. 5:13; 7:3)

Again, when Solomon consecrates the temple with sacrifices, the
Chronicler refers to the earlier time when David had given thanks, saying, "His covenant love endures forever" (2 Chron. 7:6). Once more,
after Israel's restoration from exile, this theme song of temple consecration recurs as the foundation of the restored temple is being dedicated:

He is good; his covenant love to Israel endures forever. (Ezra 3:11)

Still further, the pivotal messianic psalm of Book V celebrating
the establishment of the personalized cornerstone of the Lord's temple
(Ps. 118:22) begins and ends with the same refrain:

Give thanks to the LORD, for he is good; his covenant love endures
    forever. (Ps. 118:1, 29)

An antiphonal employment in worship of this refrain occurs
twenty-six times in one psalm in Book V (Ps. 136). Assembled in worship, God's people will declare in response to one another that from

---

3. For a discussion of the relation of the psalm in 1 Chronicles 16 to various parts of
the Psalter, see the treatment of Psalm 96 in chapter 8.

creation to redemption to consummation, "he is good; his covenant love endures forever."

The expansive usage of this phrase that apparently originated with the bringing up of the ark to Jerusalem underscores the centrality of a key feature of the Davidic covenant in the Psalter once more. The establishment of a "house," a permanent dwellingplace for the Lord's throne in Jerusalem, serves as a principal reason for the nation's giving thanks in its worship.

Third, the opening statement in Psalm 107 that the Lord has "*gathered*" his people from the lands, from east and west, from north and south (Ps. 107:3), is best understood in its full redemptive-historical context. The conclusion of the preceding psalm that ends Book IV petitions the Lord by recalling the final words of the Ark-Song: "Save us . . . and *gather* us from the nations" (Ps. 106:47; cf. 1 Chron. 16:35). The identical concept of "gathering" from the nations that ends Book IV begins Book V.[4] Yet while this "gathering from the nations" in Psalm 106 appears as a prayer for deliverance yet to come, the perspective on "gathering" in Psalm 107 is quite different. This "gathering" has already taken place.[5] Book V opens with the joyful declaration that God has "gathered" his redeemed people from east, west, north, and south (Ps. 107:3). A glorious restoration has occurred. The psalm then delineates the various situations of distress from which God's people have been redeemed.

This idea of a "gathering" from the nations has rich biblical-theological significance for Israel's prophets. Isaiah, Jeremiah, and Ezekiel all anticipate this future ingathering of God's people:

> In that day the Root of Jesse [the messianic king through the line of David] will stand as a banner for the peoples; . . . the Lord

4. Jamie A. Grant, *The King as Exemplar: The Function of Deuteronomy's Kingship Law in the Shaping of the Book of Psalms* (Atlanta: Society of Biblical Literature, 2004), 242, indicates that the purpose of Psalm 107 is "to link Book V into the Psalter as a continuum from Book IV."

5. Frank-Lothar Hossfeld and Eric Zenger, *Psalms 3: A Commentary on Psalms 101–150* (Minneapolis: Fortress Press, 2011), 2: "Whereas the exilic perspective had dominated the Fourth Book of Psalms, Psalm 107 and those that follow present the end of the exile and beginning/already begun restoration of Zion/Israel."

will . . . *gather* the exiles of Israel; he will assemble the scattered people of Judah from the four quarters of the earth. (Isa. 11:10–12; cf. Isa. 27:12–13; 56:6–8)

"And I, because of their actions and their imaginations, am about to come and *gather* all nations and tongues, and they will come and see my glory.

. . . They will proclaim my glory among the nations. And they will bring all your brothers, from all the nations, to my holy mountain in Jerusalem as an offering to the LORD . . . . And I will select some of them also to be priests and Levites," says the LORD. (Isa. 66:18–21; cf. Rom. 15:15–16)

See, I will bring them from the land of the north
    and *gather* them from the ends of the earth.
. . . .
Hear the word of the LORD, O nations;
    proclaim it in distant coastlands:
"He who scattered Israel will *gather* them
    and will watch over his flock like a shepherd."
For the LORD will ransom Jacob
    and redeem them from the hand of those stronger than they.
        (Jer. 31:8–11)

I will bring you from the nations and *gather* you from the countries where you have been scattered . . . .

. . . I will accept you as fragrant incense when I bring you out from the nations and *gather* you from the countries where you have been scattered, and I will show myself holy among you in the sight of the nations. (Ezek. 20:34–41)

The opening reference in Book V to the fact that the Lord has "gathered" his redeemed people from east and west, from north and south, should be understood in terms of this broader prophetic expectation of the "gathering" of God's people after exile. In several cases, this "gathering" brings the people to Jerusalem, to Zion, to the temple, to the place of sacrifice and worship. Not just the nation of Israel, but people from other nationalities are included among the redeemed that

God will "gather" to himself. Just as Jesus subsequently says, "Other sheep have I that are not of this fold. I must bring them also" (John 10:16). In his time, the Lord will gather his people to their land from which they had been exiled.

So the opening psalm of Book V sets the stage for the consummate realization of the gathering of Yahweh's people from all the nations to his permanent dwellingplace in Jerusalem. "Whoever is wise, and will observe these things, even they shall experience the covenant love of the LORD" (Ps. 107:43).

Basic Structural Elements in Book V

As in the case of Book I, the conjoining of a distinctively messianic psalm with a Torah psalm serves at a pivotal point in the structural formation of Book V. This repetitive pattern of Torah psalm coupled with messianic psalm appears three times across the Psalter. Psalms 1 and 2, a Torah psalm coupled with a messianic psalm, serve as two pillars demarcating the entranceway into the "temple of the Psalter." Psalms 18 and 19, a messianic psalm coupled with a Torah psalm, provide the basic structural division of the forty-one psalms of Book I (Pss. 1–41). Now in the concluding book of the Psalter, a climactic messianic psalm coupled with a climactic Torah psalm (Pss. 118–119) provides the basic structural division of the forty-four psalms of Book V.

As in Book I, Book V contains four acrostic psalms that provide additional structural elements that break down this largest of books in the Psalter into smaller segments. Acrostic Psalms 111 and 112 introduce the first structured collection of *Hallelu-YAH* psalms in Book V (Pss. 111–117). Psalm 119, the third Torah psalm of the Psalter, serves as the grand exemplar of alphabetic acrostics. Twenty-two stanzas of eight verses each follow the regular order of the Hebrew alphabet. The last acrostic of the Psalter (Ps. 145) fittingly concludes the final collection of eight Davidic psalms (Pss. 138–145) just before the Psalter launches into its *Hallelu-YAH* finale (Pss. 146–150).

In terms of additional structuring, two distinctive collections precede pivotal Psalms 118/119 in the first portion of Book V (Pss. 108–117),

189

and four distinctive collections follow pivotal Psalms 118/119 in the second portion of Book V (Pss. 120–150). As these various segments are considered more closely, it becomes quite clear that the fifth book of the Psalms has been extensively structured.

Two Collections in the First Portion of Book V (Psalms 108–117)

Three Davidic Psalms (Psalms 108–110)

These three psalms form the third collection of Davidic psalms in the Psalter, just before the first collection of *Hallelu-YAH* psalms in Book V (Pss. 111–117). As previously noted, a fourth and final collection of eight Davidic psalms stands appropriately in the penultimate position of Book V (Pss. 138–145), just before the concluding *Hallelu-YAH* finale. It could be supposed that these particular psalms of David just "happened" to be left out of the previous Davidic collections, and were "thrown in" at the last minute by an editor who could find no other convenient position for them. But it seems much more likely that these specific psalms of David were carefully chosen by a capable editorial craftsman who determined the final form of the Psalter. Each of these three psalms goes beyond the level of redemptive revelation found in the previous Davidic psalms.

Psalm 108 consists altogether of concluding sections taken from two Davidic psalms of Book II (Pss. 57, 60).[6] An analysis of the material omitted from the previous psalms discloses the distinctiveness of this newly constructed psalm. In both cases, Psalm 108 omits the agonizing struggle of David with his enemies featured in the earlier collection. A portion of the section omitted from Psalm 57 of Book II reads as follows:

6. Brevard S. Childs, *Biblical Theology of the Old and New Testaments: Theological Reflection on the Christian Bible* (London: SCM Press, 1992), 194, refers to "a former generation of French scholars" who spoke of an "anthological style" of late psalmody "to rework fragments from older psalms into new compositions which indicates both the freedom and restraint with which the psalms were adapted to new situations without losing their authority." The "reworking" of Psalm 108 clearly displays both these characteristics. On the one hand, the psalmist (whether David himself or a later editor rearranging authentic Davidic material) shows freedom in omitting certain aspects of the two original psalms, while also exhibiting restraint in modifying the portions of the original text that he has retained.

I am in the midst of lions;
I lie among ravenous beasts—
   men whose teeth are spears and arrows,
   whose tongues are sharp swords. (Ps. 57:4)

In similar fashion, the quoted portion from Psalm 60 in Psalm 108 omits the opening description of David's struggle with the Lord's chastenings of the nation:

You have rejected us, O God,
   and burst forth upon us . . . !
You have shaken the land
   and torn it open . . . .
You have shown your people
   desperate times;
you have given us wine that makes us stagger. (Ps. 60:1–3)

So what does the omission of these sections depicting deeply troublous times reveal about Psalm 108? The omissions indicate that God's people have made significant progress beyond their status as depicted in Book II. The psalmist paints a brighter picture for the nation. He is prepared to praise Yahweh among the nations, and sing of him among the peoples (Ps. 108:3). The kingdom of the Messiah is moving toward an era of peace and prosperity. The earlier struggles will indeed recur, as seen in the psalmist's plea for deliverance by the Lord's right hand (Ps. 108:6; cf. vv. 10–13). A number of psalms in the final collection of Davidic psalms will rehearse this need for divine intervention (cf. Pss. 140, 142, 143, 144). Even the immediately following psalm will display the climax of the archenemy's efforts to overcome the representative man of God's people. But the overall flow of the book of Psalms clearly moves in Book V toward the ultimate triumph over all the enemies of Messiah's kingdom.

Psalm 109 vividly depicts David's confrontation with his archenemy. Of all the imprecatory sections of the Psalter in which the psalmist prays for or pronounces curses on his evil enemies, Psalm 109 is the most extensive as well as the most intensive. Against this person David prays a judgment of reciprocity:

> He loved to pronounce a curse—
>> may it come on him;
> he found no pleasure in blessing—
>> may it be far from him. (Ps. 109:17)

The seed of Satan among humanity finds its consummate realization in this singular enemy of the Anointed One.

The justly deserved repudiation of this person finds ultimate fulfillment in the apostle Peter's pronouncement of judgment over Judas the self-cursed betrayer in the words of this psalm. The New Testament quotes only the one relevant phrase regarding the necessity of a replacement for Judas among the Twelve: "May another take his place of leadership" (Ps. 109:8; cf. Acts 1:20b). But the full context of this judgmental pronouncement provides a darker framework:

> Let an accuser stand at his right hand.
> When he is tried, let him be found guilty,
> and may his prayers condemn him.
> May his days be few;
> *may another take his place of leadership.*
> May his children be fatherless
> and his wife a widow. (Ps. 109:6–9)

Not only the man himself, but the seed of this man stands as symbolic representation of the generational lines of the "seed of Satan" that will busy itself in every age with striking blow after blow against the "seed of the woman." It is in this context that Peter clearly indicates the necessity of an apostolic replacement: "May another take his place of leadership" (Ps. 109:8; Acts 1:20b).

Psalm 110, assigned to David by both the title of the psalm and the argument of Jesus (Matt. 22:41–46), distinctly combines the offices of messianic king and messianic priest. The covenant "LORD" (*Yahweh*) makes two solemn declarations to David's "Lord" (*Adonai*), and both must be taken into consideration to fully appreciate the consummate picture of the Lord's Messiah that has been intentionally reserved for the final book of the Psalter. This "Lord" of King David sits enthroned alongside Yahweh, exercising authority over Israel's king, the highest official of the nation.

Who can this person be? What in David's understanding of Yahweh's redemptive revelation could have prepared him to portray this vision of a person who holds a position as the sovereign over God's people, far above his own kingly role?

The most obvious framework for understanding is found at the heart of the Lord's covenantal promise to David. His greater successor to the throne will be the Son of God (2 Sam. 7:14), who by his very nature is equal to God (cf. Ps. 45:6–7). So it should not be surprising to find King David referring to a regal person anointed by Yahweh who is his "Lord." But still further, this psalm reports Yahweh as taking a sovereign oath regarding this unique person. He not only will be king, but will simultaneously hold the sacred office of priest (Ps. 110:4).

So what framework for understanding a union of these offices of king and priest might David have had? In Israel's experience, a king could not hold the office of priest, and a priest could not hold the office of king. Witness the tragic experience of good King Uzziah, who dared to cross the line dividing these two offices (2 Chron. 26:16–21).

Again, the key covenantal word promised directly to David and his descendants offers a framework for comprehending this challenging concept. The essence of sonship as anticipated in the heart of the Davidic covenant (2 Sam. 7:14) provides the possibility of combining these two offices in one person. As Son of God, David's descendant naturally inherits the office of king. Likewise, as Son of God, David's descendant possesses immediate access to his Father, which is the essence of priesthood.

It is not for us to understand exactly "how" or "how much of" these redemptive truths were comprehended by David. It is not for us to determine limits for the illuminating work of the Holy Spirit that inspired the Scriptures. But we do know that this Psalm 110 was written at some point in history, and that David has been credited with its composition. We also know that the offices of king and priest were to be united in one person, according to Psalm 110.

In addition, we know that this psalm was incorporated at some point into Book V of the Psalter, which places its full realization in the context of exilic and postexilic experiences of Israel. This conclusion does not mean that the psalm was in fact composed at the very end

193

of Israel's redemptive history. But it does mean that this psalm in this grouping of psalms was suitable for the period of exile and restoration.

From David's perspective, this concept of a priesthood outside the formal orderings of Levi could be most encouraging to him at times when he was denied access to the regulated orderings of Levi at the temple/tabernacle in Jerusalem. There was the potential for another priesthood, comparable to the ancient order of Melchizedek, that combined kingship and priesthood. In his exile, perhaps during the days of Absalom's rebellion, David might have come to understand something of this other way of access to the presence of God.

At the same time, this psalm is uniquely suitable for Israel's exilic and postexilic period. The messianic expectation of this psalm introduces a new and different day in the history of redemption. Anticipating the return from exile, the people may expect a day in which their King will be their Priest. Their Sovereign will be their Supplicator.

During the days of exile when the nation had no king, no priesthood, and no temple, a King/Priest, the Son of God the Father, could answer all the people's needs. During the postexilic days in which the nation struggled to reestablish a functioning priesthood and temple even in the imposed absence of kingship, a single individual who combined both offices would provide the ideal solution to the people's challenging situation. In fact, a similar combination of offices may be found in the postexilic prophecies of Zechariah. In a unique act of symbolic ceremonialism, Israel's high priest Joshua undergoes coronation with a tiered crown placed on his head (Zech. 6:11). As explanation for this event unparalleled across Israel's history, this is what the Lord of Hosts says:

> Here is the man whose name is the Branch, . . . and he shall build the temple of the LORD, . . . and he will sit and rule on his throne. He will be a priest on his throne. (Zech. 6:12–13)

Zechariah's prophetic word closely parallels the thought patterns of Psalm 110. The future messianic Branch, the regal descendant of David, will focus on building the temple of the Lord. Even as David's son Solomon built the temple, so this Davidic descendant will build

God's temple. As he rules from his throne, he also serves as Priest. The sonship to God the Father as described in 2 Samuel 7:14 finds consummate realization in this postexilic prophecy of Zechariah.

This perception of messianic sonship to God as the foundational concept for a conjunction of kingship and priesthood in a single messianic figure is, as a matter of fact, the basis for the central argument of the book of Hebrews in the New Testament. God has now spoken by his "Son." This "Son" is the kingly "heir of all things" who has done the priestly work of providing "purification for sins." As a consequence, he "sat down at the right hand of the Majesty in heaven," where he rules as messianic king and intercedes as messianic priest (Heb. 1:2–3). The writer of Hebrews then cites Psalm 2:7 and 2 Samuel 7:14 as his first two of seven Scriptures to support his grand thesis (Heb. 1:5). As will be immediately recognized, these two passages confirm sonship to God as the primary identity of the promised Messiah originally depicted in the Davidic covenant and repeatedly reaffirmed throughout the book of Psalms.

Psalm 110 along with Psalm 118 brings to a climax the psalms of a focal messianic character in the Psalter. For this reason, they are appropriately located in the final book of the Psalms. If foundational Psalm 2 is properly positioned as one of the twin pillars providing entrance into the temple of the Psalter, then Psalms 110 and 118 are properly positioned as consummative messianic psalms in Book V.[7] These two consummative messianic psalms, along with Psalm 2, are quoted in the New Testament more than any other psalm.

Seven Psalms Featuring Six *Hallelu-YAH* Psalms Arranged in Chiastic Form (Psalms 111–117)[8]

Immediately after this third major collection of Davidic psalms (Pss. 108–110), six *Hallelu-YAH* psalms balance one another (Pss. 111–113,

---

7. For a fuller treatment of Psalm 110 as it is quoted and interpreted in the book of Hebrews, see O. Palmer Robertson, *The Israel of God: Yesterday, Today, and Tomorrow* (Phillipsburg, NJ: P&R Publishing, 2000), 57–83.

8. Psalms 113–118 by ancient Jewish tradition are called the "*Hallel* of Egypt," presumably because of the opening reference in Psalm 114 to the time that Israel came "out of Egypt." For centuries, this grouping of psalms has been read at the family celebration of

115–117) across a single non-*Hallelu-YAH* psalm inserted at their midpoint (Ps. 114):

- Two psalms *beginning* with *Hallelu-YAH* (Pss. 111–112) are followed by one psalm *beginning and ending* with *Hallelu-YAH* (Ps. 113).
- Then a non-*Hallelu-YAH* psalm appears at the midpoint (Ps. 114), balanced by two psalms that *end* with *Hallelu-YAH* (Pss. 115–116), followed by one psalm *beginning* with *Hallelu Yahweh and ending* with *Hallelu-YAH* (Ps. 117).

The chiastic arrangement of these seven psalms embodying this first grouping of *Hallelu-YAH* psalms in Book V is quite remarkable, particularly in view of the complete absence of the term *Hallelu-YAH* in Books I, II, and III as well as in the rest of the entirety of the Old Testament, except for the ending psalms of Book IV. Not until the concluding triad of Book IV (Pss. 104–106) does the term *Hallelu-YAH* ever occur in Scripture. The psalmist is obviously now moving the whole collection toward its climax. In triads echoing the pattern of Book IV,[9] the first triad of Book V (Pss. 111–113) features two psalms beginning with *Hallelu-YAH* followed by one psalm beginning and ending with *Hallelu-YAH*. Then the second triad (Pss. 115–117) features two psalms ending with *Hallelu-YAH* followed by one psalm beginning with *Hallelu Yahweh* and ending with *Hallelu-YAH*.

But why this grouping of six *Hallelu-YAH* psalms arranged chiastically about a non-*Hallelu-YAH* psalm at this point in Book V? Why

---

the Jewish Passover and at other Jewish festivals. Any effort to discover a different grouping of psalms in distinction from this ancient tradition might seem counterproductive. But structural considerations in the Scriptures themselves should be given their full weight. Primary factors include: (1) the balance of the six *Hallelu-YAH* psalms (Pss. 111–113, 115–117) around Psalm 114; and (2) the third joining of a messianic psalm with a Torah psalm (Pss. 118–119; cf. Pss. 1–2, 18–19), which has the effect of separating Psalm 118 from the previous grouping of Psalms 111–117 in terms of structure. To follow the traditional grouping, both these structural units must be denied their inherent integrity. For a full discussion of the "Egyptian *Hallel*," see Hossfeld and Zenger, *Psalms 3*, 178–79.

9. Again, in the triad that concludes Book IV, Psalm 104 ends with *Hallelu-YAH*, Psalm 105 ends with *Hallelu-YAH*, and Psalm 106 begins and ends with *Hallelu-YAH*.

should they not have been combined with the five *Hallelu-YAH* psalms that ultimately conclude the Psalter? Would not a larger grouping have made a grander impression?

These *Hallelu-YAH* psalms are placed precisely at this point to provide a proper conclusion for the first portion of Book V (Pss. 107–117).[10] As such, they anticipate the ultimate *Hallelu-YAH* finale (Pss. 146–150) that provides a proper conclusion for the second half of Book V (Pss. 120–150) as well as the entire Psalter. Messianic Psalm 118 joined with Torah Psalm 119 provides the pivotal point between the first and second halves of Book V. Again, these two pivotal psalms function in the same way as messianic Psalm 18 and Torah Psalm 19 in Book I.

This first grouping of *Hallelu-YAH* psalms in Book V (Pss. 111–117) is quite different in its substance from the second grouping of *Hallelu-YAH* psalms in Book V (Pss. 146–150). The pinnacle psalm of this "poetic pyramid" of seven psalms, the only psalm of this collection that does not use the word *Hallelu-YAH*, nonetheless climaxes this collection with its reference to Israel's coming out of Egypt from a people of "foreign tongue" (Ps. 114:1). Yet none of the prophecies concerning Israel's experience of a people with a "foreign language" refer to Egypt. Instead, they come after the exodus from Egyptian bondage and anticipate the Babylonian captivity (Deut. 28:49; Isa. 28:11; Jer. 5:15). This fact suggests that the reference to Israel's past deliverance from Egypt in Psalm 114 could intend to anticipate at the same time a similar deliverance, the deliverance from Babylon. Because of this past exodus from Egypt as well as the contemporary deliverance from Babylon, the whole earth should "tremble" at the presence of the Lord (Ps. 114:7).

A further distinction in this first grouping of *Hallelu-YAH* psalms may be seen in the fact that only once in these seven psalms is any

10. Hossfeld and Zenger, *Psalms 3*, 3, acknowledge this grouping of seven *Hallelu-YAH* psalms, but attempt to include Psalm 118 even though they emphasize the absence of a "Hallelujah" marking in Psalm 118. They do not take note of the third coupling of a messianic psalm with a Torah psalm (Pss. 118–119). Consequently, they observe that Psalm 119 "feels in its context like an erratic block." Ibid., 4. Their effort to explain away this difficulty is useful, but would be more effective if the coupling of messianic Psalm 118 with Torah Psalm 119 were recognized.

mention made of Jerusalem, the temple, the house, or the courts of the Lord. Even the one reference to "Jerusalem" could be read in terms of future anticipation (Ps. 116:19). This virtual absence of reference to the temple in Jerusalem stands in sharpest contrast with the manifold references in the second collection of *Hallelu-YAH* psalms (Pss. 146–150), in which each of these psalms but one mentions the worship of the Lord in Zion, in Jerusalem, or in his sanctuary. This paucity of reference to Zion or Jerusalem might indicate that this first collection of *Hallelu-YAH* psalms originated early in the days of Israel's return from Babylonian exile, or even before this return had actually occurred.

But an even larger consideration that marks the distinction between these two collections of *Hallelu-YAH* psalms is the frequency of the use of the word *Hallelu-YAH* as well as associated words with the same *hallel* root. Indeed, it should be underscored that this particular type of psalm belongs in a special way to the two *Hallelu-YAH* collections of Book V. As previously noted, the distinctive ejaculation *Hallelu-YAH*, using the poetically abbreviated form of *Yahweh* as the COVENANT LORD, belongs exclusively to Book V in the whole of the Old Testament, except for the three concluding psalms of Book IV (Pss. 104–106). Other forms using the root *hallel* are scattered through the first four books of the Psalms, but occur only from two to eight times in each of the first four books in reference to praising the Lord. In contrast, this same root appears thirty-eight times in this second *Hallelu-YAH* collection of five psalms (Pss. 146–150). In this final collection, the distinctive expression *Hallelu-YAH* occurs at the beginning and end of every psalm. With this obviously intentional organization of the last book of the Psalter in mind, it becomes rather clear that the final editor has arranged his collections so that they climax with the two *Hallelu-YAH* groupings in Book V.[11]

11. Patrick D. Miller, "The Beginning of the Psalter," in *The Shape and Shaping of the Psalter*, ed. J. Clinton McCann (Sheffield, UK: Sheffield Academic Press, 1993), 84, contrasts the ending of the Psalter with its beginning by speaking of the "less clear but meaningful conclusion" of the book. Yet how much more clearly could the conclusion of the Psalter be expressed than in the climactic *Hallelu-YAH* finale of Psalms 146–150? From the final triad of psalms in Book IV when the *Hallelu-YAH* ejaculation first comes to expression, through the double *Hallelu-YAH* triad of Psalms 111–117, to the finale moment

As the Psalter moves toward its conclusion, the structural significance of this first collection of *Hallelu-YAH* psalms (Pss. 111–117) is
underscored by the use of the acrostic form in the first two psalms of
the grouping (Pss. 111–112). In both cases, each half-verse of these
two psalms begins with the following letter of the Hebrew alphabet.
No letter of the alphabet is omitted. These two psalms are completely
regular in their acrostic form, except that in both cases verses 9 and 10
contain words beginning with three consecutive letters of the Hebrew
alphabet rather than the normal two.

This first collection of *Hallelu-YAH* psalms offers many reasons
that should call forth corporate adoration of the COVENANT LORD.
The Lord must be praised, for "his righteousness endures forever" (Ps.
111:3). He should be praised because of the power of his redemptive
works (Ps. 111:6). He should be praised because his gracious and righteous nature can and will be reflected in those who trust him. Remarkably, the same phrase applied to the Lord in Psalm 111 is repeated
twice in Psalm 112 to describe the man who fears the Lord: "His
righteousness endures forever" (Ps. 111:3; cf. Ps. 112:3, 9). According
to the psalmist, this reflection of Yahweh's righteousness in the life of
those who trust him deserves repeating: "His righteousness"—that is,
the righteousness of those who trust Yahweh—"endures forever" (Ps.
112:9). The comparison is taken even a step further. Just as the Lord
is "gracious and compassionate," so the man who fears the Lord will
be "gracious and compassionate" (Pss. 111:4; 112:4).

When Paul the apostle wishes to encourage generosity in the early
Christian community of Corinth, he appeals to this very principle.
God's surpassing grace has been given to them by his indescribable
gift (2 Cor. 9:14–15). As a consequence, the believer should "abound
in every good work" (2 Cor. 9:8), just as it is written, "He has scattered abroad his gifts to the poor, his righteousness endures forever"
(Ps. 112:9; cf. 2 Cor. 9:9).

The COVENANT LORD'S care for the poor, the needy, the barren,
and the dying provides additional reasons for continually declaring,
"*Hallelu-YAH*" (Pss. 113:7, 9; 115:17; 116:3, 15). Climactically, he

---

of Psalms 146–150, the psalmist summons the people not to a mere acknowledgment of
Yahweh's kingship but to the spontaneous celebration of his sovereignty.

should be praised by all the nations because his love and faithfulness endure forever (Ps. 117:2). The words of praise in this *Hallelu-YAH* collection are also quoted by Paul to underscore the inclusion of all nations among those who praise the Lord (Rom. 15:11; cf. Ps. 117:1).

But what is the special significance of this spontaneous ejaculation of corporate praise? What new dimension does it add to the message of the Psalter, reserved as it is to the last three psalms of Book IV (Pss. 104–106), the two special collections that conclude the two major sections of Book V (Pss. 111–117; 146–150), and a single psalm that serves as a distinctive connector in the second major portion of Book V (Ps. 135)? More particularly, what is the origin of this poetic abbreviation for *Yahweh*, and what is its ongoing significance?

The term *YAH* as a poetic abbreviation for *Yahweh* appears in Scripture for the first time in the opening phrase of the Song of Moses at the crossing of the Red Sea:

> My strength and my song is *YAH*!
> He has become my salvation. (Ex. 15:2)

The song proceeds to declare that the Lord will guide his people to his "holy abode," to the mountain of his inheritance, to the place where he "sits [enthroned]," to the "sanctuary" that his hands have established (Ex. 15:13, 17). Moses concludes by declaring that Yahweh "will rule [as King] forever" (יְהוָה יִמְלֹךְ לְעֹלָם וָעֶד). It is quite striking to note that the kingship of Yahweh as well as his permanent dwelling-place plays a prominent role in Moses' ancient poem, in view of the permeating character of these two themes in the Davidic covenant, and consequently throughout the Psalter.

The only other appearances of *YAH* in the Old Testament outside the Psalms are found in one additional passage in Exodus, and two passages in Isaiah. Amalek and his nation oppose the Israelites at the time of their exodus. The uplifted hands of Moses are memorialized by the phrase "A hand upon the throne of *YAH*" (Ex. 17:16). By reference to the "throne of *YAH*," the kingship of Yahweh is associated once more with the term *YAH*, as it appeared originally in the Song of Moses at the Red Sea (Ex. 15:2, 17). When Isaiah the prophet subsequently

200

speaks in anticipation of the return of Israel's exiles, he declares that "in that day" the Root of Jesse will stand as a banner for the peoples, referring to the Davidic Messiah's coming kingship. His "place of rest" will be glorious, alluding to the restoration of Yahweh's permanent dwellingplace in Zion (Isa. 11:10). Then in quoting the Song of Moses at the Red Sea, the prophet notes that "in that day" the people will chant the poetic name of Yahweh as they declare:

> YAH, Yahweh is my strength and song;
> he has become my salvation. (Isa. 12:2; cf. Ex. 15:2)[12]

Once again, both *dynasty* and *dwellingplace*, Jesse's *Root* and his glorious *restingplace*, are associated with deliverance by *YAH* the King.

This poetic abbreviation for *Yahweh* occurs only five times in four passages of the Old Testament outside the Psalter,[13] and forty-one times in thirty-eight different verses within the Psalter.[14] The first appearance of *YAH* in the Psalter describes his procession to the chosen place of his dwelling on Mount Zion. There he receives gifts from the nations as they acknowledge his sovereignty (Ps. 69:18).

Yet the majority of appearances of *YAH* occur in conjunction with the spontaneous praise-word *Hallelu-YAH*. This summons for the community to "Praise *YAH*" is introduced only after the *Yahweh Malak* psalms of Book IV (Pss. 92–100). Only after Yahweh has been clearly declared "King" even in the context of Israel's exile in these *Yahweh Malak* psalms are the people summoned to shout, "*Hallelu-YAH*." In the final psalms of Book IV (Pss. 104–106) and in the concluding collections of both portions of Book V (Pss. 111–117; 146–150) along with a single psalm (Ps. 135), this distinctive summons appears for the first and last times in the Old Testament. Always in a patterned grouping of multiple psalms with the exception of Psalm 135, these climactic ejaculatory summonses to praise *YAH* go one step beyond

---

12. The second passage in Isaiah quotes the complaint of King Hezekiah on his sickbed as he repeats the name of *YAH* (Isa. 38:11).

13. As already indicated, the passages are Ex. 15:2; 17:16; Isa. 12:2; 38:11 (2×).

14. Places in the Psalms where *YAH* appears other than in the *Hallelu-YAH* phrase are Pss. 77:12; 89:9; 94:7, 12; 102:19; 118:5, 14, 17–19; 122:4; 130:3; 135:4. These passages deserve careful consideration.

the declaration that "Yahweh is King." Beyond declaration is exclamation and celebration. Because Yahweh rules, the people can exclaim, "*Hallelu-YAH!*"

Quite remarkably, this climactic celebratory designation of Israel's Lord in the *Hallelu-YAH* ejaculation of the final collections of Book V has taken the dominant position even over the covenant name of *Yahweh*. In all subsequent ages, across all differing cultures and languages, *Hallelu-YAH* prevails. With all reverent respect, the term *Yahweh* simply does not seem natural in so many languages. Substitutions for the tetragrammaton (*YHWH*) prevail even in the Hebrew language. Instead of attempting to pronounce the revered name of God, *Adonai* ("Lord") or *HaShem* ("the Name") is substituted. In English translations, the linguistic hybrid *Jehovah* is frequently found, which combines the consonants of *YHWH* and the vowels of *Adonai*.[15] Other English translations may substitute LORD, a title for God but not an identifying name, with small capital letters, in distinction from *Lord*, which normally stands in translation for *Adonai*.

In contrast with the difficulty of vocalizing *YHWH*, what is the English equivalent of the Hebrew phrase *Hallelu-YAH*? It's simply *Hallelu-YAH*. How do you say the Hebrew phrase *Hallelu-YAH* in Greek? in Spanish? in German? in French? in Swahili? in Chichewa? in Luganda? It's all the same in all these languages, with minor differences in spelling. No translation is necessary. Indeed, the phrase may be rendered as "Praise the LORD." Yet it has achieved spontaneous universality.

The Psalter has shown the way for the universe to praise its Creator and Redeemer. The Psalms consummate with *Hallelu-YAH*, and all nations and peoples can join in this joyful, spontaneous celebration. Even the ease with which the expression can be articulated deserves notice. In a remarkable way, the word *Hallelu-YAH* is particularly

15. Cf. Christian D. Ginsburg, *Introduction to the Masoretico-Critical Edition of the Hebrew Bible* (London: Trinitarian Bible Society, 1897), 367–68. Ginsburg notes that throughout the Hebrew Bible, wherever *YHWH* occurs by itself, it has the vowels of *Adonai* ("Lord"). But when *Adonai YHWH* occur together, *YHWH* has the vowels of *Elohim* ("God").

suitable for opening wide the mouth, dropping the jaw, and loudly shouting God's praise. Try it!

So it should not be surprising that the completed Scriptures conclude with a fourfold use of this universal phrase, originally written in Greek but readily adaptable to any and all families of languages:

After this I heard what sounded like the roar of a great multitude in heaven shouting: "*Hallelu-YAH!* Salvation and glory and power belong to our God." (Rev. 19:1)

"True and just are his judgments. He has condemned the great prostitute who corrupted the earth by her adulteries. He has avenged on her the blood of his servants." And again they shouted: "*Hallelu-YAH!*" (Rev. 19:2–3)

The twenty-four elders and the four living creatures fell down and worshiped God, who was seated on the throne. And they cried: "Amen, *Hallelu-YAH!*" (Rev. 19:4)

Then I heard what sounded like a great multitude, like the roar of rushing waters and like loud peals of thunder, shouting: "*Hallelu-YAH!* For our Lord God Almighty reigns. Let us rejoice and be glad and give him glory! For the wedding of the Lamb has come, and his bride has made herself ready." (Rev. 19:6–7)

By the Lord's good appointments, no one in heaven will have any trouble praising the Lord for his great salvation in his or her mother tongue. All together we will exclaim, "*Hallelu-YAH!*"

The Third Coupling of a Messianic Psalm with a Torah Psalm (Psalms 118–119)

As previously indicated, a messianic psalm in Book V (Ps. 118) stands coupled with the third and longest of the three Torah psalms (Ps. 119; cf. Pss. 1, 19). Just as in Book I messianic Psalm 2 is joined to Psalm 1 as the first Torah psalm, and messianic Psalm 18 is joined to Torah Psalm 19, so in Book V messianic Psalm 118 is coupled with

Torah Psalm 119. As a consequence of this threefold coupling of a Torah psalm with a messianic psalm, the principal point is repeated three times over in the Psalter: both Torah and Messiah are essential for God's people. Law cannot function properly in the life of God's people without Messiah, and Messiah can be properly appreciated only in the context of the Lord's law. Law and gospel must be joined together if God's people are to experience the full "blessed" condition that comes from the Lord (Pss. 1:1; 2:12; 119:1–2).[16]

The Messianic "Cornerstone" of Psalm 118

The similarity of subject matter and mode of expression between messianic Psalms 18 and 118 deserves notice. The title of Psalm 18 refers to the point in time at which the Lord gave his king great victories over all his enemies (Ps. 18:50). Similarly, Psalm 118 vividly depicts the "shouts of joy and victory" in the tents of the righteous over the triumphs of the Messiah (Ps. 118:15). In both psalms, the righteous person is the one rewarded by the Lord. By use of an internal refrain, Psalm 18 repeats this theme:

> The LORD has dealt with me
>> according to my righteousness;
>> according to the cleanness of my hands
> he has rewarded me. (Ps. 18:20)

> The LORD has rewarded me
>> according to my righteousness,
>> according to the cleanness of my hands
> in his sight. (Ps. 18:24)

---

16. Hans-Joachim Kraus, *Theology of the Psalms* (Minneapolis: Augsburg, 1986), 34, presses for a fuller concept of *Torah* than simply "law." He asserts that "under no circumstances" should *Torah* be translated as "law." Though overstating his case, he offers a useful observation by promoting the translation of *Torah* as "instruction": "While 'law' is connected with the impression of something fixed, rigid, and static, instruction arouses the impression of something living, dynamic, in which directions, suggestions, commands, orders, and advice are imparted. The original meaning of Torah as guidance formulated and then orally transmitted by a priest remained preserved even where it refers to commands fixed in writing." Ibid. While Kraus properly enlarges on the significance of Torah, he too rigidly minimizes the value of something "fixed" in the form of a "law."

Similar emphasis appears in Psalm 118. Rejoicing emerges from the tents of the "righteous," the gates of the "righteous" will be opened, and the "righteous" will enter through the gate of the Lord (Ps. 118:15, 19–20).

Additionally, both Psalms 18 and 118 vividly depict deliverance from death (Pss. 18:4–5; 118:17–18). Furthermore, it becomes climactically clear that Messiah, the anointed king, is the focal figure in these two psalms. The Lord gives great victories to "his king," to "his anointed," to "David and his descendants" (Ps. 18:50). With similar emphasis, the messianic king is "the stone the builders rejected" that has become "the cornerstone," and is identified by the messianic designation as "he who comes" (הַבָּא) in the name of the Lord (Ps. 118:22, 26).

The magnificently structured Psalm 118 features multiple participants interacting with three progressive speeches made by a singular figure threatened with death who is finally identified as the messianic "stone" that the builders have rejected. He has become the "head of the corner" or the "chief cornerstone" of the kingdom of God on earth (Ps. 118:22). He is the messianic king of Yahweh's kingdom. The climactic refrain of the psalm appeared earlier when David brought up the ark of the covenant to Jerusalem, symbolizing the union of God's throne with Messiah's throne: "Give thanks to the LORD, for he is good; *his covenant love endures forever*" (Ps. 118:1–4, 29; cf. 1 Chron. 16:34). The poetic structure repeatedly calls on the assembled congregation to respond to their messianic king as his developing circumstance unfolds. First the congregation affirms:

> It is better to take refuge in the LORD
>   than to trust in man.
> It is better to take refuge in the LORD
>   than to trust in princes. (Ps. 118:8–9)

Then they declare:

> The LORD's right hand
>   has worked mightily!
> The LORD's right hand
>   is exalted.

> The LORD's right hand
> has worked mightily! (Ps. 118:15–16)

Then climactically they announce:

> The stone the builders rejected
> has become the chief cornerstone;
> The LORD has done this thing,
> it is marvelous in our eyes.
> This is the day the LORD has made,
> let us rejoice and be glad in it. (Ps. 118:22–24)

When Jesus quoted the words of this psalm regarding the rejection of the chief cornerstone by the builders, the teachers of the law and the chief priests could not avoid identifying themselves with the "builders" who were rejecting their "chief cornerstone." Yet they proceeded to fulfill this prophetic poem about themselves by intensifying their plots to arrest Jesus (Luke 20:17–19).[17]

The Third Torah Psalm (Psalm 119)

The first Torah psalm (Ps. 1) described the two great groupings of people who respond either by loving and obeying the Lord's teachings or by rejecting his Torah and opposing all those who observe its decrees. Psalm 19, the second Torah psalm, presents God's glory as it appears first in the general revelation found in creation (Ps. 19:1–6) and then in the special redemptive revelation of his Word (Ps. 19:7–14).[18] This second Torah psalm designates the COVENANT LORD'S redemptive revelation as "law," "statutes," "precepts," "commands," "fear," and "ordinances." By this variety of terminology, Psalm 19 anticipates the fuller exposition of the role of Torah in the life of God's people as developed in Psalm 119, one hundred psalms later. Though a number

---

17. For a fuller exposition of this psalm by the present author, see O. Palmer Robertson, *Psalms in Congregational Celebration* (Darlington, UK: Evangelical Press, 1995), 341–56.

18. Walter Brueggemann, *The Message of the Psalms: A Theological Commentary* (Minneapolis: Augsburg, 1984), 38, enlarges on the significance of Torah as it functions in closest relation to creation as depicted in Psalm 19: "Thus creation and torah are understood together, the torah articulating God's intention for Israel in the creation."

of psalms refer to the Torah of the Lord, only Psalms 19 and 119 employ all six of these specific terms for *Torah*.

So the three Torah psalms are similar in their terminology and their strategic positions in the Psalter. Yet the overwhelming uniqueness of Psalm 119 cannot be overlooked.[19] Consisting of 176 verses divided into twenty-two stanzas of eight verses each in an alphabetic acrostic, this masterpiece of poetic perfection can be compared with nothing else in the entire book of Psalms for magnitude. With no more than three exceptions, each and every one of the 176 verses hails the incomparable glories of the Lord's Torah, his law, his statutes, his commandments, his ordinances, his testimonies, his Word.[20]

But why? Why this massive memorial to the law of the Lord (not at all intending to suggest that God's law does not deserve every word of praise it receives)? Why here and now in Book V of the Psalter does this unique piece of poetry appear?

As has been indicated, the coupling of Psalm 119 with a distinctively messianic psalm as the major dividing point in Book V explains its literary position. As in the case of the first book of the Psalter, the joining of a messianic psalm with a Torah psalm marks the major dividing point in this last book of the Psalter. But still, the question lingers: Why such an extended discourse in its extremely developed poetic form?

The poem was almost certainly composed for memorization. Its form with eight lines in each stanza following the order of the Hebrew

---

19. Grant, *King as Exemplar*, 171–75, argues that the *I* of Psalm 119 is the king, which has the effect of tying this psalm even more closely to Psalm 118. But the greater likelihood is that the *I* of Psalm 119 corresponds to the "man," the "person," the "*ish*," the "Everyman" of Psalm 1:1: "Blessed is the 'man'" (i.e., "Everyman") who delights in the Torah of Yahweh. By conjoining Everyman's obligation to the Torah in Psalm 1 to Messiah and his rule in Psalm 2, the obligation of Messiah as well as Everyman to observe Torah is effectively established.

20. James Luther Mays, *Psalms*, Interpretation, A Bible Commentary for Teaching and Preaching (Louisville: John Knox Press, 1994), 381–82, notes that Psalm 119 uses a "thematic vocabulary" of eight terms for *Torah*, with a few variations such as "ways," "paths," and "faithfulness." Mays suggests that the psalmist "used the [entire] alphabet to signal completeness and the whole vocabulary to represent comprehensiveness." Ibid., 382. For a brief overview of the eight different terms for "law" in Psalm 119, see Gordon J. Wenham, *Psalms as Torah: Reading Biblical Song Ethically* (Grand Rapids: Baker Academic, 2012), 86–88. In making connection with Deuteronomy, Grant, *King as Exemplar*, 158–59, notes that all the terms used for *Torah* in Psalm 119 appear in Deuteronomy, with one exception. In a single passage, Deuteronomy 4:1–6, five of the eight terms appear.

alphabet would make memorization an achievable task. In addition, as many language groups would have it, dealing with a subject from *A* to *Z* means comprehensive coverage.

But there may be yet more. The time of the composition of Psalm 119, judging by its setting in Book V of the Psalter, points to the age of exile. It was the time when no temple, no sacrifice, no priesthood functioned in faraway Jerusalem. So what are the pious, displaced people to do? How can they carry on with their worship? So far as current historical investigation is concerned, little or nothing is known of the life habits of the exiles in Babylon.[21] Their *modus vivendi* completely eludes us. Yet it is unimaginable that they would live without regulated worship.

Something of a comparable situation has prevailed for many decades, even centuries and millennia after the second destruction of Jerusalem in A.D. 70. For some time, the Romans would not allow a Judean survivor to even enter Jerusalem. Not one stone of the temple had been left on top of another. So what has the Diaspora done to fill the void of no temple, no sacrifices, no priesthood over the past two thousand years?

It did not take long for the dispersed Judeans to find a way. According to rabbinic tradition, the pious substituted Torah for temple. The study of the law took the place of the offering of sacrifice.

Regarding this development, Jewish tradition states:

> The Mishnah (Pe'ah) . . . declares that the study of the Law transcends all things, being greater than the rescue of human life, than the building of the temple, and than the honor of father and mother (Meg. 16b).[22]

> R. Samuel b. Inia stated in the name of Rab: The study of the Torah is more important than the offering of the daily continual sacrifices (b.Erub 63b).[23]

21. Cf. the comments of John Bright, *A History of Israel*, 4th ed. (Louisville: Westminster John Knox Press, 2000), 236: "Of the further fortunes of the exiles we know almost nothing." "A new community did, in fact, begin to emerge, though the details are almost wholly obscure." Ibid., 349.

22. Ludwig Blau, "Torah," in *The Jewish Encyclopedia* (New York: Funk and Wagnalls, 1906), 12:197.

23. Ibid.

According to one Jewish scholar, the exiles who returned from Babylon to Jerusalem soon began to substitute Torah for temple:

> In the course of time the Temple worship, which centered around the sacrificial rites, lost some of its position as the sole means by which the religious and communal life of the nation could find expression. To a considerable extent the center of gravity shifted to the study of the Torah.[24]

It is admittedly impossible to know the exact circumstances surrounding the composition of Psalm 119. Yet given the strong possibility that it was written during the Judean exile in Babylon or shortly thereafter, it may well be that this psalm developed in part as a substitute for worship at the temple in Jerusalem. The Torah took the place of the temple. The study of the law replaced the offering of sacrifice.

From a new covenant perspective, this transition may be perceived as a positive development. The Word replaces the ritual. "Solomon . . . built the house" for the Lord, according to Stephen, one of the first Christian deacons. "However, the Most High does not live in houses made by men. . . . You . . . have received the law . . . but have not kept it" (Acts 7:47–48, 53). So keeping God's law must always have its place above externalized worship practices at the temple.

Thus, it may well be that this poetic edifice of Psalm 119 was a product of Israel's exile that provided a better way of worship than the offering of sacrifices at the temple. Quite interestingly, no mention is made in the 176 verses of Psalm 119 regarding the law as it relates to temple worship, priesthood, or sacrifice. This silence regarding the laws of temple worship could provide a further indicator that the psalm was composed during and for the time of Israel's exile.

In any case, Psalms 118 and 119 were situated to serve as the pivotal point in Book V, just as Psalms 18 and 19 provided a similar structure to Book I. The materials of Book V coming after these two psalms are quite distinctive when compared to the materials before them, as the subsequent analysis may indicate.

24. Shmuel Safrai, "Temple," in *Encyclopedia Judaica* (Jerusalem: Keter Publishing House, 1972), 15:983.

Four Collections in the Second Portion of Book V (Psalms 120–150)

Book V manifests significant evidence of intentional arrangement beyond this pivotal point of the third messianic-Torah psalm coupling. Four distinct groupings of psalms provide the basic structure of this portion of the Psalter.

Fifteen Psalms of Ascents Echoing the Priestly Benediction (Psalms 120–134)

This distinctive collection of psalms vividly anticipates the movement of God's people toward the permanently established focal point of their worship in Mount Zion, in fulfillment of the covenantal promise to David concerning a permanent dwellingplace for God's house.[25] Each of these psalms is entitled "A song of ascents" (שִׁיר הַמַּעֲלוֹת). The phrase has been interpreted as referring to the fifteen steps leading up to the temple in Jerusalem, to a literary connection moving step by step through the fifteen psalms, or to the ascent of pilgrims to Jerusalem, either during the three annual feasts (cf. Deut. 16:16) or as the Israelites returned from exile to their own land (cf. Ps. 126:1). There seems to be no good reason not to understand the phrase as arising out of both the annual pilgrimages to Jerusalem and the return to Jerusalem from the exile. One psalm specifically refers to the "going

---

25. Zenger, in Hossfeld and Zenger, *Psalms 3*, 286–99, offers a number of stimulating observations regarding these Songs of Ascents, usefully analyzing the contributions of other people in relation to his own understanding. These insights include items such as: (1) certain key words in the Psalms of Ascents that repeatedly echo the Aaronic benediction of Numbers 6:24–27, including "may he bless you," "may he keep you," "may he be gracious to you," and "peace" (see the discussion above); (2) the shortness of these psalms, with the exception of Psalm 132, which is less than half the average length of all other psalms; (3) the repetition of liturgical formulas, such as "Maker of heaven and earth," "from now to eternity," and "peace be on Israel"; (4) the extensive use of figures of speech, such as "like a city bound firmly together," "as the eyes of a maid to her mistress," "like a bird from the snare of the fowler," "like those who dream," "like arrows in the hand of a warrior," and "like a weaned child with its mother"; (5) a contrast between God as Sovereign King over the nations as developed in Psalms 45–48 and Yahweh's intimate concern for barren women, children in the home, and brotherly relationships; and (6) the different placement in Qumran of Psalm 119 after Psalms 120–132, so that the end of the people's pilgrimage is not Jerusalem but the law and the sacrifice of "lifting up the lips," so that the Torah becomes their temple.

up" to Jerusalem (Ps. 122:4). An exilic and postexilic editing of the "pilgrim" songs seems evident in view of the inclusion in Book V of psalms clearly composed both during and after the exile (Pss. 137, 126). No mention is made in these fifteen psalms of a king, but numerous references are made to Zion and Jerusalem, which suits well both an exilic and a postexilic setting.

This collection features four Davidic psalms (Pss. 122, 124, 131, 133), one psalm of Solomon (Ps. 127), and one psalm specifically referring to the return after exile (Ps. 126). The suitability of the choice of psalms originating with David but also appropriate for a time during Israel's exile or return is quite remarkable, considering all the psalms of David that could not have functioned in this manner. A suitability for pilgrim recitation is found in their length, which is shorter than the typical psalm. At the same time, the content of each selection suits both David's day and the journey to Jerusalem of later generations. Psalm 122:1 declares, "I rejoiced with those who said to me, 'Let us go to the house of the LORD.'" Who could say these words with greater fervor than David, the one who danced "with all his might" before the ark as he brought it up to Jerusalem (2 Sam. 6:12–15)? Who more than David could rejoice when the community recognized his "place" on Mount Zion as the proper location for the building of the "house of the LORD"? Yet returning exiles must have been equally ecstatic as they approached the holy city. Psalm 124 testifies, "If the LORD had not been on our side . . . , they would have swallowed us alive . . . . We have escaped like a bird out of the fowler's snare" (Ps. 124:1–7). These words encapsulate the bulk of David's lifetime experience; yet they also capture the relief of those who "escaped" from exile. Psalm 131:1 declares, "My heart is not proud . . . . I have stilled and quieted my soul . . . like a weaned child with its mother." This sensitive imagery of childlike trust leads to the strong admonition, "O Israel, put your hope in the LORD both now and forevermore" (Ps. 131:3). King David was constantly required to put his hope only in the Lord, which also had to be the posture of those who ventured from exile. Psalm 133:1, 3 exclaims, "How good and pleasant it is when brothers live together in unity! . . . It is as if the dew of Hermon were falling on Mount Zion." For David, the unity of Hermon to the extreme north with Jerusalem to the south must have been first among his priorities as the king responsible for uniting peoples separated by years of bitter tribal warfare. At the same time, unity in a restored community after decades of scattering would be among the greatest blessings that could be imagined for a people returning from exile.

One biblical scholar, laboring years before current efforts to discover structures within the Psalms, notes several things about the refined organization of this collection of fifteen psalms (Pss. 120–134):

> The whole is grouped around Psalm 127, which was composed by Solomon, which stands in the middle between the first and the last of the pilgrim poems. On both sides there stands a heptade [a grouping of seven] of pilgrim songs, consisting of two psalms composed by David, and five new ones, which have no name. . . . Each heptade contains the name of *Yahweh* twenty-four times.[26]

This arrangement of fifteen individual psalms in a symmetrical form with seven psalms balancing one another on either side of a centralized focal psalm cannot be purely accidental, any more than the weights at either extremity of a tightrope walker's pole "just happen" to balance one another. The intricacies display the care of a final editor of the Psalter in determining the precise composition of the book. The placement of Psalm 127 at the pinnacle of a fifteen-psalm arrangement may be regarded as a significant structural factor of the Psalter that deserves further exploration. The excursus at the conclusion of this chapter examines several possible "poetic pyramids" similar to this one that appear in the various books of the Psalter.

This precise placing of a definitive psalm may be clearly seen at other critical moments in the Psalter, particularly at the "seams" where the various books of the Psalter are joined.[27] The only other psalm "by Solomon" appears just at the end point of Book II (Ps. 72) with its summation of the extension of Messiah's kingdom to include all

---

26. Ernst Wilhelm Hengstenberg, *Commentary on the Psalms* (Edinburgh: T&T Clark, 1954), 3:409.

27. Cf. Gerald Henry Wilson, *The Editing of the Hebrew Psalter* (Chico, CA: Scholars Press, 1985), 208, who notes that the occurrence of "royal" psalms at the "seams" connecting books in the Psalter has "all the indications of intentional arrangement."

kings and kingdoms of the earth. In a similar way, the editor of the Psalter strategically positions the one grand psalm of Moses as the opening hymn of Book IV (Ps. 90). There it stands as the perpetual response to the depressed conclusion of Book III, in which the crown of David's descendants has been cast to the dust: "O Lord, *you* have been our dwellingplace through all generations" (Ps. 90:1). Kings and kingdoms may wax and wane, even the king and kingdom of Israel. But the Lord remains as his people's permanent dwellingplace through all generations.

Not only the placement of Psalm 127 but also the substance of this short five-verse psalm underscores its focal significance. This psalm speaks of the "house" that Yahweh builds, the "city" that Yahweh guards, and the "sons" that are Yahweh's reward (Ps. 127:1, 3). Placed deliberately at the pinnacle of the fifteen Psalms of Ascents, the principal terms of this psalm must be interpreted "by the interest of the collection."[28] So the "house" to which this psalm refers is the house of the Lord, as specified in Psalms 122:1 and 134:1. The "city" of this psalm is not simply any city that any person proposes to build, but Jerusalem the locale of the Solomonic temple, as mentioned in Psalm 122:3. In similar fashion, the "sons" that are a heritage of the Lord are first of all the "sons of David," as more fully developed in Psalm 132:11–12, another member of the Psalms of Ascents collection:

> Yahweh swore an oath to David . . . :
>
> . . . .
>   "If your sons keep my covenant
>   and the statutes I teach them,
>   then their sons will sit on your throne
>   for ever and ever."

The strong rehearsal of the two principal elements of the Davidic covenant in Psalm 132 must not be minimized. This psalm vivifies the pilgrimage to Zion by a clear echo of the directive given to the Israelites in their wilderness trek toward their ultimate destination at Yahweh's own "restingplace":

28. Mays, *Psalms*, 402.

Rise, O Yahweh, and come to your restingplace,
you and the ark of your might. (Ps. 132:8; cf. Num. 10:35–36)

This psalm is replete with references to both the dynasty of David and the dwellingplace of Yahweh. The ultimate merger of David's rule with Yahweh's rule receives climactic expression. Yahweh's house, his dwelling, his restingplace, is the locale of David's perpetual kingship. "Here" is the very place where the Lord will establish a "horn" for David, a "lamp" for his anointed one, and a "crown" for his head— the very "crown" that had previously been "defiled . . . in the dust" (Ps. 132:17–18; cf. Ps. 89:39). Any effort to say that the Davidic covenant has failed because of the exile could hardly have considered this testimony in the last half of the final book of the Psalter in this majestic collection of Songs of Ascents.

Solomon is credited by its title with the composition of Psalm 127, the pinnacle psalm of these fifteen Psalms of Ascents.[29] In the psalm, he speaks about the completion of these two building projects, the "house" and the "sons," which correspond to God's *dwellingplace* and David's *dynasty*. The psalmist clearly credits Yahweh and Yahweh alone with the success of both endeavors. The same principle applies to guarding the "city," which in this case would be the Lord's chosen city of Jerusalem. If he chooses not to guard the city, as in the case of Israel's exile, all the armaments in the world are in vain. The

29. The distinctive term for "beloved" (יְדִידָה) that appears in the phrase "he gives his beloved sleep" (Ps. 127:2c) occurs only four times in the Psalms. Outside the Psalter, it refers to little Benjamin as the "beloved of Yahweh" (Deut. 33:12), to the nation of Israel as the Lord's "Beloved" (Isa. 5:1; Jer. 11:15), and to Solomon who received this special name from the Lord as his "beloved" (2 Sam. 12:25). In the plural form, it occurs twice in the Psalter in reference to the people whom the Lord loves (Ps. 60:7; 108:7). It also refers in the plural to the "lovely" dwellingplaces of the Lord (Ps. 84:1). It has been proposed that the attributing of Psalm 127 to Solomon was based on the assumption that this term in the psalm applied specifically to him. Franz Delitzsch, *Biblical Commentary on the Psalms* (Grand Rapids: Eerdmans, 1959), 3:291, says that the "By Solomon" heading was added later because an allusion was found in the phrase from Psalm 127:2 (שֵׁנָא יִתֵּן לִידִידוֹ—"he gives his beloved sleep") to Solomon's designation as "Jedidiah" (יְדִידְיָה—"Beloved") by the prophet Nathan, "because the LORD loved him" (2 Sam. 12:25). The connection with Solomon is quite likely, particularly since this designation is given to him by the Lord. In addition, the concerns of Psalm 127 for the "house," the "city," and the "sons" all have immediate relevance to Solomon as David's successor, with the expectation that he would build the house of the Lord and provide for his dynastic successors.

permanence of the dwellingplace of the Lord and his Messiah hinges altogether on the Lord's working.

This same principle applies to the "building" of the perpetual dynasty of David. "Sons," acknowledges Solomon, "are a heritage from the LORD," "children a reward from him" (Ps. 127:3). The covenant promise of sons seated on David's throne must forever be perceived as the working of God's grace.

A further application of this psalm to an ordinary domestic scene is perfectly appropriate. The Creator always manifests his concern for the humbler elements of human life. In the immediately preceding psalm, the commonplace activity of sowing and reaping (Ps. 126:5–6) relates directly to the larger drama of international exile and restoration (Ps. 126:1–4). Yet these everyday elements find fullest realization in the macrocosmic realm of Yahweh's great work as Redeemer.

Eight of these fifteen Psalms of Ascents specifically mention "Zion" or "Jerusalem" (Pss. 122, 125, 126, 128, 129, 132, 133, 134). In addition, the reference to the "hills" in Psalm 121 is very likely to the hills surrounding the city of Jerusalem. This concentrated focus on the exaltation of Mount Zion and Jerusalem reinforces the centrality of the Davidic covenant as it appears in the Psalter from beginning to end. A place for the Lord's throne alongside David's throne on Mount Zion in Jerusalem pervades the Psalms as a key factor of their message.[30]

At the same time, the paucity of references to "Zion" and "Jerusalem" in the first segment of Book V (Pss. 107–117) may be noted. The "sanctuary" and "Zion" are each mentioned only once, and both instances occur in psalms attributed to David, which is understandable (Ps. 108:7; 110:2). "Jerusalem" is also mentioned once in a psalm not attributed to David (Ps. 116:19). But the few references in the collection of Book V before pivotal Psalms 118 and 119 contrast significantly with the pervasive character of these references in the second portion of Book V (Pss. 120–150).

Quite remarkable is the permeation of this collection of psalms by four key phrases from the classic Aaronic benediction dating back to the

---

30. See Mays, *Psalms*, 386, for insightful suggestions regarding "some recurring features that are consistent with their use by pilgrims."

days of Moses (Num. 6:24–27).[31] As the people approach the restored temple, the wording in twelve of the fifteen Songs of Ascents reminds the pilgrims of the priestly benediction that awaits them as they make their trek to Jerusalem.[32] The four key phrases are "may he bless you"; "may he keep you"; "may he be gracious to you"; and "[may he give you] peace." Their appearance in these Songs of Ascents is as follows:

"May Yahweh Bless You" (יְבָרֶכְךָ יְהוָה—Numbers 6:24)

The exact wording of this ancient priestly blessing recurs twice in the Songs of Ascents. The psalmist employs these very words to declare Yahweh's blessing from Zion for all the days of his people's life (Ps. 128:5). This blessing from Zion comes from none other than Yahweh, the Maker of heaven and earth (Ps. 134:3). In addition, unity among Yahweh's people is compared to the dew of Mount Hermon falling on Mount Zion, which is where Yahweh commands the blessing (Ps. 133:3). In each of these cases, the blessing specifically comes "from Zion," where the priests would stand ready to bless with the threefold pronouncement of the Name, *Yahweh*.

"And Keep You" (וְיִשְׁמְרֶךָ—Numbers 6:24)

Psalm 121 is for all intents and purposes an exposition of this single phrase from the priestly benediction: "and keep you."[33] Yahweh is "the one keeping you" (Ps. 121:3). He is "the one keeping Israel" (Ps. 121:4); he "keeps you" (Ps. 121:5); he will "keep you from all harm" and will "keep your soul" (Ps. 121:7); Yahweh "will keep your going and coming from now unto eternity" (Ps. 121:8). Six times in five verses the psalmist uses the same key word from Numbers 6:24 to affirm that Yahweh "keeps" his people.

31. Cf. the brief but stimulating article of Leon J. Liebreich, "The Songs of Ascents and the Priestly Blessing," *Journal of Biblical Literature* 74 (1955): 33–36. Many of the observations in this section are taken from Liebreich's article.

32. Ibid., 33n1, notes that Franz Delitzsch in his commentary had observed this connection in certain isolated verses of the Songs of Ascents.

33. The connection with the priestly benediction is obscured by some translations, which render the term as "watch over you." But the word is the same as found in the priestly benediction, "keep you."

"And Be Gracious to You" (וִיחֻנֶּךָ—Numbers 6:25)

The root for "to be gracious" serves as a key concept in two of the Songs of Ascents. The eyes of the people look to Yahweh their God "until he is gracious to them" (Ps. 123:2). They repeatedly plead, "Be gracious to us, O Yahweh, be gracious to us" (Ps. 123:3). In desperation, the psalmist pleads for the Lord to "be gracious" in response to his prayers (Ps. 130:2).

"And Give You Shalom [Peace]" (וְיָשֵׂם לְךָ שָׁלוֹם—Numbers 6:26)

The term *shalom*, representing the blessing of wholeness of life in peace, occurs seven times in the Songs of Ascents. The collection opens with a recognition of the difficulty of achieving peace in this present world order. Too long the psalmist has lived among people who "hate peace." He is for "peace," but they are for war (Ps. 120:6–7). He encourages people to "pray for the peace of Jerusalem" even as he offers his own twofold prayer for its peace (Ps. 122:6–8). He declares Yahweh's peace on Israel (Ps. 125:5). An ultimate blessing of peace can even reach across generations (Ps. 128:6).

So twelve of the fifteen Songs of Ascents include a representation of at least one of the four different elements of the ancient priestly benediction. The omission of any reference to the fifth and sixth elements, "make his face shine upon you" and "turn his face toward you," is something of a mystery. It could be that because the *shekinah* never returned to Israel's restoration temple, the psalmist concluded that this benediction could not be pronounced legitimately. Because Yahweh's presence had not been manifested in the postexilic temple as in the case of Moses' tabernacle and Solomon's temple,[34] the priest could not pronounce the blessing of God's face shining on them. In any case, this collection of Songs of Ascents is made even more meaningful when the approach of the pilgrims to Mount Zion and Jerusalem is connected to the restored priestly blessing that they could expect to receive upon arrival.[35]

---

34. Ex. 40:34; 2 Chron. 5:13–14.
35. Liebreich, "Songs of Ascents," 36, proposes that the three psalms added to this collection that do not specifically include any of these benedictory words (Pss. 124, 126,

Three Transitional Psalms of Historical Recollection (Psalms 135–137)

These three psalms follow the fifteen Psalms of Ascents (Pss. 120–134) and lead to the fourth and final collection of psalms attributed to David (Pss. 138–145). The first two of these psalms offer praise and thanksgiving to the Lord for creation (Ps. 136:5–9), redemption (Pss. 135:4, 8–12; 136:10–22), and providence (Pss. 135:6–7; 136:25). The third of these transitional psalms recalls the sad days when the people of God languished "by the rivers of Babylon" (Ps. 137:1).

Psalm 135 begins and ends with *Hallelu-YAH*, the distinctive ejaculatory exaltation of the COVENANT LORD found almost exclusively in Book V. It is the only psalm that stands alone outside a grouping of this type of psalm. In addition, it is the only psalm with *Hallelu-YAH* appearing in the body of the psalm rather than exclusively at the psalm's beginning and/or ending (Ps. 135:3). The summons to "you who minister in the house of the LORD" (Ps. 135:2) echoes the admonition in the immediately preceding psalm to "you ... who minister by night in the house of the LORD" (Ps. 134:1). Beginning with the Lord's choice of Israel as his treasured possession (Ps. 135:4), the psalmist rehearses God's work in providence (Ps. 135:6–7), in the exodus (Ps. 135:8–9), in the conquest (Ps. 135:10–12), and in his superiority over all worthless idols (Ps. 135:15–18). This psalm concludes with a threefold call to the house of Israel, the house of Aaron, and all God-fearers to praise the Lord from Zion and Jerusalem (Ps. 135:19–21).

Psalm 135 represents a reformulation of Psalms 113 and 115, both of which belong to the initial grouping of *Hallelu-YAH* psalms that conclude the first portion of Book V. The first adapted portion is taken from Psalm 113, which is the final psalm of the first triad in this earlier collection of *Hallelu-YAH* psalms (Pss. 111–113):

Hallelu-YAH!
Praise, O servants of Yahweh.
Praise the name of Yahweh. (Ps. 113:1)

---

131) might have been inserted to bring the number to fifteen, in accord with the fifteen words of the Aaronic benediction.

Except for a reversal in the order of phrases, the introductory verse of Psalm 135 is identical:

Hallelu-YAH!
Praise the name of Yahweh.
Praise, O servants of Yahweh. (Ps. 135:1)

The second adapted portion is taken from Psalm 115, which is the opening psalm of the second triad in this earlier collection of *Hallelu-YAH* psalms (Pss. 115–117). The adapted materials in Psalm 135 abbreviate the mockery of the various inanimate limbs of the idols, omitting reference to noses, hands, and feet. Rather than noting that idols cannot "utter a sound" (Ps. 115:7b), Psalm 135 underscores their lifelessness by substituting the more dramatic "there is no breath in their mouth" (Ps. 135:17).

This latter psalm expresses an even stronger confidence in Yahweh's redemptive purposes. In Psalm 115, the unidentified poet responds to a mocking gibe of the nations: "Where is their God?" (Ps. 115:2). He answers with an affirmation regarding his God's locale in heaven:

Our Elohim is in heaven;
he does whatever pleases him. (Ps. 115:3)

The context of Psalm 135 is different, and the response of the psalmist different. No one from the "nations" in Psalm 135 asks, "Where is your God?" Instead of affirming that their Elohim is (merely) in heaven (Ps. 115), the psalmist now affirms his confidence in Yahweh his COVENANT LORD with greater fullness:

I know that Yahweh is great,
    that our Lord is greater than all gods.
Yahweh does whatever pleases him,
    in the heavens and on the earth,
    in the seas and all their depths. (Ps. 135:5–6)

He then expands on this affirmation by a strong remembrance of the way in which Yahweh "struck down the firstborn" of men and animals

219

in Egypt, even presuming to address Egypt directly (Ps. 135:8–9). Of all the passages in the Psalms referring to Egypt, in these verses alone does the psalmist turn and speak directly to this foreign nation: "He sent signs and wonders in *your* midst, O Egypt" (בְּתוֹכֵכִי מִצְרָיִם). Could it be that the psalmist stands among those who have recently returned to the land of Palestine, and casts his eye toward Israel's ancient oppressor, reminding the Egyptians of the earlier time when Yahweh subdued their mighty pharaoh by the repeated wonders of the plagues? The psalmist next turns his gaze toward Transjordan and reminds those people how the Lord had once destroyed "Sihon king of the Amorites" and "Og king of Bashan," as well as all the kings of Canaan (Ps. 135:10–12).

In exposing the consequences of idolatry and the importance of trusting only the Lord, Psalm 135 quotes the words of the earlier psalm:

> Those who make them
>> will be like them,
>> and so will all who *trust* in them. (Ps. 115:8; cf. Ps. 135:18)

But in making direct application to its readers, Psalm 135 carefully alters the wording of Psalm 115. Instead of a threefold admonition addressed to the house of Israel, the house of Aaron, and fearers of Yahweh to *trust* in the Lord, Psalm 135 admonishes the house of Israel, the house of Aaron, *the house of Levi*, and fearers of Yahweh to *praise* the Lord (Ps. 115:9–11; cf. Ps. 135:19–20). Beyond *trust* is *praise*. The final verse of Psalm 135 indicates that the altered situation of God's people should inspire their praise:

> Praise be to the LORD
>> *from Zion,*
>> to him who dwells
>>> *in Jerusalem.* (Ps. 135:21)

The psalmist now resides with his people in Zion, in Jerusalem. Quite dramatic is the statement that Yahweh once more "dwells in Jerusalem" and that his people are to bless him "from Zion."

One further factor of Psalm 135 structure must be observed in relation to the first collection of *Hallelu-YAH* psalms in Book V (Pss. 111–117). Again, this earlier grouping consists of two triads of *Hallelu-YAH* psalms balanced around a psalm without *Hallelu-YAHs* that celebrates the exodus from Egypt (Ps. 114). Now Psalm 135 opens with an adaptation from Psalm 113, the final psalm of the first *Hallelu-YAH* triad of Book V (Pss. 111–113), and closes with an adaptation from Psalm 115, the beginning psalm of the second *Hallelu-YAH* triad of Book V (Pss. 115–117). In a further point of parallelism, the middle section of Psalm 135 rehearses the events of the exodus from Egypt (Ps. 135:8–9), just as Psalm 114 does in its function as the center of the two *Hallelu-YAH* triads (cf. Ps. 114:1).

As a consequence, Psalm 135 serves as a concentrated mirror of the initial collection of *Hallelu-YAH* psalms of Book V in all three of its segments. In addition, Psalm 135 with its multiple use of the term *Hallelu-YAH* serves as a connecting link to the climactic finale of the entire book of Psalms (Pss. 146–150). As previously indicated, only in Psalm 135 is the *Hallelu-YAH* exclamation found within the body of the psalm (Ps. 135:3). All other appearances of *Hallelu-YAH* occur either at the beginning or at the end of a psalm. Not without reason, Psalm 135 has been included in some Jewish traditions as "The Great *Hallel*," in comparison with "The *Hallel* of Egypt" in Psalms 113–118.

So some progress appears to be represented in this arrangement of the Psalter. Instead of continuing in exile, the people of God have returned to their native land in accord with the promises of God. In the complex structures of the Psalter, not all subsequent psalms will assume this different perspective. But clearly, the blessing of the Lord now comes once more "from Zion" and "Jerusalem."

Psalm 136 is arranged antiphonally according to the general instructions previously prescribed by David.[36] This psalm begins

---

36. Note the reference to the antiphonal reading of the Psalms going back to the instructions of David, but still practiced five hundred years later in the postexilic period: "And the leaders of the Levites . . . stood opposite them to give praise and thanksgiving, one section responding to the other, as prescribed by David the man of God" (Neh. 12:24).

and ends with a summons to give thanks to the Lord, "for his covenant love endures forever" (Ps. 136:1, 26). The psalm surveys the faithfulness of the Lord's love in the process of creation (Ps. 136:5–9), in the various phases of redemption (Ps. 136:10–24), and in providence (Ps. 136:25). The final circumstance of the redeemed presumes the nation's return from exile. The Lord has "remembered us in our low estate" and has "freed us from our enemies" (Ps. 136:23–24). Each new remembrance of God's faithfulness calls for an antiphonal response by a repeated refrain that occurs twenty-six times over: "His covenant love endures forever."[37] This phrase reminds of the Lord's faithfulness through the ages, even up to the time of the restoration of the Israelites to their land after the exile (cf. Ezra 3:10–11).

Psalm 137 presents the plaint of Israel's captives "by the rivers of Babylon." But why, it may be asked, should this psalm deal specifically with Israel in exile some several psalms after a previous psalm has dealt just as specifically with the restoration after exile (Ps. 126)? Why should a chronological order be so obviously ignored by the organizer of the Psalter?

In response to this legitimate question, it may first be observed that Psalm 126 has been appropriately placed among the Psalms of Ascents. The "restoring to Zion" of the opening phrase of Psalm 126 properly suits the liturgical framework of these Psalms of Ascents in view of the return of the Israelites to Zion after their exile. Psalm 137's depiction of a people in exile would not be a suitable addition to a collection of psalms focusing on pilgrimage to Jerusalem. Clearly, the prevailing consideration of the Psalter's arrangement is not primarily chronological but biblical-theological.

From a positive perspective, Psalm 137 appears as the third and final member of this triad of psalms of historical recollection that provide a transition between the Psalms of Ascents (Pss. 120–134) and the final Davidic collection (Pss. 138–145). This placement of Psalm 137

---

37. This antiphonal arrangement of a significant portion of many of the psalms achieves cosmic dimensions in Psalm 148, where heaven (vv. 1–6) and earth (vv. 7–12) praise the Lord antiphonally. A recapturing of this feature of the Psalter could aid greatly in the revival of worship practices in the universal church today.

may be best understood by considering its role as an introduction to the final collection of Davidic psalms (Pss. 138–145), which have been appropriately saved for the penultimate position in the Psalter.

In Psalm 137, God's people are situated "by the rivers of Babylon" (Ps. 137:1). Yet even though the people have been banished from their devastated city, Jerusalem and Zion remain prominently as the perpetual center of Israel's life:

> If I forget you, O Jerusalem,
>> may my right hand forget its skill.
> May my tongue cling to the roof of my mouth
>> if I do not remember you,
>> if I do not consider Jerusalem my highest joy. (Ps. 137:5–6)

It may be remembered that only a small remnant numbering a total of approximately forty-nine thousand responded positively to the decree of Cyrus that the Judean captives could return to their native land (Ezra 2:64–65). The great majority of Israelites chose to remain in Babylon, and were admonished by the prophet Zechariah to "flee Babylon" (Zech. 2:6–7). In this context, the psalmist reminds the people of the sadness associated with their exile from the land specially promised to them (Ps. 137:1). Above all else, they must not forget Jerusalem (Ps. 137:5–6).

Jerusalem was repeatedly called "the City of David" (2 Sam. 5:7, 9; 6:10, 12, 16; 1 Kings 2:10; 8:1; 9:24; 1 Chron. 11:5, 7; 15:1, 29; 2 Chron. 5:2; 24:16; Isa. 22:9). It was the personally chosen locale for David's own residence as well as the Lord's permanent dwelling-place. This key feature of the Davidic covenant retained its position of prominence throughout the Psalter. Though Jerusalem is currently envisioned as being totally overpowered by her overlords, this last psalm that precedes the Davidic collection declares Jerusalem's ultimate enemy, the "daughter of Babylon," to be "doomed to destruction" (Ps. 137:8). Fitting it is, then, for this psalm to anticipate the final collection of Davidic psalms to be employed as proper expressions for a people struggling with their perpetual enemies, though with the ultimate expectation of deliverance.

The Fourth and Final Collection of Davidic Psalms
(Psalms 138–145)

This special collection of psalms attributed to David is appropriately reserved for the penultimate position in the book of Psalms. In contrast with the earlier Davidic collections in Books I and II, only one of these psalms refers to a specific life experience of David, "when he was in the cave" (Ps. 142 title), which is a rather general notation indicating a state of displacement for David similar to Israel's situation in exile.

But why are these psalms of David reserved for the final book of the Psalter? Why were they not included along with the previous collections of Davidic psalms in Books I and II? Why, indeed, were these particular psalms of David chosen as the last collection of his psalms, and not some others? What sense does it make to reintroduce these perpetual "enemies" of David when the Psalter has already declared in Book IV, "*Yahweh Malak*" (Pss. 93:1; 96:10; 97:1; 99:1), and repeated *Hallelu-YAH*s have been loudly shouted in the earlier portion of Book V (Pss. 111–117)?

Perhaps the final editor of the Psalms wanted to retain a strong dose of realism at the very end of the book. It may well be that God is established as King in Zion, and that Yahweh rules the nations. Yet the tension between the *already* and the *not yet* must be fully acknowledged. The final blow of destruction for the enemy has not yet been struck. The struggles that David had in bringing forth the messianic kingdom continue until today. Even in the midst of victories, including the prospect of restoration after exile, the angst continues. So the editor of the Psalter is compelled to include this final collection of Davidic psalms for the sake of the well-being of God's people in every subsequent generation.

In any case, these specific psalms are suitable to the final phase of the Psalter collection. During the days of Israel's exile, the Psalter most likely began to take on its final form. Given this historical and biblical-theological setting, psalms appropriate for application to the period of Israel's exile properly constitute this final Davidic collection. While no good reason exists to deny their Davidic authorship, these psalms are simultaneously suitable for the time of Israel's exile as

224

well as for the period of their original composition. This is, after all, the manner in which the church as well as individual believers have applied the Psalms to their various historical situations across the ages.

Indicators of Appropriateness for an Exilic Application of These Final Davidic Psalms

Insight into the appropriateness of these final Davidic psalms in relation to Israel's exile becomes clearer through noting certain distinctive phrases:

1. Psalm 141:2 reads:

> May my prayer before you
> be *like* incense;
> may the lifting up of my hands
> be *like* the evening sacrifice. (Ps. 141:2)

For those living in the context of new covenant realities, this comparison of prayer to incense and sacrifice might not appear so remarkable. Yet surprisingly, of the many references to sacrifice in the Psalms, only a very few passages possibly liken prayer to sacrifice. "Sacrifices of righteousness" (Ps. 4:5) might refer to morally righteous actions as sacrifices, though the phrase could call for the offering of literal sacrifices in conformity to the law, or even sacrifices offered by a righteous person.[38] The "sacrifice" of a "broken spirit" is described as being acceptable to God (Ps. 51:17). The psalmist asks the Lord to accept the "freewill offerings" of his mouth (Ps. 119:108), but this psalm also gives significant evidence of being exilic in origin. Indeed, obedience to God is presented as being more desirable than sacrifice (Ps. 40:6–8; cf. 1 Sam. 15:22; Isa. 1:11; Jer. 6:20; Hos. 6:6; Amos 5:21–24; Mic. 6:6–8). But these passages do not describe this desired obedience as an actual "sacrifice." Elsewhere in the old covenant Scriptures outside the Psalter, two passages from the Prophets could allude to spiritual sacrifices. Jonah refers to his "song of thanksgiving"

---

38. Cf. Bruce K. Waltke and James M. Houston, *The Psalms as Christian Worship* (Grand Rapids: Eerdmans, 2010), 237.

as a "sacrifice" (Jonah 2:9). At the very end of the old covenant era, the prophet Malachi refers to incense brought in the Lord's name from the rising of the sun to its setting (Mal. 1:11). But even he might have been anticipating actual material sacrifices.[39]

So specific comparisons of prayer to sacrifice in the Psalms are rare if not nonexistent. Yet this likening of prayer to sacrifice in Psalm 141:2 suits perfectly a situation in which the temple in Jerusalem has been destroyed and material sacrifice cannot be offered. Prayer must substitute for sacrifice in the context of exile. At the same time, by his exclusion from the possibility of approach to the temple/tabernacle complex, David could also be perceived as praying in this same way.

2. Psalm 142:5 declares, "You are . . . *my portion* in the land of the living." This imagery of God's being the portion of his people finds expression only rarely in Scripture. The Lord is the "portion" of Israel's priests instead of a specific block of territory (Num. 18:20). The concept appears occasionally in the Psalms (cf. Pss. 16:5; 73:26; 119:57). But in a distinctive way, of necessity the Lord must be the "portion" of a people driven from their land into exile. This fact is underscored by the book of Lamentations when, in the midst of Judah's devastation by the Babylonians, the message is proclaimed: "The LORD is my portion; therefore I will wait for him" (Lam. 3:24). Again, David in exile may be conceived as praying in this same manner.

3. Psalm 143:3 employs a striking phrase to express the despair of the psalmist: "You have made me dwell in darkness like those long dead" (הוֹשִׁיבַנִי בְמַחֲשַׁכִּים כְּמֵתֵי עוֹלָם). This distinctive phrase appears in only one other passage in the Old Testament. The book of Lamentations expresses grief over Israel's exile by this identical phrasing, though with a slight difference in word order: "In darkness you have made me dwell like those long dead" (בְּמַחֲשַׁכִּים הוֹשִׁיבַנִי כְּמֵתֵי עוֹלָם—Lam. 3:6). As a consequence, Psalm 143 may be read as an appropriate expression of the Israelites in the extremities of their exile, as well as of David in his days of despair.

4. Psalm 144:5–8 calls for a manifestation of God's redemptive powers similar to David's descriptions (2 Sam. 22:8–20) as the only

---

39. References to "spiritual" sacrifices in the New Testament occur much more frequently. They may be found in Rom. 12:1; Eph. 5:2; Phil. 2:17; 4:18; Heb. 9:26; 10:10, 12, 14; 13:16; 1 Peter 2:5; 1 John 2:2; 4:10.

hope for deliverance from "foreigners." This plea for divine intervention finds emphasis through poetic repetition:

Deliver me and rescue me
from the mighty waters,
from the hands of "foreigners" (מִיַּד בְּנֵי־נֵכָר)
whose mouths are full of lies,
whose right hands are deceitful. (Ps. 144:7–8)

Deliver me and rescue me
from the hands of "foreigners" (מִיַּד בְּנֵי־נֵכָר)
whose mouths are full of lies,
whose right hands are deceitful. (Ps. 144:11)

In the psalm just preceding this final collection of Davidic psalms,
Israel's captives in Babylon exclaim, "How can we sing the LORD's
songs in a 'foreign' land?" (עַל אַדְמַת נֵכָר—Ps. 137:4). While Psalm 144
is attributed to David, this distinctive reference to "foreigners" makes
it simultaneously appropriate for rehearsal in a time of exile.[40]

The fact that four of the first seven of these final Davidic psalms
contain distinctive phrasings appropriate to the time of Israel's exile
as well as David in flight could provide a clue to the reason for
their position in the Psalter. Since the final form of the Psalter probably took shape in the time of Israel's exile and restoration, both
temporal and biblical-theological reasons existed for positioning
these specific psalms just before the Psalm-book's *Hallelu-YAH* finale
(Pss. 146–150).

The Placement of Acrostic Psalm 145 as the Last of the Davidic Psalms

The reason for the placement of Psalm 145 as the last of this
fourth Davidic collection appears in its title. Not a single other of

---

40. A totally different perspective on "foreigners" is found in the first collection of
Davidic psalms (Book I, Pss. 3–41). After the Lord had delivered David from all his enemies,
he declared: "Foreigners cringe before me. They all lose heart; they come trembling from
their strongholds" (Ps. 18:44–45).

David's seventy-two psalms is called "a psalm of praise," as the title of Psalm 145 indicates. This last Davidic psalm has been set in its place in preparation for the final crescendo of praise in the Psalter. The acrostic nature of the psalm underscores its significance in the structure of Book V. It is the last of four acrostic psalms in Book V, and completely regular in following the alphabet except that the letter *nun* is omitted.[41] For the first time since Book I, a psalm specifically indicated as Davidic hails Yahweh as King (Ps. 145:1). The psalm underscores this kingship of Yahweh by a fourfold reference to his kingdom at the focal point of the psalm (Ps. 145:11, 12, 13 [2×]), and interestingly finds its echo on the lips of mighty King Nebuchadnezzar of Babylon, who experienced the glory of Yahweh's kingdom as greater than his own:

> His kingdom is an eternal kingdom;
> His dominion endures from generation to generation. (Ps. 145:13;
>   cf. Dan. 4:3b)

In a glorious "generational antiphony" that lifts this psalm above a single moment frozen in redemptive history, future generations are expected to respond antiphonally to David's praise:

> One generation will commend your works to another;
>   *they* will tell of your mighty acts.
> *They* will speak of the glorious splendor of your majesty,
>   and *I* will meditate on your wonderful works.
> *They* will tell of the power of your awesome works,
>   and *I* will proclaim your great deeds.
> *They* will celebrate your abundant goodness
>   and joyfully sing of your righteousness. (Ps. 145:4–7)

Four times over, the psalmist (David) refers to "all" that the Lord has made, in anticipation of a final summons for all creation to praise the Lord:

41. The effort of the LXX to supply the missing letter is not convincing. Hengstenberg, *Psalms*, 3:535, makes a good case for a threefold division of the psalm with seven verses for each section.

He has compassion
  on all he has made.
  All you have made
shall praise you. (Ps. 145:9–10)

The LORD is . . . loving toward all he has made (Ps. 145:13b)

The LORD is . . . loving toward all he has made (Ps. 145:17b)

The last verse of this final Davidic collection anticipates the climax of the entire Psalter: "Let every creature praise his holy name for ever and ever" (Ps. 145:21). Its obvious echo appears in the closing words of the book of Psalms: "Let everything that has breath praise the LORD" (Ps. 150:6). For these several reasons, the positioning of Psalm 145 as the final Davidic psalm of the Psalter, appearing immediately before the finale of praise (Pss. 146–150), is altogether appropriate.

The *Hallelu-YAH* Finale (Psalms 146–150)

This climactic grouping consists of five psalms, each beginning and ending with *Hallelu-YAH*. These five psalms form the *Hallelu-YAH* finale of the book of Psalms.[42] Just before these five *Hallelu-YAH* psalms, two psalms of David first describe the Lord as the One who subdues peoples under messianic King David (Ps. 144:1, 2c) and then exalts the Lord himself as the King whose kingdom is an everlasting kingdom, and whose dominion endures through all generations (Ps. 145:1, 13a).

This concept of God as King appears in the most ancient traditions of God's people. In the Song of the Sea, Moses declares:

Yahweh will reign as King
  forever and ever [יְהוָה יִמְלֹךְ לְעֹלָם וָעֶד]. (Ex. 15:18)[43]

---

42. Frank-Lothar Hossfeld and Eric Zenger, *Psalms 2: A Commentary on Psalms 51–100* (Minneapolis: Fortress Press, 2005), 1, speak of Psalms 146–150 as "a grand hymnic finale."

43. See also Num. 23:21; Deut. 33:5. Despite the apparently ancient character of all three of these poetic affirmations of the kingship of Yahweh, Kraus, *Theology*, 26, opts for the skepticism of A. Alt without arguing his case. He indicates that he wants to "advance the hypothesis" (without proof or argumentation) that the designation of Yahweh as King

Now in this conclusion to the book of Psalms, God is exalted once more as King among the nations. In addition, just as God is King, so David is empowered by him to serve as king-Messiah over his people, including peoples from all nations as well as from Israel.

Conclusion to Book V

The end of the book of Psalms reflects its beginning. The vision portrayed in the two "pillar psalms," Psalms 1 and 2, is depicted as having been realized. A kingdom of righteousness that is wholly in accord with the Torah of Yahweh finally exists, and will continue throughout eternity. The two kings and the two kingdoms have been united. Nations and peoples are ruled jointly and unitedly by Yahweh and his Messiah.

The various circumstances that bring forth this climactic praise in this *Hallelu-YAH* finale echo major themes of the Psalter:

> *The Lord is Creator of this entire world.* He is "the Maker of heaven and earth, the sea, and everything in them" (Ps. 146:6). Sun, moon, and stars should praise him, "for he commanded and they were created" (Ps. 148:3, 5). The people of Israel are summoned to "rejoice in their Maker" (Ps. 149:2). *Hallelu-YAH!*

> *The Lord is Sustainer of the universe.* He "gives food to the hungry" and "sustains the fatherless and the widow" (Ps. 146:7, 9). He "supplies the earth with rain and makes grass grow on the hills. He provides food for the cattle and for the young ravens when they

---

first appeared at Shiloh in connection with the "stories about the Ark." Ibid., 27. Why material regarded by Kraus himself as "stories" should have greater significance than the ancient poetic forms of Scripture is not made clear. Kraus insists that the idea of Yahweh as King over all the other gods actually derived from the widespread influence of the ancient Near East, and particularly from Ugarit, Babylon, and Egypt. Ibid., 28–29. But then in explaining the distinctiveness of this idea in Israel, he notes that "all the powers and deities were totally stripped of their power" when Yahweh was declared King over all other "gods." Ibid., 30. At this point it must be questioned what evidence is actually present in Israel's Scriptures of the process of transformation of a borrowed idea, or whether it might be more likely that from the most ancient origins of Israel's faith this radical affirmation of the exclusiveness of Yahweh's existence as God and King had always been present. Once the uniqueness of revelational experiences in Israel is recognized, no need remains for the absorption and transformation of naturalistic, foreign religious concepts.

call" (Ps. 147:8–9). Lightning and hail, snow and clouds, fruit trees and all cedars, small creatures and flying birds all do his bidding (Ps. 148:8–10). He "determines the number of the stars and calls them each by name" (Ps. 147:4). *Hallelu-YAH!*

The Lord is Redeemer of his people. He is the God of Jacob who upholds the cause of the oppressed, loves the righteous, and frustrates the ways of the wicked (Ps. 146:5, 7, 9). He sustains the humble but casts the wicked to the ground, for he delights in those who fear him (Ps. 147:6, 11). He has "revealed his word to Jacob, his laws and decrees to Israel" (Ps. 147:19). *Hallelu-YAH!*

The Lord is King, and has joined Messiah's kingship to his own. The Lord reigns forever (Ps. 146:10). He has raised up for his people a "horn," a sovereign, beneficent ruler (Ps. 148:14). His people should rejoice in their King (Ps. 149:2). *Hallelu-YAH!*

The Lord has established his permanent dwellingplace on earth, which reflects his dwellingplace in heaven. The Lord reigns in Zion across all generations (Ps. 146:10). He builds up Jerusalem (Ps. 147:2). Jerusalem and Zion must praise their God, for he strengthens the bars of their gates (Ps. 147:12–13). The earthly Mount Zion rejoices in the One who rules as their King (Ps. 149:2). His heavenly hosts praise the Lord from the heavens and in the heights above (Ps. 148:1–2). His splendor is above the earth and the heavens (Ps. 148:13b). His sanctuary is in his mighty heavens (Ps. 150:1). By this dual representation of God's permanent dwellingplace, these concluding psalms underscore the union of the Lord's rule in heaven with his kingdom on earth. *Hallelu-YAH!*

Excursus 2: The "Poetic Pyramids" of the Psalter

Introduction: An Initial Exploration of a Possible Structural Element in the Psalter

A possible structural element in the Psalter that has received little or no recognition may be characterized as the *poetic pyramid*. The following observations represent an initial exploration of this structural element in the Psalter. No effort will be made at this point to explore interconnections across the various psalms in each collection.

Several different poetic pyramids deserve careful consideration in the various books of the Psalter. These collections take on a similar form in that they each feature a centrally positioned psalm that serves as the peak or pinnacle of the grouping. The same number of psalms on either side of the pinnacle psalm supplies balance to the collection. A common theme regularly provides unity of substance. More convincing examples appear in the later books of the Psalter. Possible poetic pyramids beginning with these later books may be noted as follows:

Psalms 120–134

Of the several collections of this sort, the Songs of Ascents (Pss. 120–134) represent the most elaborate example of a possible poetic pyramid. Psalm 127, designated in its heading as being "by Solomon," serves as the pinnacle psalm of this collection. As noted earlier, this psalm contains the major emphases of the Davidic covenant, including the building of the "house" in terms of both the construction of the temple and the perpetuating of the Davidic dynasty. Balancing this central psalm are seven psalms on either side, making a total of fifteen psalms in the grouping. Two psalms "by David" and five additional psalms without attribution of authorship appear on either side of Psalm 127. In addition, the divine name *Yahweh* appears exactly twenty-four times on either side of this "pinnacle psalm."

But why this concentration on the divine name *Yahweh*? Earlier it was noted that no fewer than twelve of the fifteen Psalms of Ascents reflect some aspect of the priestly benediction recorded in the book of Numbers. After rehearsing the threefold pronouncement of the name *Yahweh*, the book of Numbers provides a summary explanation of the significance of this benediction: "So shall they *set my name* on the sons of Israel, and I shall bless them" (Num. 6:27). The apex of blessing expected by the people as they made their "ascent" to the temple in Jerusalem was that the priest would "set [Yahweh's] name" on them. So, appropriately, these Psalms of Ascents focus repeatedly on the name *Yahweh*, the covenantal name of the God of Israel. It is not merely a curious interest in balanced word count that lies behind the twenty-four uses of the name *Yahweh* on either side of pivotal Psalm 127. Instead, a focus on the ultimate blessing associated with the Name lies beneath this preciseness in the pronouncement of the divine Name. The collection may be graphically depicted as shown in figure 9.1.

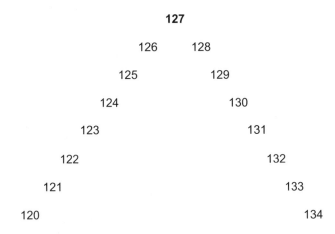

Fig. 9.1. Psalms 120–134

Psalms 111–117

A second possible poetic pyramid may be observed in the first collection of *Hallelu-YAH* psalms of Book V (Pss. 111–117). This grouping consists of seven psalms, with Psalm 114 as the pinnacle psalm of the collection. As previously noted, on either side of Psalm 114 is a triad of *Hallelu-YAH* psalms, with both triads featuring a comparable arrangement. In the first triad, Psalms 111 and 112 begin with *Hallelu-YAH* followed by Psalm 113, which begins and ends with *Hallelu-YAH*. In the second triad, Psalms 115 and 116 end with *Hallelu-YAH*, while Psalm 117 begins with *Hallelu Yahweh* and ends with *Hallelu-YAH*. Psalm 114 with its celebrated reference to Israel's coming "out of Egypt" (Ps. 114:1) serves as the pinnacle of this collection by providing the focal purpose of praise, even though this central psalm contains no *Hallelu-YAH*. This poetic pyramid may be depicted as shown in figure 9.2.

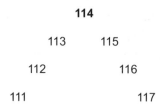

Fig. 9.2. Psalms 111–117

Psalms 92–100

A third possible poetic pyramid may be observed in Book IV, embracing the nine psalms of the *Yahweh Malak* grouping. Psalm 96 serves dramatically as the pinnacle psalm of this collection. Three psalms in this collection begin with the same *Yahweh Malak* declaration (Pss. 93:1; 97:1; 99:1). In its totality Psalm 96 mirrors the central portion of the psalm in Chronicles that defines the origin of the "*Yahweh Malak*" jubilation outburst. This phrase perpetually rehearsed the celebratory climax originating at the bringing up of the ark of the covenant to Jerusalem, effectively uniting Yahweh's throne with David's throne (1 Chron. 16:31). The inclusion of Psalms 92 through 100 in this grouping was discussed earlier. The structure of this collection may be depicted as shown in figure 9.3.

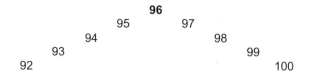

Fig. 9.3. Psalms 92–100

Psalms 77–83

A fourth possible poetic pyramid appears in Book III, with its collection of seven psalms describing the devastations and deliverances

234

of "Jacob" and "Joseph," representing the southern and northern tribal groups. Deliverance for the southern tribe of Judah appears in Psalm 78, which recalls the historic divine choice of Zion and David (Ps. 78:68–72). But Psalm 79 follows immediately with its vivid description of the destruction of Jerusalem by the Babylonian invaders (Ps. 79:1–4). At the same time, a climax of this grouping of seven psalms focuses on centered Psalm 80 with its depiction of the devastation and deliverance of the northern tribes represented by Joseph and Benjamin, sons of Jacob and his beloved wife Rachel, along with Joseph's twin sons Ephraim and Manasseh (cf. Ps. 80:1–2). All references to "Joseph" in the Psalter appear in this collection of seven psalms (Pss. 77–83), with the single exception of the recounting of the Joseph-history in Psalm 105:17–22. The first mention of Joseph in the Psalter occurs in the initial psalm of this grouping (Ps. 77:15). Psalm 80 as the pinnacle psalm of this grouping climaxes with the appearance of the "son," the "son of man," the "man of the right hand" (a play on the name *Ben-Yamin*, "Son of the Right Hand," Ps. 80:15, 17). As previously discussed, this singular saving hero, later identified in Jewish tradition as "Messiah ben Joseph" or "Messiah ben Ephraim," provides hope of deliverance for the northern tribes despite their devastation by Assyrian armies. Psalm 80 serves not only as the pinnacle of this grouping, but as the central psalm of the Psalter, since, according to traditional Jewish calculations, Psalm 80 contains the central letter of the entire book of Psalms. This collection of seven psalms, with Psalm 80 serving as its pinnacle, concludes with references to prior deliverances among the tribes of Ephraim and Manasseh, descendants of Joseph, in the days of the judges (Ps. 83:9–12). This possible pyramid grouping may be envisioned as shown in figure 9.4.

Fig. 9.4. Psalms 77–83

Psalms 20–24

A fifth possible poetic pyramid may be noted in Book I with its grouping of five kingship psalms (Pss. 20–24). In this instance, Psalm 22 serves as the pinnacle psalm of the collection, with two kingship psalms on either side of this central psalm. As previously discussed, Psalm 22 depicts both the kingship of Messiah and the kingship of Yahweh. On the one side of the pinnacle, Psalms 20 and 21 present Messiah as king. On the other side, Psalms 23 and 24 present Yahweh as King. This poetic pyramid may be diagrammed as shown in figure 9.5.

Fig. 9.5. Psalms 20–24

Conclusion on the Poetic Pyramid as a Possible Structural Element in the Psalter

So several poetic pyramids appear to provide a distinctive structural element in various books of the Psalter. Further exploration is required to confirm these structures, and to uncover the precise relationships of specific psalms within these particular groupings.[44]

But what is the significance of this unique arrangement in the Psalter? Why did the editor(s) apparently make rather extensive use of this form?

As in the case of the acrostic psalms discussed previously, the purpose may well have been for facilitating a significant grasp of a larger portion of the Psalter. As a consequence of this arrangement, if a person were to memorize the pinnacle psalms of each of these groupings (Pss. 22, 80, 96, 114, 127), he or she would possess strong anchors for attaining a fuller comprehension of four books of the Psalter. These five poetic pyramids embrace no fewer than forty psalms, or more than

44. Additional groupings worth exploring include Psalms 11–17, 26–32, 54–60, and 146–150.

one-fourth of the entire Psalter. Understanding the strategic position of the pinnacle psalms would enable a person to grasp much more effectively the substance of the Psalter as a whole. If this awareness of the pinnacle psalms were joined to a comprehension of the acrostic psalms along with an identity of the "seam" psalms connecting the various books, a person would have no trouble possessing adequate material for meditating on the Torah of Yahweh "day and night."

10

Concluding Observations

So the flow of the book of Psalms may be traced from its beginning to its end.[1] Though not purely chronological, a relative ordering in time sequence is apparent. Though not topical, the various collections of psalms display clear content-groupings. Beginning with David's struggle against personal enemies opposed to his establishment as the Covenant Lord's reigning Messiah, the Psalter moves through repeated confrontations that eventually include international enemies, climaxing with assaults by world-conquerors Assyria and Babylonia. Throughout these developments, the Psalter envisions the full merger of the Davidic messianic kingdom with the rule of Israel's Covenant Lord. Built on the foundation of God's lordship manifested in creation and throughout his providential ordering of the world, God's covenant with David and his sons will eventually consummate in this messianic kingship that comes to realization through conflict. In the end, the Psalter summons peoples of all nations along with inanimate creation to offer united praise to the Covenant Lord with a resounding *Hallelu-YAH*!

In reviewing this flow of the Psalter from Psalm 1 to Psalm 150, four matters will be presented: (1) diagrams depicting the structure of

1. Jamie A. Grant, *The King as Exemplar: The Function of Deuteronomy's Kingship Law in the Shaping of the Book of Psalms* (Atlanta: Society of Biblical Literature, 2004), 262, says that nothing required a division of the Psalter. Yet if there is a flow, a movement of redemptive-historical circumstance from *confrontation* to *communication* to *devastation* to *maturation* to *consummation* across the five books, an inherent reason exists for the Psalter's division. Even if many individual psalms do not exactly follow this "flow," the overall progression in structure and circumstance nonetheless provides an essential explanation for the division of the Psalter.

the Psalter; (2) a structural overview designed to aid in the memorization of the substance of the Psalter; (3) distinctive themes that recur across the five books; and (4) the impact of Psalter structure on the New Testament's perspective on the Psalms.

Diagrams Depicting the Structure of the Psalter

Intentional structure is apparent across the Psalter, as a number of recent studies have shown. This inherent structure may be observed in part through considering groupings among various authors as indicated in the Psalter headings. The "seam" psalms that join the various books also make a contribution to the intentional arrangement of the materials, as do collections according to specific genres, such as the kingship psalms or the Psalms of Ascents. But the substance of the psalms themselves supplies the most basic indicator of the Psalter's structure. This aspect of psalm arrangement overrides all other considerations of structure. The following diagrams depict the basic structure of the Psalter as it unfolds across the five books, in light of various structural elements.

Introductory Diagram: Overall Structure of the Psalter

In this diagram, the five books of the Psalter can be clearly perceived in terms of their relative length and thematic focus. Clearly, Books I and V are the largest of the five books, encompassing over forty psalms each. Books III and IV each contain only seventeen psalms, which represent only slightly more than one-third the number of psalms included in the opening and concluding books. Book II is mediating in size, with thirty-one psalms.

This initial diagram also indicates the overarching theme of each of the five books. These five major theme-words obviously cannot represent the substance of each psalm in the various books. But they can bring into focus the major thrust of each successive book as well as its role in the progression of the Psalter as a whole. See "Introductory Diagram: Overall Structure of the Psalter" in the color figures at the end of the book.

239

Diagrams 1 through 5: Structure in Each of the Five Books

The following five diagrams depict the basic structure within each of the five books of the Psalter. These diagrams include indicators of authorship, coupling of Torah and messianic psalms, acrostic psalms, creation psalms, significant groupings or themes, and possible poetic-pyramid psalms.

Diagram 1. Book I (Psalms 1–41): Confrontation

Book I begins with the coupling of a Torah psalm with a messianic psalm (Pss. 1–2). These two psalms introduce the major themes that will be developed across the whole of the Psalter. Book I consists essentially of the first Davidic collection of the Psalter (Pss. 3–41*[2]). Virtually all the psalms of this book are attributed to David by their titles.

The relative size of the various books has significance for structural considerations. If the authors/editors of the various portions of the Psalter intended to make it possible for people to learn the entire substance of the Psalter, the larger books needed to be broken down into smaller sections. So Books I and V are divided into two major segments by the coupling of a messianic psalm with a Torah psalm in these two larger books (Pss. 18–19; Pss. 118–119). In addition, the eight acrostic psalms of the Psalter are distributed across these two books, with four acrostic psalms in Book I and four in Book V. The effect of their placement is to subdivide these books into even smaller units.

An interesting feature of Book I is the positioning of its three creation psalms immediately before an acrostic psalm. Creation Psalm 8 precedes acrostic Psalm(s) 9/10; creation Psalm 24 precedes acrostic Psalm 25; and creation Psalm 33 precedes acrostic Psalm 34.

Two groupings of possible poetic-pyramid psalms are represented in the diagram. These special collections feature a prominent "pinnacle psalm" at the center of the grouping, with an equal number of related psalms on either side of the central psalm.

---

2. As elsewhere, the asterisk (*) indicates a grouping of psalms whose titles might not all specifically refer to a particular individual.

At least three significant thematic groupings of psalms appear in Book I. Five kingship psalms occur just after the coupling of messianic Psalm 18 with Torah Psalm 19 (Pss. 20–24). These five kingship psalms are positioned so that they respond to messianic Psalm 18. In this first kingship collection, Psalms 20 and 21 present the messianic king; Psalms 23 and 24 present Yahweh as King; and Psalm 22 combines these two kingships in a single psalm. As an additional structural factor, Psalm 25 with its tenfold underscoring of the significance of the "teaching" of the Lord responds to Torah Psalm 19. The fourfold confession of sin in Psalm 25 indicates a further response to Torah Psalm 19.

A grouping of seven psalms may be viewed as possibly responding to the second major aspect of the Davidic covenant alongside the "perpetual dynasty" theme: the "permanent dwellingplace" for the Lord. Each one of Psalms 26–32 refers to the Lord's dwellingplace with a variety of phrases. Psalm 29 of this grouping serves as the pinnacle psalm, with its dramatic representation of the thunderous "voice of the LORD" speaking from his regal dwellingplace in heaven.

Book I concludes with a grouping of eight psalms depicting the psalmist in his suffering. Four psalms report the plight of the innocent sufferer (Pss. 34–37). Two acrostic psalms bracket this collection (Pss. 34, 37). Four psalms following this collection describe the condition of the guilty sufferer (Pss. 38–41). As one other structural feature of Book I, two quasi-acrostics "bracket the brackets" of the innocent sufferer (Pss. 33, 38).

So all these various factors inherent in the psalms of Book I provide meaningful structure to this opening portion of the Psalter. With these factors in mind, the "average Israelite" who memorized the two introductory psalms, the second Torah-messianic coupling, and the four well-positioned acrostic psalms, along with their immediate contextual connections, would have mental "hooks" to readily bring to mind the major thrust of twenty-five of the forty-one psalms of Book I. With a strong grasp of these twenty-five psalms, it would not be difficult to "fill in the gaps" of the remaining psalms of Book I.

The same results should follow the study of these psalms today. Diagram 1, "Book I (Psalms 1–41): CONFRONTATION," in the color figures at the end of the book, depicts the basic structure of the forty-one psalms of Book I.

Diagram 2. Book II (Psalms 42–72): Communication

If the theme of Book I is *confrontation*, the overarching theme of Book II is *communication*. In Book I, David confronted a multitude of enemies as he attempted to establish the Lord's kingdom of righteousness and peace. This ongoing struggle continues in Book II. But now a new phase of communication with foreign nations and peoples of the world emerges. The psalmist displays his desire to communicate with non-Israelite peoples by his majority use of *Elohim*, the general name for God, instead of *Yahweh*, the special name of Israel's COVENANT LORD. He also invites the nations to join with him in worshiping the one true Elohim.

In terms of authorship indicators in the titles of Book II, a one-third to two-thirds relationship develops between psalms attributed to the Sons of Korah (Pss. 42–49*) followed by a single psalm of Asaph (Ps. 50), and psalms constituting the second Davidic collection (Pss. 51–71*) followed by a single psalm of Solomon (Ps. 72).

Significant groupings in Book II include two introductory psalms (Pss. 42/43, 44); four kingship psalms consisting of an initial messianic kingship psalm joined to a triad of Elohim kingship psalms (Pss. 45, 46–48); four psalms involving a divine summons to judgment with the designation of appropriate respondents (Pss. 49–52); a psalm revisiting atheism (Ps. 53; cf. Ps. 14); seven psalms indicating specific enemies (Pss. 54–60); eight psalms of dialogue between the kings, with four cries from Israel's king and four responses affirming Elohim's kingship (Pss. 61–64, 65–68); three psalms of ongoing struggle (Pss. 69–71); and a final psalm describing Messiah's ultimate universal rule (Ps. 72). Near the beginning and at the ending of Book II is a psalm proclaiming the glories of the messianic king who is identified as Elohim, and whose rule embraces all time and space (Pss. 45, 72). This messianic figure also endures scorn and shame on the Lord's behalf (Ps. 69). Diagram 2, "Book II (Psalms 42–72): COMMUNICATION," in the color figures at the end of the book, displays the structure of Book II.

Diagram 3. Book III (Psalms 73–89): Devastation

Only seventeen psalms constitute Book III. The first two-thirds of these psalms are attributed by their titles to Asaph (Pss. 73–83), and the final one-third to the Sons of Korah (Pss. 84–89*). As in Book II, an individual and a corporate psalm introduce the distressful circumstance of the book (Pss. 73–74). Before finally plunging the nation into the dark days of the exile, the psalmist affirms Elohim's kingship over all earthly kings (Pss. 75–76). But then seven psalms report the devastation that comes to both the southern and the northern kingdoms of Israel, accompanied by pleas for deliverance (Pss. 77–83). The psalms of the Sons of Korah offer a positive perspective on the state of the nation's salvation, though the book concludes with psalms expressing both individual and corporate distress (Pss. 84–87, 88–89). One pinnacle psalm arises at the central point of Book III, which is also located at the center of the Psalter as a whole (Ps. 80). This focal psalm directs the devastated people's faith to a suffering and glorified "Messiah ben Joseph." Diagram 3, "Book III (Psalms 73–89): DEVASTATION," in the color figures at the end of the book, shows the structural diagram of Book III.

Diagram 4. Book IV (Psalms 90–106): Maturation

Book IV, like Book III, consists of only seventeen psalms. The context is set at the time of Israel's exile, which would be four to five hundred years after David. Yet both introductory psalms in Book IV speak of the blessings of prosperity and length of life (Pss. 90–91). For in the gracious purposes of God, exile brought *maturation*.

The psalm opening this book is attributed to none other than Moses. This psalm presents the eternal God as the One in whom we live and move and have our being (Ps. 90). Despite the nation's distressing circumstances, the core of the book is summarized in its distinctive declaration: "*Yahweh Malak*" ("Yahweh is King"). He has always been King, he is King, he will always be King. This triumphant declaration leads the whole earth to praise, to give thanks, and to shout for joy (Pss. 92–100). Psalm 96, in its entirety replicating the central core of the psalm celebrating David's triumphant bringing up of the ark of the covenant to Mount Zion (1 Chron. 16:23–33), serves as the pinnacle psalm of the *Yahweh Malak* collection. Following this collection, three Davidic psalms anticipate the rejuvenation of a Davidic kingdom based on the righteousness, the eternality, the graciousness, and the sovereignty of Yahweh's kingship (Pss. 101–103). In anticipation of the climax that will come in Book V, this book concludes with the first *Hallelu-YAH* triad, which includes two psalms of historical recollection (Pss. 104–106). Diagram 4, "Book IV (Psalms 90–106): MATURATION," in the color figures at the end of the book, shows the basic structure of Book IV.

Diagram 5. Book V (Psalms 107–150): Consummation

Book V is the largest of the books of the Psalter, containing forty-four psalms. David is designated as author of fifteen of these psalms, including an opening triad, four of the Psalms of Ascents, and a final collection of eight psalms attributed to him (Pss. 108–110, 122, 124, 131, 133, and 138–145). Rather than supposing that these psalms represent later non-Davidic psalms that have been "davidized" to give them greater acceptance, it may be assumed that the final editors selected genuinely Davidic psalms whose contents were appropriate for the exilic period, though originally composed in response to the circumstances of David's own day. The complete absence of any historical situation in the titles of these psalms, with the exception of one generalized reference to David's being "in the cave" (Ps. 142), indicates the suitability of a later application to exilic times. A central psalm attributed to Solomon serves as the pinnacle of the poetic pyramid that shapes the fifteen Psalms of Ascents (Ps. 127).

This book contains the final Torah/messianic coupling, which provides a major structural division within this largest of the five books of the Psalter (Pss. 118–119). The four acrostic psalms introduce and/or conclude various collections within Book V, with twin acrostic Psalms 111 and 112 introducing the first *Hallelu-YAH* grouping of Book V, acrostic Psalm 119 serving as the climactic Torah psalm, and acrostic Psalm 145 concluding the final Davidic collection just before the *"Hallelu-YAH* finale" (Pss. 146–150). Significant groupings in Book V include introductory Psalm 107, a Davidic triad (Pss. 108–110), the initial *Hallelu-YAH* grouping of seven psalms (Pss. 111–117) arranged as a poetic pyramid with Psalm 114 as its pinnacle, the third and final coupling of a messianic psalm with a Torah psalm (Pss. 118–119), the Psalms of Ascents (Pss. 120–134), three transitional psalms of historical recollection (Pss. 135–137), the final Davidic collection (Pss. 138–145), and the *Hallelu-YAH* finale (Pss. 146–150). Psalm 148 may be viewed as the pinnacle of this climactic collection. Psalms 110 and 118 both provide climactic revelations of Messiah in his sufferings and glory, and along with Psalm 2 are quoted more extensively in the New Testament than any other psalms. See diagram 5, "Book V (Psalms 107–150): CONSUMMATION," in the color figures at the end of the book.

Summary

Several factors may serve to summarize the significance of these basic structures within the Psalter:

First, the division into five books is by no means arbitrary. Instead, a clear progression may be observed in the substance of the various books, and not merely on the basis of uncertain verbal connections. *Confrontation, communication, devastation, maturation,* and *consummation* have significant value in defining the substance of each of the books.

Second, each of the five books begins with one or two introductory psalms. These opening psalms generally serve to set the stage for the substance of their respective books.

Third, the threefold placement of coupled Torah and messianic psalms plays a significant role in the structure of the Psalter. The positioning of eight acrostic psalms provides an additional breakdown of the two larger books within the Psalter. These acrostic psalms also serve to introduce or conclude special collections at various points in Books I and V.

Fourth, thematic or topical considerations often determine specific collections within the Psalter. Kingship psalms as well as psalms of the innocent sufferer and psalms of the guilty sufferer form special collections. The collection of four psalms featuring judicial summonses with designated respondents (Pss. 49–52) encompasses psalms by three different authors, demonstrating that thematic substance takes precedence over common authorship in Psalter groupings. A distinctive grouping of psalms focusing on the northern tribal community provides unique substance to the central core of the Psalter. *Hallelu-YAH* psalms always occur in groupings, with the single exception of Psalm 135. These psalms anticipate consummate realization of the kingdom of God and his Messiah as the Psalter moves toward its climactic conclusion.

Fifth, poetic-pyramid psalms, each with a centered pinnacle psalm, appear in four of the five books. These psalms provide a significant structural element while also enabling an easier comprehension of the totality of the Psalter.

All these various elements of structure offer a meaningful framework for the interpretation of individual psalms. Awareness of these thematic and structural elements can only enrich the appreciation of this glorious book of divinely inspired and God-glorifying Scripture.

In addition, awareness of this internal structuring based on the essential substance of the Psalter makes *memorization* of the entire Psalter a realizable possibility. It has already been noted that memorizing the two opening psalms and the four acrostic psalms of Book I and understanding the coupling of messianic Psalm 18 with Torah Psalm 19, along with an awareness of connected psalms, provides access to the substance of twenty-five of the forty-one psalms of Book I. Recognizing the inherent structures of the five books makes memorization of the essential substance of the Psalter an attainable goal. The following overview of Psalter structure is designed to aid a person desiring to commit the substance of the Psalms to memory.

A Structural Overview Designed to Aid in the Memorization of the Substance of the Psalter

Though memorization has become a lost discipline, believers in the modern age would do well to commit to memory some basic biblical truths that would provide a solid foundation for their faith and life. Martin Luther's "Little Bible" of the Psalter could be memorized as a step toward enabling a person to experience the rich blessing of meditating on the Lord's Torah "day and night." The following summary of the basic structural elements of the five books of the Psalter is designed to assist in the memorization of the substance of the Psalter.

Book I (Psalms 1–41): Confrontation

[Forty-one psalms with two psalms introducing the entire Psalter, followed by the first Davidic collection.]

Introductory psalms: Torah Psalm 1 and messianic Psalm 2

(1) The first Davidic collection, divided into two sections by the coupling of messianic Psalm 18 with Torah Psalm 19 (Pss. 3–17,* 18–41*).
(2) Acrostic Psalm(s) 9/10 subdividing the first section of Book I.
(3) Five kingship psalms in response to messianic Psalm 18 (Pss. 20–24), with Psalm 22 as the pinnacle.
(4) Acrostic Psalm 25 in response to Torah Psalm 19.
(5) Seven "regal dwellingplace" psalms, with Psalm 29 as their pinnacle (Pss. 26–32).
(6) Acrostic Psalms 34 and 37 bracketing four "innocent sufferer" psalms (Pss. 34–37) and subdividing the second section of Book I (Pss. 18–41).
(7) Four "guilty sufferer" psalms (Pss. 38–41) following the four "innocent sufferer" psalms.
(8) Three creation psalms (Pss. 8, 24, 33), each preceding an acrostic psalm (Pss. 9/10, 25, 34).
(9) Two quasi-acrostic psalms (Pss. 33, 38) "bracketing the brackets" of acrostic Psalms 34–37.

Book II (Psalms 42–72): Communication

[Thirty-one psalms with one-third attributed to the Sons of Korah (Pss. 42–49*), followed by a single psalm attributed to

Asaph (Ps. 50), and two-thirds constituting the second Davidic collection (Pss. 51–71*), followed by a single psalm attributed to Solomon (Ps. 72). This book opens with two introductory psalms followed by seven segments.]

Introductory psalms (Pss. 42/43, 44)

(1) Four kingship psalms (Pss. 45–48).
(2) Four psalms of judicial summons and response (Pss. 49–52).
(3) Atheism revisited (Ps. 53).
(4) Seven specified enemies (Pss. 54–60).
(5) Eight psalms representing the dialogue of the kings (Pss. 61–68).
    Cry of the messianic king—four psalms (Pss 61–64).
    Undisturbed reign of the Divine King—four psalms (Pss. 65–68).
(6) Ongoing struggle (Pss. 69–71).
(7) Messiah's triumphant rule (Ps. 72).

Book III: (Psalms 73–89): Devastation

[Seventeen psalms with two-thirds attributed to Asaph (Pss. 73–83) and one-third attributed to the Sons of Korah (Pss. 84–89*), opening with two introductory psalms, followed by four segments. In this book, four psalms specifically report the devastation of the northern and southern kingdoms (Pss. 74, 79, 80, 89).]

Introductory psalms (Pss. 73–74)

(1) Elohim's kingship over all earthly kings (Pss. 75–76).
(2) Devastation and deliverance (Pss. 77–83), with Psalm 80 as the pinnacle.
(3) Positive perspective of the Sons of Korah (Pss. 84–87).
(4) Individual and corporate distress (Pss. 88–89).

Book IV (Psalms 90–106): Maturation

[Seventeen psalms opening with two introductory psalms followed by three segments.]

Introductory psalms (Pss. 90–91)

(1) *Yahweh Malak* psalms (Pss. 92–100), with Psalm 96 as their pinnacle.
(2) A Davidic triad (Pss. 101–103*).
(3) First *Hallelu-YAH* triad (Pss. 104–106), concluding with two psalms of historical recollection (Pss. 105–106).

Book V (Psalms 107–150): Consummation

[Forty-four psalms, with an introductory psalm followed by seven segments.]

Introductory Psalm 107

(1) A Davidic triad (Pss. 108–110).
(2) A *Hallelu-YAH* grouping of seven psalms (Pss. 111–117), introduced by twin acrostic Psalms 111 and 112, with Psalm 114 as the pinnacle of this collection.
(3) The third coupling of a messianic psalm and a Torah psalm, with Psalm 119 also being an acrostic psalm (Pss. 118–119).
(4) Fifteen Psalms of Ascents, with Solomonic Psalm 127 as the pinnacle (Pss. 120–134).
(5) Three transitional psalms of historical recollection (Pss. 135–137).
(6) The final Davidic collection of eight psalms, concluding with acrostic Psalm 145 (Pss. 138–145).
(7) The *Hallelu-YAH* finale of five psalms (Pss. 146–150), with Psalm 148 as its pinnacle.

Distinctive Themes Recurring across the Five Books of the Psalter

Several familiar themes permeate the Psalter. Generally recognized themes include: (1) the struggle of the righteous with the wicked; (2) the glories of God in his knowledge, power, faithfulness, and grace; (3) God's creation and providential care of the world; (4) the sin of humanity and the call for repentance and faith; (5) the need for redemption and forgiveness as provided by the promised messianic king; (6) the summons of all peoples to praise and thank the Lord; and (7) the coming eschatological day in which God will exercise judgment and his redeemed people will shout, "*Hallelu-YAH.*"

But beyond these regularly recognized emphases, certain distinctive themes recur across the various books of the Psalter that are not always perceived. This analysis will consider three of these emphases: (1) the intimate friend who becomes an archenemy; (2) the sufferings of Messiah transformed into praise; and (3) the multiple grouping of kingship psalms across the Psalter.

The Intimate Friend Who Becomes the Archenemy

Quite remarkably, three psalms from three of the five books of the Psalter contain vivid passages describing a close friend of God's Messiah who becomes his vicious enemy. These three passages are all specifically quoted in the New Testament. Psalm 41:9 in Book I speaks of "my close friend, whom I trusted, he who shared my bread, [who] has lifted up his heel against me" (quoted in John 13:18; cf. Matt. 26:23). Psalm 69:8–9 in Book II declares, "I am a stranger to my brothers, an alien to my own mother's sons; for zeal for your house consumes me" (quoted in John 2:17). Psalm 109:4–5, 8 in Book V says, "In return for my friendship they accuse me . . . . They repay me evil for good, and hatred for my friendship. . . . May his days be few; may another take his place of leadership" (quoted in Acts 1:20). Though not quoted in the New Testament, Psalm 55:12–14 of Book II also speaks in this same tone: "If an enemy were insulting me, I could endure it; if a foe were raising himself against me, I could hide from him. But it is you, a man like myself, my companion, my close friend, with whom I once enjoyed sweet fellowship as we walked with the throng at the house of God."

What is the significance of this theme, and why does it recur so regularly in the Psalms? Its appearance in three books of the Psalter is quite striking. Even more remarkable is the fact that three of these four passages find explicit acknowledgment in the New Testament. But why is this theme so prominent and so pervasive in the Psalter?

This theme takes on a focal dimension because it represents the climax of the struggle depicted throughout the Psalms. The struggle between the righteous and the wicked climaxes with one representative man opposed by Satan himself. It represents a repetition of the struggle between the first man, Adam, and the devil as the archenemy. This struggle finds its antitype in the contest between David and Goliath, between the covenantal head of Israel and the appointed hero of the Philistines. The victory of the one man achieves victory for all who are united to him.

This concept of one man representing the many corresponds to the structure inherent in the divine covenants. One man functions as the covenantal head of a people. It is the role of Adam, Noah, Abraham, Moses, David—and Christ. In the Psalter, the focus is on David as covenantal head of the nation. If he achieves victory, his people triumph. If he is overcome, the whole nation is defeated.

This collection of passages echoes the hand-to-hand combat of Satan with the promised seed as anticipated in the first gospel proclamation found in Genesis 3:15. Satan will crush his heel, and he will crush Satan's head (cf. Rom. 16:20).

So even today, the focus of faith must be on our Champion, the Lord Jesus Christ. Apart from him, there is no victory for God's people. No salvation, no forgiveness, no prosperity, no perfection. But in his triumphs, all who believe in him become "more than conquerors" through him who loved us and gave himself for us (Rom. 8:37). Not without good reason does this theme recur so regularly in the Psalter. In this theme may be found a healthy dose of redemptive reality. Without a singular saving hero, we would have no hope. Without the mortal conflict of the Christ, the Messiah—Jesus—with Satan, there would be no salvation, no singing, no *Hallelu-YAHs*.

The Sufferings of Messiah Transformed into Praise

This distinctive pattern recurs in four of the five books of the Psalter. The theme of a suffering Messiah has not always been appreciated or even understood. All forms of triumphalism stumble over this perspective. A triumphant Messiah delights everyone. But the joining of suffering to triumph is a concept most difficult to grasp. Yet key psalms in the various books of the Psalter develop this theme:

Book I. Psalm 22: "My God, my God, why have you forsaken me?" is the puzzling question that opens this psalm (Ps. 22:1). But in the end, the suffering Messiah declares: "Praise him! . . . Revere him . . . ! For he has not despised or disdained the suffering of the afflicted one . . . but has listened to his cry for help" (Ps. 22:23b–24).

Book II. Psalm 69: The psalm begins with the desperate cry of a drowning man. "Save me, O God, for the waters have come into my soul" (Ps. 69:1). But in the end, this same person exclaims, "I will praise God's name in song and glorify him with thanksgiving" (Ps. 69:30).

Book III. Psalm 80: God's people have been fed with "bread of tears," vividly describing their devastation at the hands of the invading Assyrians (Ps. 80:5). Though the "vine" identified as the "son" is cut down and burned with fire, he is the "man at [God's] right hand," the "son of man" that God has made strong for himself (Ps. 80:14–17). Though identified with them in the totality of their calamity, he is the One by whom they will be raised to newness of life (Ps. 80:18).

Book V. Psalm 118: All nations swarm about the messianic king like menacing bees (Ps. 118:10–12). But Yahweh has done the marvelous thing of establishing this stone rejected by the builders as the defining cornerstone of his kingdom (Ps. 118:22–23).

This theme of Messiah's suffering in humiliation and then being exalted in glory has puzzled the interpreters of Scripture in every age. Yet it permeates the Psalms and provides a realistic perspective on the Christian gospel and the life of faith. Messiah suffers and is glorified. The Christian suffers and is glorified. The regular recurrence of this distinctive theme in the various books of the Psalter provides a properly defined object for faith in the "real" Messiah. It warns against all false messiahs, and depicts the expected scope of life for every disciple of the Messiah.

The Grouping of Kingship Psalms across the Psalter

Kingship psalms are widely distributed across the five books of the Psalter. No other theme has such a broad spectrum in psalm collections than this message of the Lord's and Messiah's kingship. Not only do the three pivotal messianic psalms conjoined with a Torah psalm focus on kingship (Pss. 2, 18, 118). In addition, at least five significant collections of kingship psalms appear in at least four of the five books of the Psalter. Each of these kingship collections has its own distinctive flavor suitable to its respective context. The following observations regarding the various groupings may capture something of the significance of this defining element in the Psalter:

Book I. Psalms 20–24: As previously discussed, this first collection of five kingship psalms is strategically placed to respond to messianic Psalm 18. Two psalms presenting the messianic king's dependence on prayer for Yahweh's interventions in his struggles (Pss. 20–21) are balanced over against two psalms depicting Yahweh's glorious kingship that provides Messiah with his needed reassurances (Pss. 23–24). Joining these two groupings is a mediating psalm that presents both kingships (Ps. 22). This entire collection is well suited for the days of David's early struggles to establish the messianic kingdom of righteousness and peace.

Book II. Psalms 45–48: This second collection of kingship psalms begins with the startling identification of the messianic king as *Elohim* (Ps. 45:6). While continuing efforts have been made to minimize this assertion, the text stands undisturbed. As previously indicated, the remaining psalms of this second kingship collection repeatedly affirm God's exalted lordship over the nations (Ps. 46:10). This Great King over all the earth has subdued nations under the feet of his people (Ps. 47:2–3). He resides in unperturbed peace even when the nations advance against Zion his holy city, for when they see her they flee in terror (Ps. 48:2–5). Clearly, this picture of kingship in Book II has progressed beyond the days of David's constant struggles against his multitudinous enemies.

Book II. Psalms 65–68: This third collection highlights the Divine King's response to David's pleas for help in facing his enemies. The psalmist summons the peoples of all nations to sing, to rejoice, and to praise God for his rule over nature and the world (Pss. 65:1, 5, 7, 9; 66:1, 7; 67:3–4; 68:32). Conflict continues, but God the King has processed from Sinai to enthronement at his holy mountain in Jerusalem (Ps. 68:17–18, 24).

Book III. Psalms 75–76: Before plunging both the southern and the northern kingdoms of Israel into the darkness of exile (Pss. 79, 80, 89), Book III affirms that God as Judge of all nations is the only One who can bring down one and exalt another (Ps. 75:7). In vivid depiction of the defeat of alien invaders, the psalmist declares:

> Valiant men lie plundered,
> > they sleep their last sleep;
> not one of the warriors
> > can lift his hands. (Ps. 76:5)

In the midst of this third book's message of national devastation by invading armies, God's kingship takes on a distinctive character. He rules these unruly nations. He warns the arrogant not to lift up their horns against heaven:

> For in the hand of Yahweh is a cup full of foaming wine
> > mixed with spices;
> he pours it out and all the wicked of the earth drink it down
> > to the very dregs. (Ps. 75:8)

Book IV. Psalms 92–100: Only a matured faith can declare, "*Yahweh Malak*" ("The LORD is King") in the midst of a comprehensive national disaster such as Israel's exile. Clearly, this extended pronouncement that the Lord has always been and will always be King moves in a different paradigm of thought from the earlier kingship collections that also affirm his sovereignty. But the pressing need in the hour of exile is this faith-declaration of the psalmist that God remains on his throne perpetually. He rules uninterruptedly in behalf of the well-being of his people, whatever may be their outer circumstances.

Book V. Psalms 111–117, 135, 146–150: Is there a collection of psalms in this climactic book of the Psalter that supports God's sovereignty as in all the previous books? If a collection of kingship psalms appears in Books I, II, III, and IV, would it not be expected that this final book would also contain its own unique collection of kingship psalms?

Nothing will be gained by pressuring Scripture to declare more than it intends to affirm. But it may well be that the *Hallelu-YAH* collections of Book V intend to affirm—even to celebrate—Yahweh's consummate kingship. Tracing the roots of this explosive exclamation to its origin at the shores of the Red Sea, we find that the people shout the poetic abbreviation *YAH* for *Yahweh*, God's sacred name (Ex. 15:2). Then they proclaim, "Yahweh will *reign as King* forever and ever" (Ex. 15:18). In the second appearance in Scripture of this term *YAH*, Moses celebrates victory over Amalek by memorializing Yahweh's kingship over the nations when he declares, "A hand upon the *throne of YAH!*" (Ex. 17:16). In both these original appearances of *YAH*, his sovereign kingship over opposing nations serves as the focal point of the narrative.

Not until the approaching climax of the Psalter is the celebrative *Hallelu* joined to *YAH*. The initial triad of this combination-word occurs in the final three psalms of Book IV (Pss. 104–106). Psalms 111–117 form the first *Hallelu-YAH* collection of Book V. Acrostic Psalm 145, the final psalm of David positioned to precede the *Hallelu-YAH* finale (Pss. 146–150), opens with the messianic king's exaltation of "my God the King" (Ps. 145:1). Four times in three verses of this psalm, David describes the glories, the splendors, the eternality of God's kingdom (Ps. 145:11–13). This concluding psalm of David, situated just before the Psalter's finale, is uniquely designated by its title as a *Hallel* psalm, using the same root for "praise" found in the word *Hallelu-YAH*.

With these considerations in mind, it may well be concluded that the *Hallelu-YAH* psalms distinctly featured in the fifth book of the Psalter intend to acclaim the Lord's kingship in climactic fashion. He is indeed Lord of all. As *Hallelu-YAH* Psalm 149 declares:

> Let Israel rejoice
> in their Maker;
> let the people of Zion be glad
> in their King. (Ps. 149:2)

This multiple collection of kingship psalms recurring through-out the various books of the Psalter should be given appropriate recognition. Their full force should be acknowledged in terms of the exaltation of Yahweh as King, and Messiah as king in his behalf. From this perspective, the student of Scripture will be better prepared to appreciate the exalting declarations of the New Testament that so strongly affirm this dual kingship:

> Now to the King eternal, immortal, invisible, the only God, be honor and glory for ever and ever. Amen. (1 Tim. 1:17)

> Keep the commandment unstained and free from reproach until the appearing of our Lord Jesus Christ, which he will display at the proper time—he who is the blessed and only Sovereign, the King of kings and Lord of lords, who alone has immortality, who dwells in unapproachable light, whom no one has ever seen or can see. To him be honor and eternal dominion. Amen. (1 Tim. 6:14–16 ESV)

> Then I saw heaven opened, and behold, a white horse! The one sitting on it is called Faithful and True, and in righteousness he judges and makes war. His eyes are like a flame of fire, and on his head are many diadems, and he has a name written that no one knows but himself. He is clothed in a robe dipped in blood, and the name by which he is called is The Word of God. And the armies of heaven, arrayed in fine linen, white and pure, were following him on white horses. From his mouth comes a sharp sword with which to strike down the nations, and he will rule them with a rod of iron. He will tread the winepress of the fury of the wrath of God the Almighty. On his robe and on his thigh he has a name written, King of kings and Lord of lords. (Rev. 19:11–16 ESV)

The Impact of Psalter Structure on the New Testament's Perspective on the Psalms

The New Testament's usage of the Psalms may be reconsidered in view of the many structural aspects of the Psalms. Were the New Testament writers aware of these structures? Did they have structural considerations in mind when they quoted certain psalms? Did their awareness of Psalter structure influence their quotations from the Psalms?

Formal quotation is not the only indicator of the significance of an Old Testament passage for the New Testament. Yet an investigation of the structural elements in the Psalms as a factor for New Testament quotations from the Psalms has special significance. For by quoting an external source, an author lays down his own creative pen because someone else has spoken better or more significantly than he himself could have done alone. The quotation of an Old Testament passage doubly underscores the significance of that particular passage to the authors of the New Testament. In investigating the possible significance of Psalter structure for New Testament authors, this analysis will consider (1) quotations from the three messianic psalms coupled with the three principal Torah psalms; (2) quotations from the eight acrostic psalms; (3) quotations from the focal messianic psalms; and (4) quotations from the *Hallelu-YAH* psalms.

Quotations from the Three Messianic Psalms Coupled with the Three Principal Torah Psalms

Three messianic psalms coupled in the Psalter with three principal Torah psalms stand out at primary points of structure in Books I and V: Psalms 2, 18, and 118. How are these psalms viewed by New Testament writers?

All three of these messianic passages are quoted in the New Testament. Psalm 2 plays a recognized role in the developing theology of the new covenant. Three elements of this key psalm function very early and very significantly in the life of the new covenant people of God. In response to the threats of the prevailing officials of Judaism, the apostles appeal to the opening words of Psalm 2 as the basis for understanding their abuses. As Herod, Pontius Pilate, and the world's people along with the people of Israel maltreated God's holy Son, Jesus, so his apostles can experience their similar maltreatment (Acts 4:24–28; cf. Ps. 2:1–2). Because these oppositions were anticipated in Psalm 2, the apostles conclude that these enemies of the Christ have done "what your power and will had decided beforehand should happen." Clearly, the apostles are not treating the Psalter's description of Messiah's role in facing the enemies of God's kingdom as merely "mythopoetic language." Instead, the apostles read Psalm 2 as anticipating history—"real" history—in which kings of the earth and rulers of the world stand against the Lord's Messiah and his people.

In addition, the critical declaration of Psalm 2 that identifies Messiah as Yahweh's Son is quoted several times over in the New Testament, including the critical moments of Jesus' baptism and transfiguration (cf. Matt. 3:17; 17:5). The figurative "birth" of Messiah to his glorious position as Yahweh's Son depicts his exalting resurrection day (Acts 13:32–33; cf. Ps. 2:7).

The writer of Hebrews directly unites "You are my Son" from Psalm 2:7 with the antecedent promise of the covenant that the heir to David's throne will be Son to God (2 Sam. 7:14; cf. Heb. 1:5). The author of Hebrews then moves confidently in developing his main contribution to New Testament theology by declaring Jesus as "High Priest" alongside his kingship on the basis of sonship to God as established in Psalm 2:7. For if he is Son to God, he will clearly have the ready access to the Father necessary to a properly functioning priesthood (cf. Heb. 5:5–6).

According to the climax of Psalm 2, Messiah as Son to God "herds" or "rules" the nations with a rod of iron (Ps. 2:9; cf. Rev. 19:15). But just as he has received this authority from his Father, so he gives authority to his people that they might rule the nations "with an iron scepter" and "dash them to pieces like pottery" (Rev. 2:26–27; cf. Ps. 2:9).

So the critical role of Psalm 2 finds manifold reflection in the broadest theological categories of the New Testament. The key concept of Messiah as Son to God determines its perspective on history, Christology, and eschatology.

As Paul in the book of Romans comes to the climax of his gospel message that embraces all the world's nations, he quotes from Psalm 18. Just as David praised the Lord for subjecting foreign nations under his domain (Ps. 18:43), so the nations of the world that receive the gospel should praise the Christ (cf. Rom. 15:9, quoting Ps. 18:49). The full context of this quotation from pivotal Psalm 18 of Book I in the Psalter underscores the accuracy of Paul's choice in selecting this Old Testament passage to establish the propriety of all nations' praising the Messiah of the Davidic covenant:

258

You have delivered me from the attacks of the people; you have *made me the head of nations; people I did not know are subject to me.* As soon as they hear me, *they obey me; foreigners cringe before me.* They all lose heart; they come trembling from their strongholds. The LORD lives! Praise be to my Rock! Exalted be God my Savior! He is the God who avenges me, who *subdues nations under me,* who saves me from my enemies. You exalted me above my foes; from violent men you rescued me. Therefore *I will praise you among the nations,* O LORD; I will sing praises to your name. He gives his king great victories; he shows unfailing kindness to his anointed, to David and his descendants forever. (Ps. 18:43–50; cf. Rom. 15:9)

It would be difficult to find a passage from the Old Testament that reinforces Paul's point more effectively than the quotation from this strategic psalm. The Lord has given David great victory over all his enemies, so that nations and peoples gladly submit to his rule (Ps. 18:1, 43, 47). In the climactic realization of this principle in redemptive history, Jesus as David's greater Son now experiences this same sovereignty over the nations, only on a much larger scale.

Psalm 118, the pivotal messianic psalm of Book V in the Psalter, focuses on the "stone" rejected by the builders of God's kingdom. That foundational "stone" has become "the chief cornerstone" (Ps. 118:22). Just as a building can have only a single cornerstone, so only one person can qualify as the "chief cornerstone" of God's kingdom. But the people in charge of constructing this kingdom of God on earth reject the stone of God's choice. Apparently they do not favor the shape of this stone because of the definition it would give to the character of the kingdom. But despite its rejection by men, God establishes it as the defining stone of his kingdom.

Psalm 118 is quoted in the New Testament more than any other psalm. Twelve times over, six different authors of the New Testament quote this psalm, including all four Gospels, a speech in Acts reported by Luke, 1 Peter, and Hebrews.[3] This psalm answers the critical "why" concerning the rejection of Jesus as Messiah by Israel's

---

3. Quoted passages from Psalm 118 as cited in Kurt Aland et al., eds., *Greek New Testament*, 4th rev. ed. (Stuttgart: Deutsche Bibelgesellschaft, 1994), 888, include the following: Ps. 118:6 (Heb. 13:6); 118:22 (Luke 20:17; Acts 4:11; 1 Peter 2:7); 118:22–23

leaders. Corresponding to its role as pivotal psalm in the climactic Book V of the Psalter, Psalm 118 is appropriately recognized by the New Testament authors for its critical significance.

So the three messianic psalms that function as major structural markers in the Psalter play a principal role in the theology of the New Testament. The repeated quotation of these three psalms suggests an awareness by New Testament authors of their significance in the Psalter.

Quotations from the Eight Acrostic Psalms

The eight acrostic psalms distributed evenly between Book I and Book V of the Psalter function as key elements of Psalter structure. Is there any indicator that these key structural psalms receive recognition in the New Testament?

Three of these acrostic psalms are quoted in the New Testament, with two others very likely alluded to. Paul quotes acrostic Psalm(s) 9/10 to establish the depravity of humanity (Ps. 10:7; cf. Rom. 3:14). His quotation, taken from the nonacrostic section of acrostic Psalm(s) 9/10, describes the evil of this oppressor of the poor. Because of its position as the first acrostic psalm at the midpoint of several psalms in the Psalter depicting the struggle of the righteous with the wicked, this psalm offers a concentrated picture of the depravity of the wicked. As a foundational factor in Paul's universal gospel, this vivid image of wickedness is applied to the whole of humanity.

The apostle Peter quotes acrostic Psalm 34, which functions in the Psalter as the introductory bracketing-psalm of a collection of four psalms describing the plight of the innocent sufferer. Peter could have quoted any one of these four psalms. But he chooses acrostic Psalm 34, the first of this collection, to encourage Christians to live in harmony with one another and habitually do good despite the constant barrage of unjust abuses that they will inevitably receive (1 Peter 3:8–12). By citing the first of this collection of four psalms of the innocent sufferer, Peter might have been deliberately urging the readers of his letter, who could well have been conscious of the

---

(Matt. 21:42; Mark 12:10–11); 118:25–26 (Matt. 21:9; Mark 11:9–10; John 12:13); 118:26 (Matt. 23:39; Luke 13:35; 19:38).

contextual structure of the Psalter, to receive their encouragement from all four psalms of the innocent sufferer bracketed by the two acrostic psalms (Pss. 34–37).

Acrostic Psalm 112 is appropriately quoted by Paul to encourage generosity in Christian giving (Ps. 112:9; 2 Cor. 9:9). This second of the acrostic psalms in Book V is symbiotically coupled with the immediately previous psalm, which is also an acrostic psalm (Ps. 111). These twin acrostics introduce the first *Hallelu-YAH* grouping of Book V. Both psalms open with this expression of praise, often translated as "Praise the LORD!" These two psalms are closely bound together by their distinctive substance. Psalm 111 declares regarding the Lord that "*his righteousness endures forever.*" As a perfect echo, Psalm 112 declares regarding the person who fears the Lord that "*his righteousness endures forever*" (Pss. 111:3b; 112:3b). Psalm 111 speaks of the Lord's grace in redemption, while Psalm 112 describes the righteous person's gracious generosity toward the needy (Ps. 111:9; 112:9). Paul displays full comprehension of the joint message of these twin psalms in which the righteous person mirrors his Lord by his lifestyle. The apostle bases his admonition to Christian generosity on God's gracious redemption as well as Christ's self-giving. In an identical manner, the Psalter's acrostic twins (Pss. 111–112) anticipate a replication of God's generosity in the lifestyle of the Christian believer (cf. 2 Cor. 8:9; 9:9–11).

So these quotations from the acrostic psalms suggest some awareness of the significance of these psalms in the structural context of the Psalter. It cannot be clearly demonstrated that the New Testament writers consciously worked with these psalms in light of their structural role in the Psalter. Yet the general principle of contextual quotation in the New Testament encourages the observation that New Testament writers may well have had an awareness of the structural aspect of the acrostic psalms, and were therefore conscious of their special significance.

Quotations from the Focal Messianic Psalms

Focal messianic psalms quoted in the New Testament include the following:

261

Psalm 2 is quoted several times in the New Testament, as already discussed. In addition, the landmark faith-confession of Peter on behalf of all the apostles can be understood only in the context of the Davidic covenant as cited in Psalm 2: "You are the Messiah, the Son of the living God" (Matt. 16:16).

Psalm 22 is quoted repeatedly in the Gospels and also in Hebrews (Matt. 27:46; Mark 15:34; John 19:24; Heb. 2:12). Because Jesus partakes of human flesh and blood, he stands as a brother among brothers. Because of mortal flesh, he can vicariously suffer for his people even to the point of death.

Psalm 45 is quoted in Hebrews 1:8–9, affirming the deity of the messianic king. This affirmation has even greater significance when considered in the context of the collection of kingship psalms declaring God's kingship as well as Messiah's (Pss. 45–48). Messiah's role as Elohim can be fully appreciated only in this context of God's kingship.

Psalm 69 is quoted by three different New Testament authors in reference to four different segments of this psalm, as discussed previously. The fact that three different New Testament writers drew appropriate quotations from this single psalm could indicate that a general comprehension of basic Psalter structure existed in Judaism during New Testament times. This psalm has some structural prominence as the first psalm of the Davidic triad responding to the immediately preceding "dialogue of the kings" (Pss. 61–68). As a consequence, its content might have been more generally well known.

Psalm 110 is the second-most-quoted psalm in the New Testament—ten times in five different books (Matthew, Mark, Luke, Acts, and Hebrews). Coming in Book V of the Psalter, this psalm represents the maturest perspective on the coming messianic king. Not only is he "Lord" over King David, seated in ultimate honor at Yahweh's right hand, but by divine oath he has also been established as "priest forever after the order of Melchizedek" (Ps. 110:4; cf. Heb. 7:11–28). Because of its exalted Christology, this focal messianic psalm plays a major role in determining the theology of the New Testament.

Psalm 118, as previously mentioned, is the psalm most quoted in the New Testament. This magnificently structured psalm makes extensive use of antiphonal refrains to underscore the rejection and sufferings as well as the triumphs and glories of Messiah. Coming in the final book of the Psalter, this psalm appropriately presents both the sufferings and the glories of the expected messianic king in a climactic fashion for the celebration of the people of God across the generations.

So these focal messianic psalms play a significant role in the New Testament. Even beyond their immediate contribution to the specific passages that quote them, they have an impact on the formation of New Testament theology.

Quotations from the *Hallelu-YAH* Psalms

Three psalms from the first grouping of *Hallelu-YAH* psalms in Book V are quoted by the apostle Paul in the New Testament (Ps. 112:9 [2 Cor. 9:9]; Ps. 116:10 [2 Cor. 4:13]; Ps. 117:1 [Rom. 15:11]). In each case, Paul demonstrates a full understanding of the larger context of the portion of Scripture that he is quoting.

As already indicated, Paul is well aware of the connection between twin acrostic Psalms 111 and 112. The several connections between Psalms 111 and 112 with 2 Corinthians 8 and 9 support the concept that Paul had grasped the context of these twin acrostic psalms introducing the first grouping of *Hallelu-YAH* psalms in Book V.

In anticipation of his quotation from a second *Hallelu-YAH* triad of this collection, Paul describes his ministry as always carrying around in the body the "death of Jesus," as always being "given over to death" so that "death is at work in us" (2 Cor. 4:10–12). He then quotes *Hallelu-YAH* Psalm 116, in which the psalmist describes himself as being caught in the entanglement of the "cords of death," experiencing the "anguish of the grave," being "delivered from death," and finding reassurance because of the preciousness of the "death of his saints in the sight of the LORD" (Ps. 116:3, 8, 15). Despite this face-to-face confrontation with death, the psalmist exclaims, "I believed; therefore I have spoken," which becomes the focus of Paul's quotation. Despite always experiencing death, we also believe, and so we have the courage to keep speaking (Ps. 116:10; cf. 2 Cor. 4:13). Once more, the apostle displays complete awareness of the context of his quotation.

As his third quotation from this first *Hallelu-YAH* grouping in Book V, the apostle quotes the climactic psalm of this collection of seven psalms. Psalm 117 as the final psalm of this grouping opens with *Hallelu Yahweh* and closes with *Hallelu-YAH* (Ps. 117:1–2). Paul's point is that all nations may now join Israelite believers in glorifying God, which is exactly the effect of the corporate exclamation *"Hallelu-YAH"*: *"All of you,* together now, Praise *YAH."* "All you nations" and "all you peoples" must praise the Lord together because of his great love toward us and toward all other nationalities alike (Ps. 117:1–2; Rom. 15:11).

It cannot be definitively declared that Paul worked consciously with the grouping of these *Hallelu-YAH* psalms. But it may be asked: Would any other Scripture from the Old Testament have suited his purposes so well? If not, how did Paul locate these passages from the psalms that confirmed the various points he was making so perfectly? Is it not likely that the apostle had memorized at least Psalms 111 and 112, the opening acrostics of this collection, which would have given him ready access to the content of the rest of the grouping?

No specific quotations from the *Hallelu-YAH* finale (Pss. 146–150) occur in the New Testament. But the repeated *Hallelu-YAH* at the conclusion of the book of Revelation clearly echoes the consummate celebration of these consummate psalms. Babylon as the embodiment of materialism has finally been defeated. So God's redeemed people can repeatedly shout, *"Hallelu-YAH!"* (Rev. 19:1, 3–4, 6).

Analyzing the pattern of explicit quotations of the Old Testament in the New represents only one approach in understanding the relation of new covenant consummation to old covenant anticipation. A much fuller picture could be achieved by investigating allusions and verbal parallels, not to speak of the larger realm of theological categories. But even within the limited framework of quotations, a number of conclusions may be reached.

In reviewing these New Testament quotations from the perspective of key Psalter structures, observations must be stated cautiously. Evidence is not sufficient to lead to a clear conclusion that the major structures of the Psalter played a significant role in the quotations of the New Testament. New Testament authors are obviously not limited to making use of only this type of material. They habitually reach into all the treasures of God's truth embedded in the Psalter. At the same time, it could have been that an awareness of basic structural elements of the Psalter served them well in grasping the total message of the Psalter. This larger comprehension of Psalter structure as sacred Scripture might have assisted in preparing them for making good and proper use of the whole book of Psalms.

In terms of the impact that these structures should have on the related matter of current exegesis, focusing on inherent structures in the Psalter can only enrich the exegetical process. For instance, fresh insight into Shepherd-Psalm 23 will be gained when these justly familiar words are placed in the context of the five kingship psalms that define its context within the Psalter. This Good Shepherd will lead his sheep into pastures of fresh grasses so that they "lie down" because they are fully satisfied (Ps. 23:2). According to the concluding verses of the immediately preceding kingship psalm, the poor "will eat and be satisfied," while all the rich "will eat and worship" (Ps. 22:26, 29). For this Good Shepherd who makes them lie down is none other than the King of Glory, the Sovereign Lord of the universe (Ps. 24:1, 7–10). Fresh insight may be gained by reading this most familiar psalm of the Bible in the context of the five kingship psalms. In a similar way, recognizing the centralized role of Psalm 80 in the context of national devastations in Book III can only enhance the appreciation of the "man of [God's] right hand," the "son of man" that God has made strong for himself. From this perspective, the self-identification of Jesus as "son of man" experiencing humiliation and glory may enrich the appreciation of his role as the deliverer of a crushed people.

Conclusion

So a fresh reading of the Psalter in the flow of its structure may provide new insight into more of the richness of God's inspired and infallible Word as revealed in the Psalter. Rediscovering the Psalms in their fuller biblical-theological context as uncovered by the structure of the Psalter may provide rich blessings to the church of today.

All glory must be given to the God of the Scriptures for this magnificent piece of inspired literature. For the glory of this work witnesses to the glories of our God!

SELECT BIBLIOGRAPHY

Ackroyd, Peter R. *I & II Chronicles, Ezra, Nehemiah*. Torch Bible Paperbacks. London: SCM Press, 1973.

Alexander, Joseph Addison. *The Psalms: Translated and Explained*. Grand Rapids: Zondervan, 1864. Reprint, n.d.

Augustine. *Expositions on the Book of Psalms*. Edited by A. Cleveland Coxe. In *Nicene and Post-Nicene Fathers*, edited by Philip Schaff. Vol. 8. Peabody, MA: Hendrickson, 1994.

Avishur, Yitzhak. *Studies in Hebrew and Ugaritic Psalms*. Jerusalem: Magnes Press, 1994.

Blau, Ludwig. "Torah." In *The Jewish Enclyclopedia*, 12:196–99. New York: Funk and Wagnalls, 1906.

Blidstein, Gerald J. "Messiah." In *Encyclopedia Judaica*, 11:1410–12. Jerusalem: Keter Publishing House, 1972.

Bright, John. *A History of Israel*. 4th ed. Louisville: Westminster John Knox Press, 2000.

Brown, Francis. *The New Brown-Driver-Briggs-Gesenius Hebrew and English Lexicon*. Peabody, MA: Hendrickson, 1979.

Broyles, Craig C. "The Psalms and Cult Symbolism: The Case of the Cherubim-Ark." In *Interpreting the Psalms: Issues and Approaches*, edited by Philip S. Johnston and David G. Firth, 139–156. Downers Grove, IL: InterVarsity Press, 2005.

Brueggemann, Walter. *The Message of the Psalms: A Theological Commentary*. Minneapolis: Augsburg, 1984.

Buttenwieser, Moses. "Messiah." In *The Jewish Enclyclopedia*, 8:505–12. New York: Funk and Wagnalls, 1906.

Calvin, John. *Commentary on the Book of Psalms*. 3 vols. Grand Rapids: Baker, 1993.

Childs, Brevard S. *Biblical Theology of the Old and New Testaments: Theological Reflection on the Christian Bible*. London: SCM Press, 1992.

———. *Introduction to the Old Testament as Scripture*. London: SCM Press, 1979.

Craigie, Peter C. *Psalms 1–50*. Word Biblical Commentary 19. Waco, TX: Word Books, 1983.

Dahood, Mitchell. *Psalms I, 1–50*. Garden City, NY: Doubleday, 1965.

———. *Psalms II, 51–100*. Garden City, NY: Doubleday, 1968.

———. *Psalms III, 101–150*. Garden City, NY: Doubleday, 1970.

deClaisse-Walford, Nancy L. *Reading from the Beginning: The Shaping of the Hebrew Psalter*. Ann Arbor, MI: UMI Dissertation Services, 1996.

Delitzsch, Franz. *Biblical Commentary on the Psalms*. 3 vols. London: Hodder & Stoughton, 1894–89.

———. *Biblical Commentary on the Psalms*. 3 vols. Grand Rapids: Eerdmans, 1959.

Dillard, Raymond B., and Tremper Longman III. *An Introduction to the Old Testament*. Leicester, UK: Apollos, 1995.

Dodd, C. H. *According to the Scriptures: The Sub-structure of New Testament Theology*. London: Nisbet & Co., 1952.

Driver, S. R. *Introduction to the Old Testament*. 9th ed. Edinburgh: T&T Clark, 1913.

———. *A Treatise on the Use of the Tenses in Hebrew*. Oxford: Clarendon Press, 1892.

Freedman, David Noel. "Acrostic Poems in the Hebrew Bible: Alphabetic and Otherwise." *Catholic Biblical Quarterly* 48 (1986): 408–31.

———. "Acrostics and Metrics in Hebrew Poetry." In *Pottery, Poetry, and Prophecy: Studies in Early Hebrew Poetry*, 51–76. Winona Lake, IN: Eisenbrauns, 1980.

———. "Who Asks (or Tells) God to Repent?" *Bible Review* 1, 4 (1985): 56–59.

Gaster, Theodor. "Psalm 29." *Jewish Quarterly Review* 37 (1946): 55–65.

Ginsberg, Harold Louis. "A Phoenician Hymn in the Psalter." Paper presented at Atti del XIX Congresso Internazionale degli Orientalisti, Rome, 1935.

Ginsburg, Christian D. *Introduction to the Masoretico-Critical Edition of the Hebrew Bible*. London: Trinitarian Bible Society, 1897.

Goldingay, John. *Psalms, Volume 1: Psalms 1–41*. Grand Rapids: Baker, 2006.

———. *Psalms, Volume 2: Psalms 42–89*. Grand Rapids: Baker, 2007.

———. *Psalms, Volume 3: Psalms 90–150*. Grand Rapids: Baker, 2008.

Grant, Jamie A. *The King as Exemplar: The Function of Deuteronomy's Kingship Law in the Shaping of the Book of Psalms*. Atlanta: Society of Biblical Literature, 2004.

———. "The Psalms and the King." In *Interpreting the Psalms: Issues and Approaches*, edited by Philip S. Johnston and David G. Firth, 101–18. Downers Grove, IL: InterVarsity Press, 2005.

Gray, George Buchanan. *The Forms of Hebrew Poetry.* New York: KTAV Publishing House, 1972.

Gunkel, Hermann, and Joachim Begrich. *Introduction to Psalms: The Genres of the Religious Lyric of Israel.* Translated by James D. Nogalski. Macon, GA: Mercer University Press, 1998.

Hengstenberg, Ernst Wilhelm. *Commentary on the Psalms.* 3 vols. Edinburgh: T&T Clark, 1851–54.

Hossfeld, Frank-Lothar, and Eric Zenger. *Psalms 2: A Commentary on Psalms 51–100.* Minneapolis: Fortress Press, 2005.

———. *Psalms 3: A Commentary on Psalms 101–150.* Minneapolis: Fortress Press, 2011.

Howard, David M., Jr. *The Structure of Psalms 93–100.* Biblical and Judaic Studies 5. Winona Lake, IN: Eisenbrauns, 1997.

Johnston, Philip S., and David G. Firth. *Interpreting the Psalms: Issues and Approaches.* Downers Grove, IL: InterVarsity Press, 2005.

Kidner, Derek. *Psalms 1–72: An Introduction and Commentary on Books I and II of the Psalms.* London: Inter-Varsity Press, 1973.

———. *Psalms 73–150: A Commentary on Books III–V of the Psalms.* London: Inter-Varsity Press, 1975.

Klein, Ralph W. *1 Chronicles: A Commentary.* Hermeneia. Minneapolis: Augsburg Fortress, 2006.

Knohl, Israel. "The Messiah Son of Joseph." *Biblical Archaeology Review* 34, 5 (September–October 2008): 58–62.

Knoppers, Gary N. *I Chronicles 10–29: A New Translation with Introduction and Commentary.* Anchor Bible. New York: Doubleday, 2004.

Knox, Ronald Arbuthnott. *Holy Bible: A Translation from the Latin Vulgate in the Light of the Hebrew and Greek Originals, Authorized by the Hierarchy of England and Wales and the Hierarchy of Scotland.* London: Burns & Oates, 1955.

Kraus, Hans-Joachim. *Psalms 1–59: A Commentary.* Minneapolis: Augsburg, 1988.

———. *Psalms 60–150: A Commentary.* Minneapolis: Augsburg, 1989.

———. *Theology of the Psalms.* Minneapolis: Augsburg, 1986.

Lee, Seong Hye. *The Psalter as an Anthology Designed to Be Memorized.* Bristol, UK: University of Bristol and Trinity College, 2011.

Liebreich, Leon J. "The Songs of Ascents and the Priestly Blessing." *Journal of Biblical Literature* 74 (1955): 33–36.

Luther, Martin. *Luther's Works.* Vol. 35. Philadelphia: Muhlenberg Press, 1960.

Maloney, Les D. *A Word Fitly Spoken: Poetic Artistry in the First Four Acrostics of the Hebrew Psalter.* New York: Peter Lang, 2009.

Mays, James Luther. *The Lord Reigns: A Theological Handbook to the Psalms.* Louisville: Westminster John Knox Press, 1994.

———. *Psalms.* Interpretation: A Bible Commentary for Teaching and Preaching. Louisville: John Knox Press, 1994.

McCann, J. Clinton, ed. *The Shape and Shaping of the Psalter.* Sheffield, UK: Sheffield Academic Press, 1993.

———. *A Theological Introduction to the Book of Psalms: The Psalms as Torah.* Nashville: Abingdon Press, 1993.

McFall, Leslie. "The Evidence for a Logical Arrangement of the Psalter." *Westminster Theological Journal* 62, 2 (2000): 223–56.

Miller, Patrick D. "The Beginning of the Psalter." In *The Shape and Shaping of the Psalter*, edited by J. Clinton McCann, 83–92. Sheffield, UK: Sheffield Academic Press, 1993.

———. "Kingship, Tora Obedience and Prayer." In *Neue Wege der Psalmenforschung*, edited by Klaus Seybold and Erich Zenger, 127–41. Freiburg: Herder, 1995.

Mitchell, D. C. "The Fourth Deliverer: A Josephite Messiah in 4QTestimonia." *Biblica* 86, 4 (2005): 545–53.

Mowinckel, Sigmund. *The Psalms in Israel's Worship.* Two vols. in one. Biblical Resource Series. Grand Rapids: Eerdmans, 2004.

Ridderbos, N. H. "The Psalms: Style-Figures and Structure." *Oudtestamentische Studiën* 13 (1963): 43–76.

Robertson, O. Palmer. *The Christ of the Covenants.* Phillipsburg, NJ: Presbyterian and Reformed, 1980.

———. *God's People in the Wilderness: The Church in Hebrews.* Fearn, Ross-shire, Scotland: Christian Focus Publications, 2009.

———. *The Israel of God: Yesterday, Today, and Tomorrow.* Phillipsburg, NJ: P&R Publishing, 2000.

———. *Psalms in Congregational Celebration.* Darlington, UK: Evangelical Press, 1995.

Safrai, Shmuel. "Temple." In *Encyclopedia Judaica*, 15:970–83. Jerusalem: Keter Publishing House, 1972.

Sarna, Nathan M. "Acrostics." In *Encyclopaedia Judaica*, 2:229–30. Jerusalem: Keter Publishing House, 1972.

Soll, William Michael. "Babylonian and Biblical Acrostics." *Biblica* 69 (1988): 305–23.

Stec, David M. *The Targum of Psalms*. Collegeville, MN: Liturgical Press, 2004.

Stek, John H. "Psalms." In *The NIV Study Bible*. London: Hodder & Stoughton, 1985.

VanGemeren, Willem A. *Psalms*. Expositor's Bible Commentary. Grand Rapids: Zondervan, 2008.

Vincent, M. A. "The Shape of the Psalter: An Eschatological Dimension?" In *New Heaven and New Earth: Prophecy and the Millennium: Essays in Honour of Anthony Gelston*, edited by P. J. Harland and C. T. R. Hayward, 61–82. Leiden: Brill, 1999.

Waltke, Bruce K., and James M. Houston. *The Psalms as Christian Worship*. Grand Rapids: Eerdmans, 2010.

Walton, John H. "Psalms: A Cantata about the Davidic Covenant." *Journal of the Evangelical Theological Society* 34 (March 1991): 21–31.

Weiser, Artur. *The Psalms: A Commentary*. London: SCM Press, 1959.

Wellhausen, Julius. *Prolegomena to the History of Ancient Israel*. Cleveland: World Publishing, 1961.

Wenham, Gordon J. *Psalms as Torah: Reading Biblical Song Ethically*. Grand Rapids: Baker Academic, 2012.

Wilson, Gerald Henry. *The Editing of the Hebrew Psalter*. Chico, CA: Scholars Press, 1985.

———. "King, Messiah, and the Reign of God: Revisiting the Royal Psalms and the Shape of the Psalter." In *The Book of Psalms: Composition and Reception*, edited by Peter W. Flint and Patrick D. Miller Jr., 391–406. Leiden: Brill, 2005.

———. "The Structure of the Psalter." In *Interpreting the Psalms: Issues and Approaches*, edited by Philip S. Johnston and David G. Firth, 229–46. Downers Grove, IL: InterVarsity Press, 2005.

INDEX OF SCRIPTURE

285

293

Index of Subjects and Names